The Interaction of Monetary Policy and Wage Bargaining in the European Monetary Union

The Interaction of Monetary Policy and Wage Bargaining in the European Monetary Union

Lessons from the Endogenous Money Approach

Sebastian Dullien
Financial Times Deutschland

D 188

First published 2004 by
PALGRAVE MACMILLAN
Houndmills, Basingstoke, Hampshire RG21 6XS and
175 Fifth Avenue, New York, N. Y. 10010
Companies and representatives throughout the world

PALGRAVE MACMILLAN is the global academic imprint of the Palgrave Macmillan division of St. Martin's Press, LLC and of Palgrave Macmillan Ltd. Macmillan® is a registered trademark in the United States, United Kingdom and other countries. Palgrave is a registered trademark in the European Union and other countries.

ISBN 1–4039–4151–3

This book is printed on paper suitable for recycling and made from fully managed and sustained forest sources.

A catalogue record for this book is available from the British Library.

Library of Congress Cataloging-in-Publication Data

Dullien, Sebastian.
   The interaction of monetary policy and wage bargaining in the European Monetary Union: lessons from the endogenous money approach / Sebastian Dullien.
      p. cm.
   Includes bibliographical references and index.
   ISBN 1–4039–4151–3 (cloth)
      1. Unemployment–European Union countries. 2. Inflation (Finance)–European Union countries. 3. Collective bargaining–European Union countries. 4. Wages–European Union countries. 5. Monetary policy–European Union countries. 6. Banks and banking, Central–European Union countries. 7. Economic and Monetary Union. I. Title.
   HD5764.A6D85 2004
   332.4'94–dc22   2004044794

10   9   8   7   6   5   4   3   2   1
13   12   11   10   09   08   07   06   05   04

Printed and bound in Great Britain by
Antony Rowe Ltd, Chippenham and Eastbourne

To my parents

Contents

List of Figures

ix

List of Tables

Acknowledgements

This book originated as a PhD thesis at the economics department of the Freie Universität Berlin. It would not have been possible without the generous support and help of a number of people for whose assistance I am very grateful. Of course, the usual disclaimer applies. The views presented here are mine alone, and so are all possible errors.

First of all, I wish to thank my two supervisors, Waltraud Schelkle, now at the London School of Economics, and Professor Manfred Nitsch, from the Freie Universität Berlin, who always had an open ear for my problems. Moreover, Professor Stefan Collignon deserves special thanks, not only for acting almost like a third supervisor in discussing the ideas and models of this book, but also for the intellectual support he has given me in my academic work since we first met in a seminar at the Freie Universität in 1997.

I am also greatly indebted to Bob Hancké, who gave me invaluable help in formulating the research question and structuring the work within the workshops of the European Political Economy Infrastructure Consortium (EPIC). Bob Hancké also pointed out where my ideas needed more explanation to make them understandable for a broader audience. For EPIC, I wish to thank the European Commission, which funded the project, as well as all those at the London School of Economics, the Wissenschaftszentrum Berlin, the European University Institute in Florence and the Instituto Juan March in Madrid who organised the programme.

As for the financial side of writing this book, I thank my former boss Andrew Gowers at the *Financial Times Deutschland* (now editor-in-chief at the *Financial Times* in London) for giving me the possibility of working part-time during the project, as well as his successors Christoph Keese and Wolfgang Münchau for continuing the arrangements.

Discussions with participants at the EPIC workshops, but also with former colleagues at the Deutsches Institut für Wirtschaftsforschung (DIW) as well as lecturers from the Economics Department of the Freie Universität Berlin and colleagues from the *Financial Times Deutschland* on aspects of this work, helped me to focus my ideas. I would like to mention in person Karl Betz, Lioba Diez, Thomas Fricke, Ulrich Fritsche, Gustav Horn, Heike Joebges, Christiane Karweil, Andreas Krosta, Birgit Marschall, Susanne Mundschenk, Professor Hajo Riese,

Wolfgang Scheremet, Mark Schieritz, Christian Schütte, Daniela Schwarzer, Jan Strasky and Lucas Zeise. I also profited a lot from discussions in the internet forum of the so called 'gang of eight', focused on what the group calls 'creditary economics'. My brother Thomas was always at hand when I had problems with the maths and Jessica Nash made my English intelligible.

Finally, I wish to thank Andreas Langensiepen and Kristine Nienborg for their continuing emotional support during the work on this book, and Kristine for her hospitality in Belgrade and Maputo, where parts of this work were written. Indira Dupuis helped me to get through the different phases of final alteration and preparation for publication of the book.

SEBASTIAN DULLIEN

1
Introduction: The Unsolved Unemployment–Inflation Puzzle

How do wage bargainers and central banks jointly influence output, employment and inflation? This question has – with varying focal points – been a topic for economists and political scientists for decades. Yet, while the answers have changed over time, the question is far from being solved and disagreement among academics persists.

In the 1960s, it was widely agreed that aggregate demand management through monetary and fiscal policy should be used to keep unemployment low. After the breakdown of the Keynesian revolution in the early 1970s and the emergence of the problem of stagflation – the simultaneous rise in inflation and unemployment – the focus shifted. In the new consensus, it was wage setters who were responsible for setting wages in such a way that full employment could be reached. The central bank was given sole responsibility for keeping prices stable. Cracks in the consensus of the 1980s and early 1990s have now begun to appear and a shift towards an interactionary approach to wage bargaining and monetary policy institutions seems to be underway. However, from a policy perspective, the basic question is as pressing today as it was twenty-five years ago: what causes unemployment and inflation, and what can be done about it? While inflation, the main problem in the 1970s, is now well under control in the industrialised world, unemployment remains a huge challenge.

Moreover, much of what economists concluded from their theoretical models could not be confirmed by the complex economic working of the real world. The Phillips-curve trade-off between inflation and unemployment, once thought to be stable, disappeared when the attempt was made to exploit it in economic policy. The permanent increase in unemployment in Europe during times of disinflation cast doubt on the idea that inflation had no benefits and disinflation could come at no costs, as expressed in Grilli, Masciandaro and Tabellini (1991).

1

In addition, some other real-world phenomena also could not be explained sufficiently by the mainstream models. After inflation had been brought under control, some countries experienced high economic growth and were able to reduce unemployment significantly, while others did rather poorly. This is true if one compares the USA and Europe, which arguably have experienced different monetary policy stances since 1990. However, this observation is also true within the European Monetary Union (EMU) and the preceding European Monetary System (EMS), arrangements which brought rather similar monetary conditions to countries with different institutional structures: some countries did especially well after going into EMS and EMU (especially smaller countries such as the Netherlands and Ireland, but also the southern European countries Spain and Portugal), while others did comparably worse than the times before EMS and EMU (e.g. Germany).

What might be the most pressing problem, however, is not the divergence of unemployment within EMU, but the high overall level of unemployment, leading back to the question of what role monetary policy can play in improving the level of employment and output, and which part of this task is the wage bargainers' responsibility.

This book will provide a possible answer to that question. By linking (post-)Keynesian considerations about endogenous money with modern supply-side models of monopolistic competition in the goods market, it shows that the classical dichotomy between the real and monetary sectors, as well as the notion that wage bargainers are responsible for unemployment, both hinge on some dubious assumption of orthodox economic theory: namely, the notion that money is net wealth to the private sector and that the money stock is exogenously set. When relaxing these assumptions, it is wage bargainers, together with the central bank, who have responsibility for output, employment and inflation. While unions and employers influence the supply-side price level with their wage contracts, the central bank can influence demand, which translates into demand prices and aggregate output and employment.

1.1   The macroeconomic consensus after the end of the Keynesian revolution

For some twenty-five years after the breakdown of the 'Keynesian revolution', there has been a wide consensus among macroeconomists about the way the economy works. While the 'old Keynesians' had proclaimed up until the mid-1970s that there was an exploitable trade-off between unemployment and inflation (the modified Phillips-curve),[1] The followers of Lucas' rational expectation revolution insisted on a strict dichotomy between the real and the monetary sector: according to their view (which quickly found its way into economic textbooks), in the medium and long run, unemployment could not be influenced by macroeconomic policy decisions.[2]

According to Lucas' followers' dominant view, employment and real wages are solely determined in the labour market. Firms hire workers until the market real wage equals the workers' marginal productivity. At the same time, workers provide labour until their marginal disutility from working equals their marginal utility from the real wage paid. As long as the labour market is free of any institutional features that keep wages from adjusting, equilibrium will be attained. All remaining unemployment is voluntary. Aggregate output is thus determined by the agents' decisions to work.

Monetary policy in this setting consists of providing the economy with an exogenously set money supply. If the money stock grows faster than output, inflation occurs. Only unexpected changes in the money supply might have any real consequences. However, since rational agents expect any systematic attempt to inflate the economy in order to push down unemployment, this does not leave any scope for macroeconomic policy to influence unemployment in the medium or long run. Consequently, all a central bank should do is maintain a low and stable inflation; unemployment and growth are not its concern. Moreover, as politicians might be inclined to inflate in order to reap short-term gains from a temporarily lower rate of unemployment, control over monetary policy should be given to some independent central bank, preferably headed by a central banker who has a strong distaste for inflation (Rogoff 1985). Since economic agents rationally anticipate the anti-inflationary stance of such an independent central bank, they adjust their inflation expectations to lower rates of inflation. Their real decisions remain unaffected. Reducing inflation thus comes without any real costs; an independent central bank just yields more macroeconomic stability as a quasi-'free lunch' (Grilli, Masciandaro, and Tabellini 1991).

Since unemployment is thus a labour market problem, the policy conclusions for this area are, in Calmfors words (1998, p. 141):

> [E]quilibrium unemployment is determined mainly by the institutions in the labour market and . . . it can be reduced by well-designed labour-market reform.

Such reforms would include lowering the level and duration of unemployment benefits so that people have a higher incentive to increase their labour supply. Further, changes to the legal framework for wage setting with the aim of decreasing unions' bargaining power are advised, as unions could then no longer push for real wages too high for full employment.

The level of unemployment which grinds on at a given level of labour market rigidities is also called the NAIRU (the non-accelerating inflation rate of unemployment), as any attempt to increase employment beyond this point would accelerate inflation. The NAIRU has also often been dubbed as the part of unemployment which is 'structural'. It has also become a guideline for practical monetary policy, with central bankers becoming cautious as soon as actual employment approaches the estimated NAIRU.[3]

1.2   Empirical experience: challenging the consensus

Some economists have recently grown more and more uncomfortable with the consensus view of the world, as empirical experience seems to be out of line with what theory predicts. First, disinflation does not appear to be a 'free lunch' at all: during the first period of disinflation at the beginning of the 1980s, unemployment exploded in both Europe and in the USA. It took the USA almost a decade before unemployment was again reduced to the 1979 level. Europe never really recovered from this first strong rise in unemployment. The second period of restrictive monetary policy and disinflating in Germany in the early 1990s (which the other EMS countries had to follow) caused similar casualties: European unemployment rose above 10 per cent for several years.

But monetary policy also seems to play a role in the opposite direction. US monetary policy has often been credited with the longest peace-time expansion of the economy, which occurred in the 1990s. During this episode, unemployment fell well below 6.5 per cent, the level which had long been believed to be the US NAIRU – without igniting inflation (Solow 2000a, p. 157). Though, of course, only time will tell what consequences the bursting of the internet stock market bubble will hold for the US economy, this experience nevertheless remains remarkable and is not captured in the standard models.

Europe also experienced a monetary expansion, though a sadly short-lived one, at the end of the 1990s. The beginning of EMU brought all of Europe lower interest rates: first, in the Southern

European countries such as Italy, Spain and Portugal, nominal interest rates converged to the traditional low German level. Second, monetary policy switched to an expansionary stance. The European Central Bank (ECB) not only orchestrated a cut in the interest rates of all national central banks that were to become members of the euro-zone just prior to the beginning of EMU in late 1998, but also lowered interest rates again in early 1999. During the ensuing two years, growth in the euro-zone picked up and unemployment declined, in some cases, as in Spain, dramatically.

These developments came about at a time when labour market institutions remained unaltered. While union power was diminished in the USA during the Reagan years (1980–8), the late 1990s did not bring much change. That labour market institutions have played a role in the evolution of unemployment also seems highly dubious for Europe (Figure 1.1). True, at the beginning of the twenty-first century, labour markets in Europe are tightly regulated. Unemployment benefits are relatively high and centralised bargaining with strong unions is common. The European unemployment rate is well above that of the USA, where unemployment insurance indemnity periods

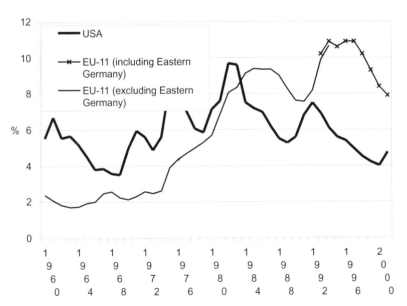

Figure 1.1   Unemployment in the USA and the euro-zone, 1960–2000
Source: European Commission (2002).

and payments are well below European standards, centralised wage contracts are hardly heard of and labour markets are said to be close to a perfect market. However, most of the European labour market institutions have been in place since the 1960s or early 1970s, but unemployment increased sharply only in the late 1970s–early 1980s and again in the early 1990s. Furthermore, European labour market regulations became increasingly more 'employment-friendly' from the mid-1970s (Blanchard and Wolfers 2000, p. C16), while unemployment in Europe continued to rise. Blanchard and Wolfers' (2000, Table 8) and Freyssinet's (2000, Table 7) indices for employment protection nicely demonstrate this fact: while employment protection strongly increased in Europe until the mid-1970s, a general downward trend can be observed since. As Solow (2000b, p. 5) notes, the timing of changes in labour market institutions and observed increases in unemployment seems to be wrong. Instead, some economists claim that there is ample evidence that macroeconomic factors played a crucial role (e.g. Fitoussi and Passet 2000).

The labour market developments which cannot be related to actual changes in labour market institutions nevertheless show up in the NAIRU estimates from the OECD (2000a) (see Figure 1.2). 'Structural' unemployment rose in most of Europe until the mid-1990s and began to fall from then on. The sharp fall in the Spanish NAIRU is particularly remarkable. The USA experienced a falling NAIRU during most of the 1990s expansion; if one includes the years 2000 and 2001 in the estimation period, a further fall should show up in the NAIRU, since US unemployment continued to fall in 2000 without inflationary pressure emerging.

1.3   Interaction between monetary policy and wage bargaining

Even in the 1970s–1990s, Keynesianism was never quite dead. Some voices remained which claimed that there was such a thing as a persistent problem of lack of aggregate demand and that this lack of demand was at the root of high European unemployment (Riese 1995; Modigliani 1997; Betz 2001b; Collignon 2002a). Many of those Keynesian authors claimed that lower interest rates could help to get to a higher employment solution.[4] And they agreed on the necessity that wage developments should remain in line with increases in labour productivity. Collignon (2002a) even draws the connection between the NAIRU and monetary policy. In his model, it is the capital stock which limits inflation-free employment growth. Lower interest rates with

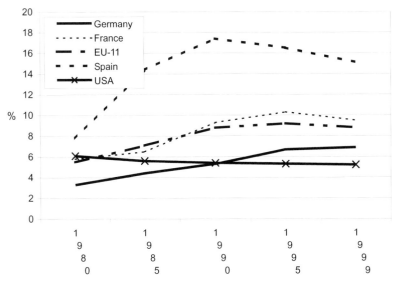

Figure 1.2   NAIRU estimates from the OECD, 1980–99
Source: OECD, *Economic Outlook* (2000a).

stable wages would lead to an investment boom, which could change the capital stock and thus help to shift the NAIRU downwards.

But the unease with the results from standard economic theory was not limited to economists of Keynesian origin, who had long disliked some of the extreme conclusions from Lucas' rational expectations revolution. As neither labour market institutions nor monetary policy seemed to live up to what standard theory had claimed, even economists not necessarily of a Keynesian background began to look for a way out. As the stagflation experience of the 1970s prevented them from returning to the simple Philips-curve Keynesianism of the 1960s and 1970s, they began to focus on the interaction of monetary policy and labour market institutions. And as one of the key features of the US expansion of the 1990s was that wage and consequently unit labour cost pressure remained low over most of the decade, the focus shifted to the question of how wages were determined. A wave of contributions following Hall and Franzese (1998) thus linked the theory of central bank independence and recent macroeconomic models with contributions which aimed at showing an influence of wage bargaining structures on macroeconomic outcomes.

To put it in a nutshell, these new contributions state that money is not neutral in the long run. As the central banks' behaviour or setup is anticipated by strategically acting economic actors, changes in monetary policy rules can change the private actors' behaviour in real terms. This change of behaviour then translates into changes in employment. Depending on the setup of the labour market – notably the number of bargaining unions and the substitutability of different types of labour – these effects vary.

This book is about these new developments in macroeconomics. But it is intended to be more than a mere survey; it also tries to ask what conclusions can be drawn from this new strand of literature for the real-world interaction of unions, employers and the central bank in EMU. To this end, this book questions some assumptions standard not only to the new interaction literature but also to textbook macroeconomic models which make their conclusions' practical relevance highly questionable. Then, linking the new literature on interaction of monetary policy and wage contracts with Keynesian considerations such as those from Riese (1995) or Collignon (2002a), it offers a new possible explanation for how the macroeconomy may work.

The book is organized as follows: Chapter 2 surveys the recent literature on interaction between monetary policy and wage bargaining. It then tries to judge which of the models are the most plausible, and contrasts their conclusions with the real- world experience of some selected European countries. Even the most plausible models do not seem able to explain the developments in all the country cases examined. Moreover, the quality of a fit between theory and empirics seems to vary with the size of the country in question: developments in small countries appear to be explained far better than those in large countries. While Soskice and Iversen (2000) and Coricelli, Cukierman and Dalmazzo (2000) (hereafter, SICCD) present a model in which falling nominal wages lead to increased aggregate demand and employment, this mechanism can be found to work only in Ireland and the Netherlands. For Germany, France, or EMU as a whole, wage deflation does not seem to bring any positive effects.

Chapter 3 then provides a possible explanation for why the models do not work for large economies. It is claimed that the heart of the problem lies with the assumption of a real balance effect. If the money supply is endogenously determined and money is not net wealth for the private sector, as can be well argued for the euro-zone, a real balance effect cannot be at work. Chapter 4 then develops *how* monetary policy can influence aggregate demand in a world without real balances, by influencing the relevant interest rates via changes of the short-term interest rate instrument. Chapter 5 then presents a macro-model of monopolistic competition without building on the real balance effect. It is shown that, in such a world, changes in the nominal wage level do not change aggregate demand or aggregate employment. Instead, monetary policy plays a central role in managing aggregate demand, while nominal wages play a key role in determining the price level.

While it is found that changes in the short-term interest rate can indeed influence aggregate demand, Chapter 6 qualifies this conclusion. It shows that in a world of endogenous money it is the holding of monetary assets which finances the macroeconomic capital stock. If the central bank does not want private investors to dump domestic monetary assets from their portfolios, it is constrained by financial markets to keep prices relatively stable. Thus as Riese (1995) puts it: the central bank has to act as a market participant. However, its degree of market power varies with the openness and size of the currency area it controls. A large central bank such as the ECB is found to have some discretion; but as nominal wages are central to price stability, the degree of this discretion is also limited by the unions' behaviour.

Chapter 7 finally returns to the question of how wage bargainers and the central bank interact. As stable (but not falling) nominal wages are a necessary, albeit not sufficient condition, for higher aggregate demand, it is only central bank and wage bargainers *together* who can guarantee stable prices *and* expanding output. A policy mix to yield optimal employment and inflation outcomes would combine stability-oriented wage demands with a monetary policy which is as expansionary as possible, given the constraints from financial markets. This final chapter further examines within a game-theoretic approach why this optimal policy mix is not necessarily reached: coordination problems, a failure to cooperate between European wage bargainers and the central bank as well as a central banker who is overly conservative and risk averse are proposed as possible explanations. It is concluded that in principle a social pact between unions, employers and the central bank could solve these problems, but that the European Macroeconomic Dialogue as initiated by the European Council at the Cologne Summit in 1999 lacks both the setup and the public acceptance to meet these ends.

Two strands are thus interwoven in this book, both of which are necessary to understand what is going on in EMU between wage bargainers and the central bank, but which might be of varying interest to different groups of readers. One strand is the narrow theory of interaction between monetary policy and wage bargainers, the other is the theoretical justification of the macroeconomic foundations used. The book is organised in a way that even those interested primarily in only one strand can read it and skip the other chapters. Those with a primarily political economic concern can read chapters 2, 5 and 7, those primarily interested in a theory of the macroeconomic mechanics of a system without exogenous outside money can read chapters 3, 4, 5 and 6. A reader with an interest in both strands should – of course – read the whole book.

2
Bargaining Structures and the Central Bank: Literature and Empirics

Economists' interest in the importance of labour market structures for macroeconomic outcomes is not new. Following Bruno and Sachs' (1985) seminal work on the negative correlation between the degree of 'corporatism' and the 'misery index' of an economy,[1] the late 1980s and early 1990s saw a tide of literature on this question. However, it was only in the late 1990s that a second tide of contributions linked the neo-corporatist literature with the economic research on central bank independence and monetary policy rules.

This chapter will trace the development from the early literature on bargaining structures and macroeconomic outcomes to the modern contributions depicting the interaction of bargaining structures and monetary policy. It will also give an overview of these interaction contributions and will judge to what extent the modern studies help us to understand the real-world policy interaction in the euro-zone. The chapter is organised as follows: Section 2.1 gives a very short overview of the early literature on bargaining structures. Section 2.2 then elaborates on the modern contributions as a special branch of this and classifies the modern branch according to the structure of the underlying economic model. Section 2.3 contrasts the modern contributions' conclusions with some empirical facts of the euro-zone economy. An Appendix (p. 46) considers issues of GDP growth and component accounting.

2.1 Early literature on bargaining structures

The early literature on bargaining structures stemmed from the experience of the oil price shocks in the mid- and late 1970s. Although the industrial countries were hit by a rather symmetric shock, the post-oil

11

shock adjustment differed widely. While some countries were able to get inflation under control quickly without too great an increase in unemployment, other countries suffered badly. As standard macro-economic models were not able to explain the international variations in the adjustments, social scientists began to examine the impact of alternative institutional structures on economic performance, finally also getting economists' attention regarding the relationship between bargaining structures and macroeconomic performance.

The corporatist hypothesis

Bruno and Sachs (1985) and others argued that 'corporatist' institutional arrangements facilitate bargaining between labour, management and the government. By producing purportedly implicit or explicit 'social con-tracts' in which unions restrained wage demands in exchange for policy concessions from the government, shocks could be dealt with more smoothly. Several empirical studies of the correlation between different indices of corporatism and macroeconomic performance seemed to underline this corporatist hypothesis. However, the literature at this point had two grave problems (Flanagan 1999, pp. 1156f.). First, as single-dimensional indexes of corporatism were often used, the empirical results were not able to show which feature of the labour market actually led to the superior macroeconomic outcome. Second, as the term 'corpo-ratism' is multidimensional and mostly only imprecisely defined,[2] this early literature did not offer economic explanations for how a certain outcome was reached.

The hump-shaped curve and standard externalities of wage increases

To escape these shortcomings, economists started to simplify their research agenda. They began to focus on the way wages were deter-mined between unions and employers, while governments largely dis-appeared from the story. Early contributions argued that wage increases in one sector (or by one union) yielded negative externalities for the rest of the economy. The more centralised unions were, the more they took these externalities into account. A real wage increase in one sector for example, would lead to increased input prices in other sectors, and thus to reduced employment in those sectors; a single cen-tralised union would take this effect into account when bargaining for wage increases, while a single-sector union would care only about its own wage increases. In their famous 'hump-shaped curve' contribu-tion, Calmfors and Driffill (1988) added to this argument the idea that only sufficiently large unions had the power to inflict macroeconomic harm; very small wage bargainers were only price-takers and did not have the bargaining power to push for wages high enough to cause unemployment. Consequently, not only very centralised, but also very decentralised unions could be expected to do well in macroeconomic terms.

The subsequent literature tried to model possible externalities of wage increases in one part of the economy on other sectors and tried to gather empirical evidence for or against the 'hump-shaped' hypothesis. While the empirical application is in most cases at least doubtful (many studies are not robust to slight changes in the ranking of single countries on the centralisation of wage bargaining scale (Flanagan 1999)), and many contributions neglect the fact that it is not the actual level of bargaining but rather the coordination of wage contracts which is important (Soskice 1990), the theoretical possibility that externalities are imposed by wage contracts remains acknowledged. In a survey, Calmfors (1993, p. 163) classifies seven types of externalities found in the recent literature:[3]

1. *Consumer price externality:* Wages are input costs for production. Wage increases thus lead to price increases, which then lead to a fall in other people's real disposable income.
2. *Input price externality:* Wage increases in firms producing intermediate goods increase input prices for other sectors, thus lowering output and employment there.
3. *Fiscal externality:* If wage increases lead to increased unemployment, tax receipts fall and costs for unemployment benefits rise. These costs have to be borne by other sectors.
4. *Unemployment externality:* Unemployment rising in one sector makes it harder for laid-off workers in other sectors to find a new job.
5. *Investment externality:* Higher wages might make new investments less profitable. This might depress future productivity and earnings of workers then employed in the company.
6. *Envy externality:* If welfare of individual workers depends negatively on the wages of others, every wage increase decreases the welfare of others.
7. *Efficiency–wage externality:* If the effort of individual workers depends on their relative wage, a wage increase in one sector might lead to decreasing work efforts in other sectors.

All of these externalities, when taken into account by wage bargainers, lead to lower wage demands and thus, according to the standard neo-classical model, both to lower real wages and to an equilibrium shift to the right along the standard negatively sloped labour demand curve, hence to increasing employment.

2.2   Monetary policy externality

However, the literature reviewed by Calmfors (1993) misses one channel of causation between wage restraint and unemployment which has been more recently emphasised by Fabrizio Coricelli, Alex Cukierman, Alberto Dalmazzo, Robert Franzese, Peter Hall, Torben Iversen and David Soskice, and which I will call the *monetary policy externality*: as money wage increases above productivity growth lead to inflationary pressure, the central bank may find itself forced to conduct a restrictive monetary policy in order to preserve the currency's internal value. This restrictive monetary policy has negative consequences not only for the single sector, but also for the whole economy. Thus one sector's wage increase might lead, via the central bank's reaction, to a contraction of aggregate demand. Given the strong effects that changes in the real interest rate empirically have on employment and output,[4] this externality might even be more important than the other externalities pointed out in the literature.

Following this argument, the magnitude of the resulting externality depends on how the central bank reacts to wage increases. At the same time, the degree to which wage bargainers take this reaction into account depends upon the bargaining structure, since the central bank's reaction gets internalised to a varying degree depending upon size and fragmentation of unions. When taking both of these dimensions into account, the new literature on the interaction of wage bargaining and monetary policy comes to an interesting conclusion, which distinguishes it from standard macroeconomic models: the way in which a central bank behaves (that is, the monetary policy rule it follows) can in fact have *permanent* real effects on output and employment even in a world in which all economic actors act completely rationally.

The unions' capacity to react to the central bank's signals

Hall and Franzese (1998) were the first to make this point, linking wage bargaining to the literature on central bank independence and disinflation. They argue that when a central bank starts to conduct a disinflationary monetary policy, the real costs in terms of output loss and unemployment might depend on the coordination of the wage setting process. As smaller wage setters might not be able to judge the consequences of their wage demands on monetary policy,[5] or might judge their own influence on the aggregate price level to be negligible, or might be afraid that other wage bargainers will push for higher wages in their respective sectors, thus putting pressure on the price level and on monetary policy, they might be less inclined to change their behaviour when the central bank signals a change in its policy stance.

In a highly coordinated wage bargaining process, on the other hand, the credible signal of the central bank to disinflate may be enough to induce employers and unions to settle for lower wage increases. Consequently, the central bank would not need as restrictive a monetary policy as in the uncoordinated case. The loss in output and employment would be lower. Thus, the more coordinated the wage bargaining, the lower the costs of disinflation.

When using cross-country econometric analysis for the years 1955–90, Hall and Franzese (1998) find strong empirical support for their claim that the combination of an independent central bank and a highly coordinated wage bargaining process yields the best results in terms of inflation and unemployment.

However, the Hall and Franzese (1998) approach has one drawback: though it nicely presents the argument in a verbal way, it does not propose a formal model with which one could approximate the actual effects of a shift either in monetary policy stance or in the coordination of wage bargaining.

Building on Barro–Gordon

This remaining gap is exactly what a set of recent literature tries to fill. The new contributions can basically be divided into two strands: one following the Barro and Gordon (1983) game-theoretic approach and the other building on macroeconomic models of monopolistic competition as presented in Blanchard and Kiyotaki (1987) or Blanchard and Fischer (1989).[6] The main contributions to the Barro–Gordon strand are Iversen (1999a)[7] (Figure 2.1), Grüner and Hefeker (1999) or Cukierman and Lippi (1999).

At the heart of the original Barro–Gordon setup lies the assumption that there is a negative relationship between real wages and employment. By *ex post* inflating the economy given a fixed nominal wage, the central bank thus would be able to increase employment (by lowering the real wage) above what would be its natural level.

The interaction between the private sector and the central bank is modelled as a two-stage game. In the first stage, the private sector contracts on a nominal wage. This nominal wage will be at a level at

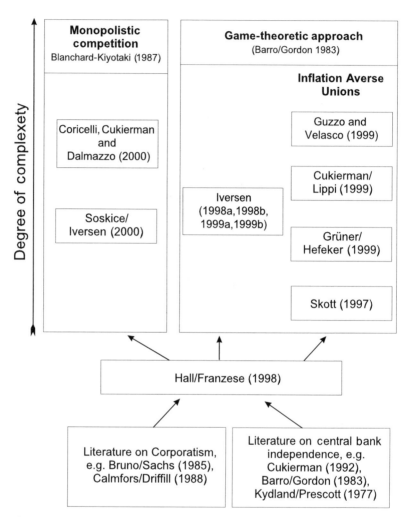

Figure 2.1 Classification of the modern literature on the interaction between wage bargainers and monetary policy

which the expected real wage (given the private sector's inflation expectations) exactly equals the marginal disutility of labour. If the private agents' expectations turn out to be correct, the resulting employment will be exactly at the natural level.

In a second stage, the central bank sets the rate of inflation. With the nominal wage known and fixed in the first stage, the central bank can set the real wage by setting the rate of inflation. With variations in the real wage, employment also changes. A short-term Phillips-curve emerges with higher inflation translating into higher employment. If the central bank is interested in high employment (that is, having a utility function which gives at least some weight to unemployment), it will inflate after the private sector has set its wages.

However, since the private sector has rational expectations, it knows by how much the central bank is going to inflate given the monetary authority's utility function. Private agents will thus set their wages in a way such that, with the monetary authority maximising its utility and choosing inflation accordingly, precisely the real wage initially desired by the private sector will result. Thus, in the end, employment will be at the natural level, while there will be inflation.

One conclusion of the basic Barro–Gordon approach is to appoint a central banker who does not care at all about employment. In this setting, the monetary authority does not have any incentive to inflate. As the private sector anticipates the conservativeness of the monetary authority, there is no need to anticipate any inflation. Consequently, wages are set so that natural employment is reached with stable prices.

In the new literature on the interaction of wage bargaining and monetary policy which builds on Barro–Gordon, the basic setup remains intact. In a first stage, unions with some monopoly power (depending on the substitutability between different types of labour and on the numbers of unions in the economy) choose their nominal wage demand. In a second stage, the central bank sets the rate of inflation at a level which maximises the bank's utility. Together with the nominal wage, this rate of inflation determines the real wage, which in turn determines output and employment in the economy. As unions are rational, they anticipate the central bank's reaction and set their wage demands accordingly.

The outcome in the new models with interaction of wage bargaining and monetary policy is more complicated than in the basic model. First, unions enter the picture, which have some monopoly power but at the same time care about unemployment. The private sector is not only concerned with 'correct' real prices as it was in Barro–Gordon, but also with employment. Guzzo and Velasco (1999) as well as Cukierman and Lippi (1999) also add inflation aversion to the unions' utility function. Besides the standard setting, Iversen (1999a) considers the possibility that unions also care about wage dispersion.

While the models' details differ from contribution to contribution, the main mechanism always remains the same within the strand building on Barro–Gordon: the highest employment outcome is the situation in which unions settle for the lowest possible real wage, as lower real wages imply higher employment via a negatively sloped labour demand curve. A setup with a certain degree of centralised wage bargaining with some degree of central bank conservatism is optimal so that this high employment point is achieved while inflation remains low.

Of the approaches reviewed here, Cukierman and Lippi (1999) is the one in which the basic features of Barro–Gordon are most easily recognisable, while at the same time it shows a vast array of results by changing the parameters of the model. In the Cukierman–Lippi setting, unions care to a varying degree for real wages and employment in their sector as well as for overall inflation. According to what they expect the central bank to do, and depending on their market position, they set a wage which consists of the full employment wage plus some wage premium. The higher the wage premium, the lower the employment – an approach which is also found in Guzzo and Velasco (1999) and Coricelli, Cukierman and Dalmazzo (2000). As unions know that a less conservative central bank would react to their wage increases by inflating the economy (which would deprive them of their real wage gain while they would have to bear the consequences of higher inflation), they are more restrained in their wage demands the *less* conservative the central bank is. A higher degree of conservatism thus leads to higher nominal wages and lower inflation, consequently to higher real wages and higher unemployment. As larger unions have to take into account the effects of their own wage demands on aggregate employment and thus the central bank's determination to inflate the economy, the more centralised wage bargaining is, the more pronounced will be this effect. A positive correlation between wage bargaining centralisation and unemployment thus emerges. This conclusion changes when unions become sufficiently inflation averse: in this case, sufficiently centralised unions constrain their wage demands so as to keep unemployment low enough for the central bank not to inflate. Consequently, the well-known hump-shaped curve emerges again.

The conclusion that unemployment is increased the more conservative the central bank is, can also be drawn from Guzzo and Velasco (1999). While their model is more complicated, adding explicitly profit-maximising firms which hire labour after unions have decided on their nominal wage rate and the central bank has reacted, the basic intuition remains the same: with inflation averse-individuals, a central bank that is more prone to inflate leads to wage restraint. Guzzo and

Velasco even conclude that the optimum output and employment are reached when the monetary authorities do not care at all for inflation. In this case, the central bank would be willing to choose any level of inflation in order to get the economy to its targeted output. As the unions want to prevent inflation, they will settle for the real wage compatible with this output target. Here inflation thus becomes the instrument with which the central bank can deter unions from higher wage demands (*sic*!).[8]

This conclusion changes in Iversen's (1999a) setting: Iversen's unions do not care about inflation, but only about real wages, employment and relative wage position. Here, it is the deterrence effect of higher unemployment which leads the unions to wage restraint. If the central bank is 'accommodating' and thus sets the rate of inflation so as to maximise employment, the standard Calmfors–Driffill hump-shaped curve emerges: in a very decentralised setting, the unions do not have price setting power, while at a very high degree of coordination they increasingly internalise the negative employment effects of their (real) wage increases.

On the other hand, when the central bank is 'non-accommodating' and unions feel a fall in demand for their labour not only because their real wages increase relative to the other sectors' real wages, but also because aggregate employment falls, the incentive for higher wage demands becomes weaker. Unions now have to internalise both effects. Consequently, the marginal benefits for a wage increase fall. Strategically reacting unions will thus exercise wage restraint. The degree of wage restraint is a function of bargaining coordination, since larger unions will have to take into account a larger effect of their own wage increases on aggregate employment.

In Iversen's (1999a) setting, this conclusion changes only when low wage dispersion additionally enters the unions' utility function. As a monopoly union might then try to bring low-skilled workers' pay closer to high-skilled workers' pay, nominal wage pressure would emerge. With a non-accommodating monetary policy, this would directly translate into real wage pressure and thus aggravate unemployment. Thus, when wage equality is the unions' aim, the positive effects of centralised wage bargaining disappear.

While Grüner and Hefeker (1999) do not discuss in detail what happens when a central bank's monetary policy changes, conclusions about this can be drawn from their analysis. They focus on the question of what changes in the transition from EMS to EMU when the central bank (Bundesbank) suddenly does not set the rate of inflation with regard to German unemployment, but with regard to unemployment in all EMU countries.[9] The setting is a basic Barro–Gordon setting, unions are inflation averse. Because the cost of a wage increase in EMU is to a certain extent externalised (with the central bank inflating the whole euro-zone in order to get employment up, which hurts all members of EMU instead of just causing unemployment in a single country), unions will bargain more aggressively under EMU than under EMS. A central bank which takes unemployment into account thus leads to higher unemployment and higher inflation than one that sets the rate of inflation regardless of unemployment. This result is close to that from Iversen's work.

Building on monopolistic competition and the real balance effect

The second strand of models tries not only to model the supply side as the ones building on Barro–Gordon do, but also explicitly to model aggregate demand. They do so by extending a Blanchard and Kiyotaki (1987) approach of monopolistic competition. So far, the contributions of Soskice and Iversen (2000) and Coricelli, Cukierman and Dalmazzo (2000) fall into this class. Here, the central bank's monetary policy is modelled by exogenously setting the nominal money stock M in reaction to the unions' nominal wage contracts. The price level is determined by how the monopolistically competitive agents choose to set their prices.[10]

Each firm i ($i = 1 \ldots n$) faces a demand function for its products y^D_i, which is a function of its own price P_i relative to the aggregate price level P and real aggregate demand y^D, which itself depends on real balances in the economy:

$$y^D_i = \frac{1}{n}\left(\frac{P_i}{P}\right)^{-\eta} y^D = \frac{1}{n}\left(\frac{P_i}{P}\right)^{-\eta}\frac{M}{P} \qquad (2.1)$$

With monetary policy being more 'conservative'[11] or more 'non-accommodating'[12] the central bank does not change the money stock when nominal wages change. Unions thus have the possibility of increasing aggregate demand by wage restraint: with falling nominal wages, prices fall and real balances increase. Increased real balances translate into higher aggregate demand, which then translates into higher employment. Unions which are able to act strategically thus have an incentive to restrain their wages, which results in lower inflation and higher employment when the central bank is sufficiently non-accommodating. Consequently, equilibrium employment in an economy with at least medium-sized wage bargainers is lower under a non-accommodating policy regime.

Under an accommodating monetary policy, on the other hand, the central bank accommodates whatever nominal wage increases unions and employers settle on. The nominal wage agreed upon thus does not have any influence on output or employment, and the unions' incentive for lower wage demands is consequently reduced.

In Coricelli, Cukierman and Dalmazzo (2000), a similar mechanism is at work. If the unions' degree of inflation aversion is sufficiently small, a higher degree of central bank conservativeness leads to lower unemployment and lower inflation: the unions can now influence aggregate employment by restraining their wage demands, just as in the Soskice–Iversen setting, and will do so. The more fragmented and thus the less centralised the wage bargaining is, the less the unions care about this monetary policy externality, and the less they are prone to restrain their wages. A special feature of Coricelli, Cukierman and Dalmazzo (2000) is the introduction of an 'ultra-conservative' central banker who not only does not react at all to wage increases as Soskice and Iversen's 'non-accommodating' central banker does, but who actually decreases money supply and thus aggregate demand when wages are rising. With such a banker, the deterrence effect is magnified and unions seek even lower wage settlements, thus increasing aggregate demand and employment while further decreasing inflation.

2.3   European empirics: does the theory fit?

Many of the contributions reviewed above offer some empirical evidence, mostly by regressing inflation and unemployment on some indices of central bank independence and bargaining coordination. The results generally give evidence for the theoretical part of the paper, thus contradicting each other as much as the underlying model. For example Iversen (1998a, 1998b, 1999a, 1999b) finds that a greater central bank conservatism leads to higher unemployment at very high degrees of coordinated wage bargaining and to lower unemployment for a medium degree of coordination. In his regressions, the effect for low degrees of coordination is not significant. Cukierman and Lippi (1999), on the other hand, find that at low levels of bargaining central-isation, unemployment increases with a more conservative central bank while at medium and high levels unemployment decreases the higher the degree of central bank conservatism.[13]

Such contradictary results are hardly surprising: the degree of wage bargaining centralisation as used by many of the studies does not always capture the relevant level of coordination. As Franzese (2001, p. 476) and Soskice (1990) document, there is disagreement over how to measure the degrees of union bargaining power and internalisation appropriately. And as Hancké (2002) shows for France, an economy with very decentralised wage bargaining structures can nevertheless show a high degree of wage bargaining coordination. For measuring central bank conservatism, we know from Mangano (1998) that indices for central bank independence also carry a high degree of subjectivity, which makes both their interpretation and their use as independent variables in econometric studies highly questionable. Viewing these uncertainties about the independent variables used in the studies together, it is not surprising that the results which emerge are not necessarily consistent.

But the lack of reliable panel regressions does not have to keep us *in principle* from using the models to explain what happens between monetary authorities and wage bargainers in Europe. However, as we cannot simply falsify the models with econometric tests as used by most of the authors (due to the data limitation caused by the subjectivity in possible indices used), we have to take a different approach. First, I will try to explore how *plausible* the chains of causation presented in the models are. In a second step, we can then see whether we manage to explain recent developments in the euro-area using the models which have not been *a priori* excluded.[14]

For the Barro–Gordon strand of literature, the first question is: how useful is the basic setup for analysing problems of the interaction of monetary policy and the private sector? What is startling is that especially active and former practitioners of monetary policy question the basic setup of the model.[15] First, it has to be assumed that the central bank which is not completely conservative has an incentive to push unemployment below its natural level. Blinder (1997, p. 14) writes:

Well, I can assure you that my central banker friends would not be surprised to learn that academic theories that assume that they seek to push unemployment below the natural rate then deduce that monetary policy will be too inflationary. They would doubtless reply, 'Of course. That's why we don't do it.' Therein lies the solution: direct the central bank to set $k = 1$ – that is, not to seek unemployment lower than the natural rate. In the world of practical central banking, this 'solution' is, I submit, adopted as if it were second nature.

And Goodhart (1994, p. 9) comments:

> [T]hat outcome seems inherently nutty, because the Central Bank itself *knows* from the outset that, if it plays this way, it will *fail* to improve employment and only generate inflation, so that it must be a stupid game for it to play at all.

Second, the Barro–Gordon simplification assumes that inflation is directly set by the central bank and is thus both target variable and instrument at the same time. This not only leaves us in the dark as to *how* monetary policy transmits to the real economy. It also abstracts from the possible problem of insufficient demand being stimulated by monetary policy, as it assumes that monetary policy influences prices and real activity *only* by changing prices and price expectations and thereby the private agents' labour supply decisions. This over-simplification leads Blinder (1997, p. 7) to conclude:

> To a practical central banker, [this assumption] seems downright silly, for it assumes away most of the uncertainties that define everyday life.

Third, deviations below the central bank's target rate of inflation can hardly be explained using Barro–Gordon. While deviations to the upside could always be the result of a central bank trying to reap gains from surprise inflation, there is no such argument for the downside: why should a central bank accept a rate of inflation below its target when it could easily choose a higher value and thereby even *increase* aggregate output and employment without further costs? Even a central bank which normally cares only about inflation should be expected to have such lexicographic preferences for increased output. The Barro–Gordon model might thus be insufficient for analysing monetary policy at times where actual inflation substantially undershoots target inflation. This is not irrelevant: if we take a look at the Bundesbank's record after 1984, when the bank moved to a 2 per cent target rate of inflation (Bundesbank 1995, p. 83), we find that over the three-year period from 1986 to 1988, inflation was sometimes significantly below the target rate of inflation (Figure 2.2). Japan experienced deflation for most of the second half of the 1990s; inflation in the

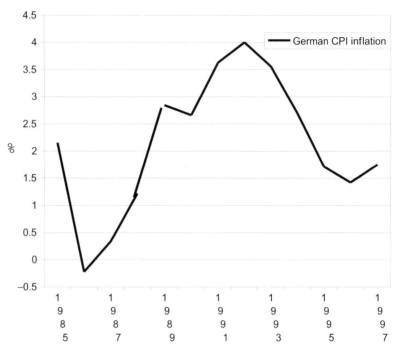

Figure 2.2   Germany: inflation, 1985–97
Source: Bundesbank (1998).

USA fell significantly below the Fed's implicit target in 2003. In late 2003, there was even a growing concern among policy makers about the dangers of deflation.[16]

So, the Barro–Gordon approach itself seems to abstract away important problems in monetary policy. This is probably the reason why in recent years, mainstream monetary theory has extensively moved away from using the Barro–Gordon approach. In Woodford's (2003) book which seems to have become the standard advanced textbook in monetary theory, not a single chapter is based on the Barro–Gordon approach. Instead, models in the tradition of Clarida, Gali and Gertler (1999) are used in which the central bank influences aggregate demand and supply not by setting inflation, but by setting the short-term interest rate.

The critique of the basic Barro–Gordon approach also applies to the augmented versions of the model. Approaches in which unions exhibit a certain degree of inflation aversion, exercising wage restraint in order to keep the central bank from inflating, would most likely cause even greater lack of understanding among practical policy makers – not only in the towers of the ECB but also at the unions' headquarters. The theoretical cause that unions are inflation averse is to a certain degree plausible:[17] first, how could policy makers be inflation averse without inflation-averse private actors? Any actual government's utility must derive from some combination of private actors' utilities. So if the central bank dislikes inflation, so must private actors. Second, as private actors hold non-fully indexed nominal assets or pension schemes, they might lose from inflation.

However, these considerations do not necessarily lead to the conclusion that unions have to behave in a way that reduces inflation. The very special results in the Barro–Gordon strand of literature on wage bargaining and monetary policy stem from the fact that the union is not able to influence real wages or employment at all since the central bank will in a second stage inflate precisely so that real wages remain at the level ensuring full employment. At the same time, inflation does not have any influence, not even in the very short run, on any real variables in the economy or on distribution. In the real world, these assumptions are problematic. Inflation does redistribute between different groups of society. If financial contracts are not indexed, creditors lose while debtors gain. As firms are usually debtors, some inflation might ease their debt burden and in the short run improve their financial position, which might lead to more employment in the very short run.

Moreover, empirically it is the holders of bonds and receivers of transfer incomes such as welfare and public pensions[18] who suffer most from inflation, as their incomes are not indexed and are usually adjusted only with a time lag. As their incomes are financed from taxes and social security contributions, unanticipated inflation would redistribute from them to active workers who carry the tax burden. Active workers, on the other hand, while of course empirically seeing their real wage position deteriorating in the process of high inflation, usually have most of their wealth invested either in their housing or in their human capital, assets the value of which should change with changes in the general price level.

Finally, a private sector inflation aversion does not necessarily imply inflation-averse wage bargainers. From a median-voter perspective, it is quite possible that pensioners, together with wealth owners and older workers, are in the majority and induce the government to install an inflation averse central banker while active union members (and thus union leaders) care far less about inflation.

It would thus be plausible that unions do not care about low levels of inflation, but become inflation averse only when the rate hits a certain threshold. The inflation a union would tolerate or even try to reach might well be above the social optimum. An ultra-liberal central bank using inflation as a deterrent could then bring inflation down only to this level preferred by the unions, not to the socially optimum level.

But the most important argument against a central bank using inflation as a deterrent against wage increases is an empirical one: the emerging conclusions as to how this influences unions' wage behaviour are highly dubious to anyone who has observed real-world interaction between wage bargainers and monetary authorities. Just imagine the Bundesbank having threatened German unions in the wake of the post-unification wage hike to lower interest rates as a punishment! As Calmfors (2001, p. 334) puts it:

> But yet the argument is an implausible one, as it would imply a situation where the typical trade union behaviour is to urge inflation-prone central banks to tighten monetary policy, so that unions would face less need to compromise on their real wage objectives. This has certainly not been the typical situation even in the Scandinavian countries, and is, of course, even less plausible in a situation with independent central banks, focusing on price stability as their prime objective.

This does not mean that unions do not care about inflation, but it seems to be more plausible that they have lexicographic preferences for low inflation – that is, preferring low inflation to high inflation, but only after their optimum solutions for unemployment and real wages have been found. This interpretation would also be in line with recent union statements: while unions stated at the advent of EMU that the euro would need to be stable, there has been no statement from labour representatives since the beginning of EMU that the ECB should tighten its monetary policy, even though inflation was running above the target ceiling of 2 per cent.

Consequently, from the approaches presented above, I will not concentrate further on those building on Barro–Gordon.[19] Instead, models building on a monopolistic competition such SICCD models seem to be better suited to explain what is going on in the euro-zone. In these models, the wage level influences the price level. It is not monetary policy alone which decides the price level or the rate of inflation. It could thus be more easily explained why monetary policy might miss its target rate of inflation even on the downside, as it is not one single economic actor who has the instrument in its hand.

But how much do those models really explain? If the SICCD analysis were correct, a shift from an accommodating to a non-accommodating monetary policy[20] should lower the equilibrium rate of unemployment in an economy with at least intermediate centralisation of wage bargaining. In addition, wage restraint should empirically lead to higher domestic demand, higher output and higher employment under a non-accommodating policy regime.

However, a closer look at a few key cases reveals that the explanatory range of this approach varies widely with the structural features of the economies examined. It especially seems to fit the empirics for small, open countries much better than rather large ones. To make my point, I will take a closer look at the macroeconomic development of the Netherlands and Ireland in the late 1990s, Italy and France in their disinflation phase prior to EMU and the German experience with wage restraint in the late 1990s. Though these cases might look like a random sample, they are carefully chosen. The Netherlands and Ireland look like model cases in which wage restraint exercised by unions led to a substantial reduction in unemployment. Italy and France provide two cases in which economies with an intermediary coordinated wage bargaining system underwent a shift from an accommodating to a non-accommodating monetary policy. Germany, finally, is a large economy under a non-accommodating monetary regime, in which the unions' wage restraint as experienced in the late 1990s should clearly yield the predicted increases in employment.

In addition, as can be seen from Table 2.1, Germany, France, Italy, Ireland and the Netherlands cover most of the cases in which unit labour costs fell relative to EU-12 from the moment the 'hard' phase of EMS began to 2001.[21] In fact, the only other cases are Austria and Finland, which have not been members of EU and EMS for all of the period but joined the European Union only in 1995.

Monetary policy: accommodating or not?

One problem with the empirics of an accommodating or non-accommodating monetary policy is that this notion is not easily measurable. It is not only the result of a legal framework, but is also influenced by the actual political landscape and the actual persons running the institution. For example, the legal framework of the German Bundesbank has not substantially changed since its

Table 2.1   Unit labour costs (ECU) in EU-11 countries, 2001, as a multiple of 1987/79 unit labour costs

Country	Unit labour costs 2001/1987	Relative to EU-11
Austria	1.29	0.97
Belgium	1.45	1.09
Finland	1.08	0.82
France	1.26	0.95
Germany	1.31	0.99
Greece	1.66	1.25
Ireland	1.26	0.95
Italy	1.22	0.92
Luxembourg	1.45	1.09
Netherlands	1.36	1.03
Portugal	2.18	1.64
Spain	1.59	1.20
EU-11	1.32	1.00
	2001/1979	
Netherlands	1.79	0.88
EU-11	2.03	1.00

Source: European Commission (2002).

foundation. However, the Bundesbank's monetary policy has varied considerably since then.

How should the degree of accommodating monetary policy be measured? Iversen (1999a) uses two alternative measures: the degree of the central bank's legal independence along the lines of indices such as that of Cukierman (1992) and a hard currency index which measures whether a currency's nominal exchange rate is relatively appreciating or depreciating.

If one takes a closer look, both indicators are highly problematic. A change in the monetary policy stance is not necessarily reflected in a change in its legal status. According to most observers, the Bank of Japan has been following a monetarist stance since the mid-1970s (Iversen 1999a, p. 59). Yet, it became fully independent only in the late 1990s. In France, monetary and fiscal policy switched to a non-accommodating *franc fort* stance in 1982 after the Keynesian experiment of the early Mitterrand years failed. Yet, the French central bank was not made fully legally independent until 1993, when France prepared to enter EMU (Kilponen 2000, p. 161).

The hard currency index has another problem: as long as inflation differs greatly among industrialised countries, one could expect that the medium or long-term inflation outlook (and thus the monetary policy stance) would strongly influence the nominal exchange rate.[22] In times when inflation converges to low and stable rates in most of the industrialised world, however, the hard currency index becomes an increasingly unreliable indicator for how non-accommodating a monetary policy is. The euro, for example, lost roughly 20 per cent of its value *vis-à-vis* the US dollar from the beginning of EMU until the summer of 2001. However, one could hardly argue that European monetary policy has been more accommodating than US monetary policy. Not only was inflation in EMU below the US figure, but the Fed also showed much more concern for output stabilisation and less concern for inflationary pressures than did the ECB. Economists offered a wide range of explanations for this depreciation of the euro. However, hardly any model works with an expectation of higher rates of inflation in the euro-area than in the USA.

Consequently, it seems most appropriate to judge monetary policy not by a single quantitative indicator, but by studying each country in detail. To this end, one should consider the following indicators, which hint at a shift to a less accommodating monetary policy stance:

1. A credible (and *ex post* achieved) shift to a lower (implicit or explicit) *inflation target*. This of course can be accompanied by changes in the central bank's legal framework. However, legal change is not a necessary condition for a change in the policy stance.
2. If a country has credibly pegged its currency to another currency: a shift by the *anchor country to a less accommodating policy stance.*
3. *Pegging the domestic currency to an anchor currency with a less accommodating policy stance.* However, such a peg is a shift to a less accommodating stance only when no use of frequent realignments is subsequently made.

Taking these points together, for European countries, the development of the EMS offers potential shifts in monetary policy. The EMS began in 1979; though symmetrically constructed, it developed towards a DM-bloc in which other members had to follow the Bundesbank's monetary policy. During the early years, however, hardly any EMS member committed to a strict pegging policy without devaluation *vis-à-vis* the German mark. The Netherlands is the remarkable exception.[23] After the first realignments in 1979,[24] the Dutch guilder followed every revaluation of the German mark within the EMS.[25]

German monetary policy itself became less accommodating in the early 1980s. Not only did the Bundesbank continuously lower the rate of inflation that they considered 'inevitable'[26] until German inflation reached what the Bundesbank considered to be price stability in 1984 (Bundesbank 1995, p. 83), it also became less concerned with output considerations. After the 1973 oil price shock, the Bundesbank disinflated only gradually. It took several years until inflation was brought back to 2 per cent. In 1974, in both their policy action and their remarks, the Bundesbank still gave more weight to developments in the real economy than it did in the 1990s. The slowing of business activity in 1974 led the Bundesbank at least partly to accommodate price increases (Bundesbank 1974, p. 17):

> Under the influence of the growing weakness of business activity and the first signs of progress in fighting inflation, a change was made in the last quarter of 1974; the target became a slightly faster rate of monetary growth, which was publicly announced towards the end of the year.

In 1990, when a demand shock from German reunification hit the German economy, the Bundesbank reacted less flexibly and thus less accommodatingly. Though as Bernanke *et. al.* (1999, p. 74) illustrate, the Bundesbank was well aware that under the exceptional circumstances, its target inflation of 2 per cent was hard to achieve, it altered neither its stance nor its target. Between the mid-1970s and the early 1990s, the Bundesbank had become less accommodating.

With their currencies being pegged to the mark, the countries of the core EMS-group followed the Bundesbank's move to a less accommodating policy. The other EMS countries, notably those who finally entered EMU together with Germany, shifted to a non-accommodating policy at the moment they joined the core of EMS (that is, at the moment they gave up the policy of frequent realigning). For most EMS members, this was the case in 1987 with the Basel–Nyborg accord. With this accord, it was agreed to use monetary policy in EMS countries with the goal of reaching convergence of inflation rates within the EMS. In addition, it was agreed to limit future realignments in both frequency and in size (Collignon 1994, pp. 36f).

Against the background of Coricelli, Cukierman and Dalmazzo's (2000) approach, who dub a central banker 'ultra-conservative' when he reacts to inflationary wage contracts with a contractory monetary policy move, one could even argue that the EMS created an ultra-conservative monetary policy environment for all countries except Germany, even if German monetary policy was merely conservative: when prices rose faster in other EMS countries than in Germany, this increased the risk of some devaluation in the country concerned. Consequently, risk premiums for that country's currency increased and the respective central bank had to raise interest rates.[27] Thus, an increase in wages and prices in countries other than Germany tightened monetary policy in this country via this market mechanism more than a merely non-accommodating monetary policy would have done.

Small European countries: the Netherlands and Ireland

Both Ireland and the Netherlands used to have unemployment performances among the worst in the European Union. Figure 2.3 shows the development of unemployment in the Netherlands: unemployment peaked in 1982 at 11.2 per cent, way above EU-11 unemployment which stood at 7.3 per cent. This peak came long before European unemployment peaked in the late 1990s. From 1982 onwards, however, unemployment fell, with the exception of a short rise in the 1994 recession. At the end of the twentieth century,

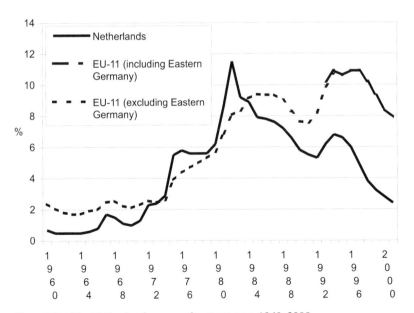

Figure 2.3   The Netherlands: unemployment rate, 1960–2000
Source: European Commission (2002).

unemployment in the Netherlands was far below unemployment in most other European countries.

Ireland (Figure 2.4) shows a similar (even if differently timed) development. Irish unemployment peaked at 16.9 per cent in 1985. While most European countries and the EU-11 as a whole experienced a steep increase of unemployment in the years prior to 1985 (when it peaked for EU-11 slightly above 10 per cent), the rise was even more pronounced in Ireland. However, while the trend for European unemployment was still upwards after 1985, Irish unemployment began a steady decline, interrupted only by the recession which followed monetary tightening by the Bundesbank in the wake of German reunification at the beginning of the 1990s. At the end of the twentieth century, Irish unemployment was far below EU-11 unemployment, with labour shortages occurring in certain sectors.

Given wage bargaining structures in both Ireland and the Netherlands, these developments seem to be nicely in line with what the Soskice–Iversen approach predicts. In the Netherlands, wage contracts are predominantly set at a sector level. In addition, institutionalised consultations between employers, unions and the governments at a national

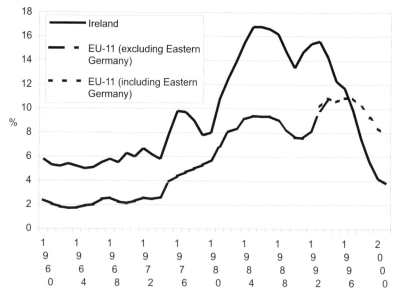

Figure 2.4   Ireland: unemployment rate, 1960–2000
Source: European Commission (2002).

level help to coordinate wage contracts (Horn, Scheremet and Ziener 1997, pp. A23ff). Consequently, most studies consider wage bargaining in the Netherlands as at least intermediately coordinated (Soskice and Iversen 2000, p. 268).

Ireland has a long history of shifts in the wage bargaining system. Until 1970, wage contracts were agreed upon predominantly at a sector level. In the 1970s, it was attempted to use centralised wage bargaining in order to align wage contracts with macroeconomic objectives. From 1970 to 1978, seven *National Wage Agreements* were concluded which were supposed to ensure the international competitiveness of Irish business. With the second oil price shock and the global recession at the beginning of the 1980s, this system seemed to be too inflexible and was abandoned. Wage bargaining was shifted to sector or even plant level. Only after a new government came into power in 1987 was wage bargaining again recentralised. Since then, *Programmes for Economic and Social Progress* commit government, employers and unions to different measures over a period of several years. The wage guidelines agreed upon in these national programmes are then modified at a plant level (Horn, Scheremet and Ziener 1997, pp. A18ff). Ireland can thus be considered to have had a highly centralised wage bargaining system from 1987 onwards.

Both Ireland and the Netherlands experienced a shift to a less accommodating monetary policy. For the Netherlands, this period can be considered as beginning some time between the first realignment of EMS currencies in 1979, in which the guilder did not follow the German mark's appreciation, and the realignment in late 1981, in which the guilder followed the German mark's appreciation of 5.5 per cent. For Ireland, the shift can be dated to the time just before the last large EMS realignment in 1987.[28]

Just as the Soskice–Iversen model would predict, wage contracts began to moderate as soon as monetary policy became non-accommodating. As Figure 2.5 shows, Dutch unit labour costs relative to the rest of the EU-11 fell from 1978 onwards. In Ireland, unit labour costs started to fall in 1987 (see Figure 2.6). As we can see in Figures 2.3 and 2.4, this was also roughly the time when unemployment in the Netherlands and Ireland started to develop more favourably than in the rest of the EU-11. NAIRU estimates as from the OECD (2000b) show that the equilibrium unemployment in the Netherlands and Ireland shifted downwards a few years after the shift to a less accommodating monetary policy. Only when unemployment was so low in 2000 that serious labour shortages in certain sectors became evident did relative unit labour costs rise again. Thus, the Netherlands and Ireland seem to be nice examples illustrating the mechanisms at work in the Soskice–Iversen model.

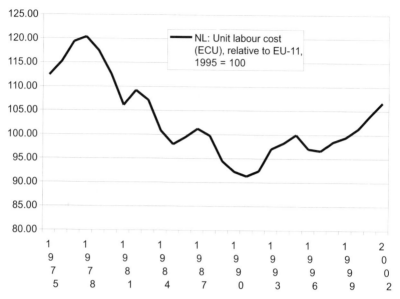

Figure 2.5   The Netherlands: development of unit labour costs (ECU) relative to the EU-11, 1975–2002
Source: European Commission (2002).

This conclusion also seems to be underscored when we take a look at the correlation of unit labour cost developments and output gaps in the years following the respective wage development in the two countries. Figures 2.7 and 2.8 plot on the horizontal axis annual changes of nominal unit labour costs and on the vertical axis the average output gap[29] in the two years following the respective change in unit labour costs. As we can see, in both countries unit labour cost increases below 2 per cent (which can be seen as the Bundesbank's target rate of inflation) are generally associated with higher (positive) output gaps. The relationship seems to be both strongers and more significant in Ireland, where unit labour cost changes explain almost half of the output gap.

Disinflation in France

Ireland and the Netherlands have not been the only countries in Europe in which a shift to a less accommodating monetary policy has induced unit labour costs to fall relative to other European countries.[30] After the adoption of the *franc fort* policy in the early 1980s, France

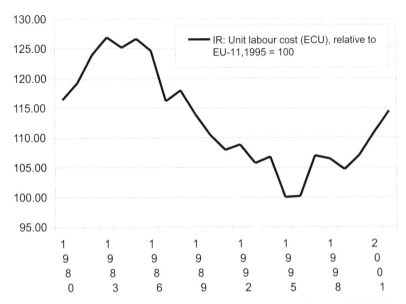

Figure 2.6   Ireland: development of unit labour costs (ECU) relative to the EU-11, 1980–2001
Source: European Commission (2002).

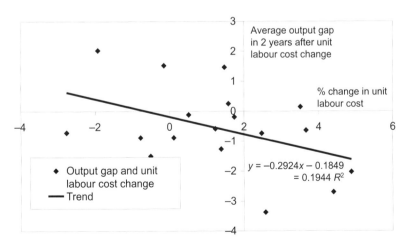

Figure 2.7   Unit labour cost developments and output gaps, The Netherlands, 1980–97
Source: European Commission (1998).

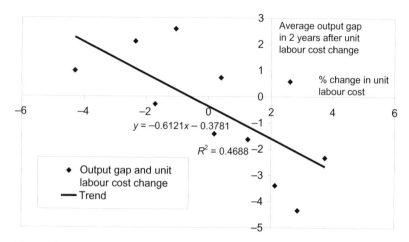

Figure 2.8   Unit labour cost developments and output gaps, Ireland, 1987–97
Source: European Commission (1998).

regained competitiveness through internal adjustment rather than frequent devaluations of the French franc. Thus, France could also be a case that fits nicely into the Soskice–Iversen explanation.

Though most older studies would consider France as having a relatively uncoordinated wage bargaining system, this is not necessarily the best description. As Hancké (2002) argues, wage setting in France is indeed *de facto* strongly coordinated even though bargaining takes place at the plant level. A relatively small number of large, internationally operating companies cover a large part of the workforce. Those companies set wages[31] for their employees in line with labour cost developments in plants which the firms are operating abroad. The rest of the respective sector in France then broadly follows these wage agreements. As many large French companies are often operating in the same foreign markets, and a large part of the foreign labour cost developments stem from exchange rate movements, the resulting wage agreements are more coordinated than uncoordinated. The overall level of coordination in French wage bargaining is thus at least intermediate.

This result would also help to explain unit labour cost developments for France (see Figure 2.9). From the adoption of the *franc fort* policy in 1982, unit labour costs started to fall relative to the EU-11.[32] This would be in line with wage setters being able to react strategically to the new policy stance. However, if one considers the French unemployment per-

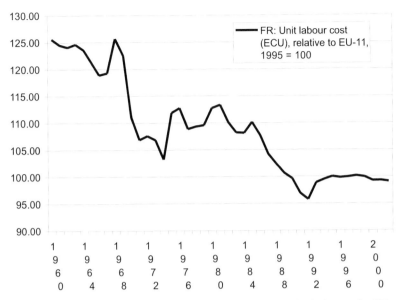

Figure 2.9 France: development of unit labour costs (ECU) relative to the EU-11, 1960–2000
Source: European Commission (2002).

formance (see Figure 2.10), one cannot see any improvement compared to the EU-11 performance. Instead, French unemployment, which used to follow EU-11 unemployment rather closely, actually began to top EU-11 unemployment in the mid-1980s. Somehow, wage restraint in France did not produce the favourable effects which should have been expected given the Soskice–Iversen model.

Plotting the output gaps for France against changes in unit labour cost (Figure 2.11), one can see that the relationship is less strong than in the case of Ireland and the Netherlands, and by far less significant. Moreover, the two data points showing the large positive output gaps represent the years 1988 and 1989, after which German reunification followed in 1990, bringing strong positive output gaps for most European countries as demand suddenly surged.

Disinflation in Italy

Another example of deflating unit labour costs relative to the rest of the EU-11 is Italy (Figure 2.12). Having had an experience of rapidly rising nominal wages and rising unit labour costs following the oil price shock in 1973, with GDP inflation topping 20 per cent, Italy managed to bring

38

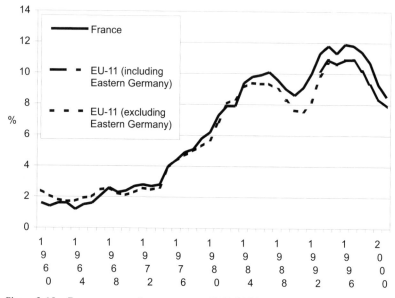

Figure 2.10 France: unemployment rate, 1960–2000
Source: European Commission (2002).

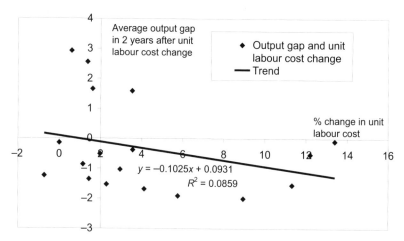

Figure 2.11 Unit labour cost developments and output gaps, France, 1980–97
Source: European Commission (1998).

down both inflation and unit labour cost increases until it entered EMU in 1999. With the advent of EMU, however, the country's labour costs were still rising faster than those of its partner countries. Italy consequently had frequently to devalue within the EMS. As wages were linked to inflation via an indexation clause (*scala mobile*) and a devaluation usually causes import prices to rise, competitiveness gains from devaluation usually quickly diminished. In addition, the chaotic, fragmented and hardly institutionalised bargaining process (Horn, Scheremet and Ziener 1997, p. A22) regularly led to wage increases incompatible with price stability and growth. This situation changed only with the Agreement on Wage Performance in July 1992 and July 1993 (Padoan 1998, p. 112). Not only was the *scala mobile* abandoned, but clear rules for wage bargaining were also established. In addition, a regular, bi-annual meeting between unions, employers and the government was established. This new setup made it possible for Italy to devalue sharply in 1992, when it dropped out of the EMS[33] without re-igniting a wage–price spiral. In the years to come, wage demands were low enough to keep Italy's unit labour costs from rising again.

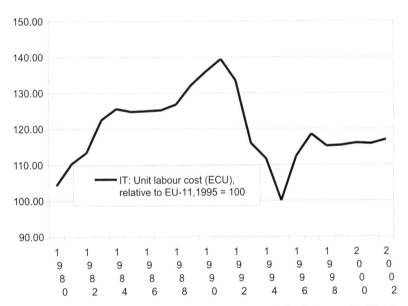

Figure 2.12   Italy: development of unit labour costs (ECU) relative to the EU-11, 1980–2002
Source: European Commission (2002).

It is difficult to tell when precisely Italy shifted to a non-accommo-dating monetary policy regime. On the one hand, real interest rates rose sharply at the beginning of the 1980s (Collignon 1998, p. 124), hinting at a tightening of the monetary policy stance. On the other, fiscal policy remained very expansive until the beginning of the 1990s (Padoan 1998, p. 110). In terms of accommodating policy, one could interpret these facts as a non-accommodating monetary policy from the early 1980s on and a compensating fiscal policy until the early 1990s. It is also possible that lax fiscal policy partly covered up unemployment, which would have emerged had fiscal policy been non-accommodating as well. Wage bargainers would have antici-pated this fiscal policy stance. Thus, in terms of the Soskice–Iversen model, we can speak of a non-accommodating macroeconomic policy environment from 1990 on.

If we now take a look at unit labour cost developments in Italy (Figure 2.12), the picture so far again fits the Soskice–Iversen explana-tion. Italy, from the early 1990s on a country with an at least interme-diately coordinated wage bargaining system, experienced a fall of unit labour costs relative to its European trading partners as soon as the macroeconomic environment shifted to a non-accommodating stance. However, again as in the case of France, the macroeconomic rewards were not as anticipated. Unemployment did not develop more favourably than in the rest of the EU-11 (Figure 2.13). Instead, in 1999 it was still above the euro-zone average, though it had pretty much converged to that average in earlier years.

Wage restraint in Germany

At last, a look at Germany might be illustrative (Figure 2.14). Though Germany did not experience a clear shift in its monetary policy stance, one could argue that monetary policy became less accommodating over time. In addition, Germany shows a parallel development to that of France and Italy: unit labour costs relative to EU-11 were falling in the late 1990s (see Figure 2.15), but the employment situation deterio-rated. Though wage developments were more than moderate (in fact, during some years, unit labour costs were not only falling relative to trading partners, but were doing so even in absolute terms), unemploy-ment in the late 1990s even deteriorated compared to EU-11 partners (Figure 2.16).

With German wage bargaining as a classical case of relatively highly coordinated wage bargaining (even if not centralised), at least the fall in unit labour costs could be explained by unions trying to increase

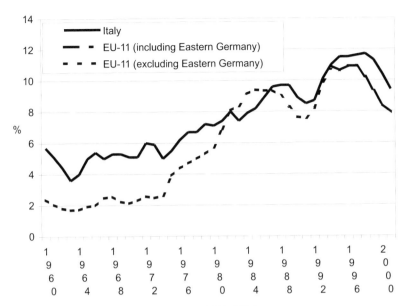

Figure 2.13   Italy: unemployment rate, 1960–2000
Source: European Commission (2002).

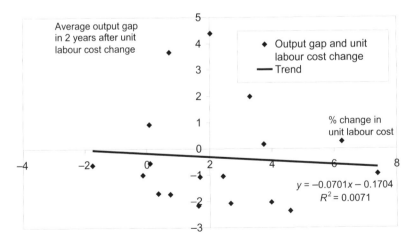

Figure 2.14   Unit labour cost developments and output gaps, Germany, 1980–97
Source: European Commission (1998).

employment. However, somehow aggregate demand (and thus output) does not seem to have picked up as one would suspect given the Soskice–Iversen approach. A look at the relationship between unit labour cost developments and subsequent output gaps underscores this point (Figure 2.14): the correlation between unit labour cost developments and the output gap for Germany is extremely weak and not very significant. The two points showing positive output gaps with wage restraint represent the wage development in the years 1988 and 1989, the reaction thus including 1990, the year in which Germany was reunited. It is hard to argue that the surge in demand in 1990 was due to wage restraint in the two preceding years. Instead, one would have to admit that the reunification shock caused most of the increase in domestic demand.

Explanatory range of the Soskice–Iversen approach

Thus, the Soskice–Iversen model (and thus also the Coricelli–Cukierman–Dalmazzo model, if one views monetary policy in the EMS as sufficiently conservative) seems to explain the performance in terms

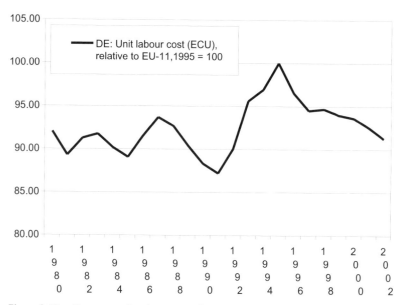

Figure 2.15 Germany: development of unit labour costs (ECU) relative to the EU-11, 1980–2002
Source: European Commission (2002).

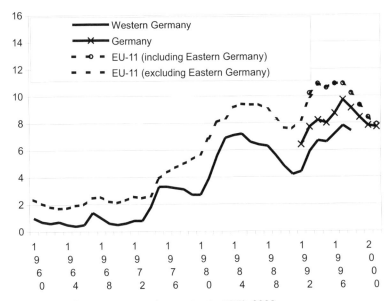

Figure 2.16   Germany: unemployment rate, 1960–2000
Source: European Commission (2002).

of employment nicely for small open economies in which unions exercise wage restraint. With falling nominal labour costs (relative to the rest of EMU), equilibrium employment in these economies seems to have increased. At the same time the approach seems to do much worse in explaining the development in large economies such as France, Italy or Germany.

A possible explanation for this selective performance of the approach becomes evident if one takes a closer look at the current account development of the small countries in which wage costs have declined: their current account surpluses exploded in line with their unemployment reduction. Figure 2.17 illustrates the importance of the current account development for the growth performance of small EMU countries.[34] Almost half of Ireland's admittedly impressive growth performance stems from increased current account surpluses. For the Netherlands, the figure is roughly 25 per cent. However, for the latter, one has to take into account that most of the Netherlands' real devaluation and improvement in the unemployment situation took place during the late 1980s and not during the 1990s. Still, if the Netherlands had not experienced the current account stimulus and thus growth contributions from abroad during the 1990s, growth would not have been much higher than in Germany.

Hence, a large part of the reduction of unemployment in Ireland and the Netherlands was not brought about by an increase in domestic demand, as would have been the case if the real balance effect modelled by Soskice and Iversen (2000) had been at work. Instead, the progress in battling unemployment was brought about by simple real devaluation against the trading partners in EMU! Ireland and the Netherlands have just been engaging in a beggar-thy-neighbour policy. As nominal exchange rates are fixed within EMU, this has taken place not by nominal, but by real devaluation.

This would also explain why the results to be expected from Soskice and Iversen's model did not show up in the cases of Germany, Italy and France: as those countries have too big a weight in EMU (or earlier, in EMS) relative to their trading partners to be involved successfully in competitive (real) devaluation, even under 'non-accommodating' monetary policy, wage restraint does not necessarily lead to increased aggregate demand and increased employment here. Instead, wage restraint here might even depress domestic demand. Empirically, the proclaimed real balance effect simply does not seem to be at work. This

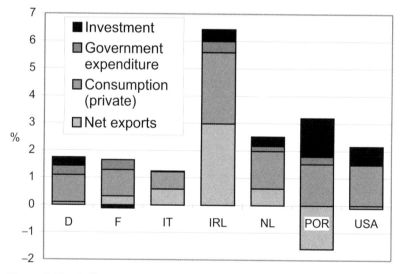

Figure 2.17 Different components' contribution to GDP growth, various countries, 1990–8
Source: OECD, *Economic Outlook*.

claim is further strengthened if one regards unit labour cost development ments and subsequent output gaps in the euro-zone as a whole (Figure 2.18). Only once, for the wage development of 1988, was wage restraint followed by a positive output gap (and we have to remember that the reaction to the 1988 wage restraint as plotted includes the extraordinary year 1990). In all other occasions, wage restraint was followed by negative output gaps.

Before I turn to the question of why the real balance effect does not work in the real world as envisioned by Soskice and Iversen (and many standard macroeconomic models), I will briefly underline for which cases (and why) the Soskice–Iversen approach is a suitable analytical tool.

At the centre of SICCD reasoning is the wage bargainers' capability to increase demand for their products (and thus labour) by restraining their wage demands. This is clearly the case for a small, very open economy. In an economy which is closely integrated in the world market (and/or has a large share of imports and exports in its GDP), the price level is to a large extent determined by the world price level and the exchange rate. If the central bank now credibly pegs its currency to the currencies of the country's main trading partners, the rate of inflation is to a large extent determined by the trading partners' rates of inflation. In this setting, unions can easily change the relative price of their labour *vis-à-vis* their trading partners' price of labour simply by lowering their wage demand. In this case, a change in

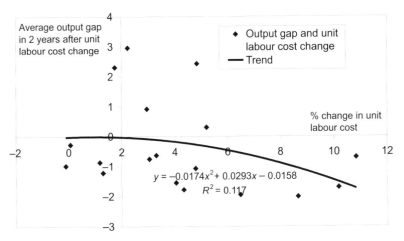

Figure 2.18   Unit labour cost developments and output gaps, EU-11, 1980–98
Source: European Commission (1998).

nominal wages translates to a large extent into a change in real wages. With real wages (and thus relative prices of the country's products) falling, foreign demand for the country's goods and labour increases.

Thus, one could also interpret real balances in the aggregate demand function as in Soskice and Iversen (2000) as a parable for international demand for domestic goods being a function of those goods' relative (and hence in a fixed exchange rate regime nominal) price. While the model thus becomes a suitable analytical tool for the case of a small open economy with fixed exchange rates, one should be very careful in drawing conclusions for a large, relatively closed economy with flexible exchange rates such as EMU. A surplus in the current account of the euro-zone in the magnitude of the Netherlands' 2001 surplus in the current account of 5.3 per cent of GDP or Ireland's 2001 surplus in the trade of goods and services of 14.7 per cent of GDP would not only provoke serious disputes with the rest of the world, which would inevitably have to run an accordingly high trade balance deficit. If one believes in a long-term adjustment of nominal exchange rates towards a balanced current account, such a situation would not be sustainable since a real depreciation would be counteracted by a subsequent gradual nominal appreciation, and the current account would balance again.

Appendix 2.1:   GDP Growth and Component Accounting

Component accounting of GDP growth, as it is used in this chapter, is a method of showing from which demand component an observed increment in GDP stems. If one adheres to a supply-side perspective of the economy, component accounting can be used to show how additional output is used – as investment, government or private consumption, or for a change in the current account. This way of breaking down growth into its determinants is widely used in applied economics as in the regular growth estimations of German economic research institutes for the German economy. However, as component accounting is not part of the general economics curriculum, I will describe in this appendix how growth components are computed and how the figures thus obtained are to be interpreted.

Starting from

$$Y_t = C_t + I_t + G_t + CA_t \qquad (A.1)$$

with Y as output, C as consumption, I as investment, G as government consumption and CA as the current account position or net exports, one can derive the growth contribution of each of GDP's components X (C, I, G or CA) as:

$$growth^X = \frac{X_t - X_{t-1}}{Y_{t-1}} \tag{A.2}$$

From (A.1) it follows that one can add up the single growth components to obtain GDP growth:

$$\hat{Y} = \frac{Y_t - Y_{t-1}}{Y_{t-1}} = growth^C + growth^I + growth^G + growth^{CA} \tag{A.3}$$

In steady-state growth, the contribution from private consumption, government consumption and investment would exactly equal their share of GDP. However, the contribution from changes in the current account would be 0 as on a steady-state growth path the current account itself would be balanced all the time (otherwise, the economy would accumulate ever-growing external debt or external assets) and thus not change.

Contributions to GDP growth from the current account can come about only if the absolute current account deficit or surplus changes. Thus, if one country experiences over a longer period a large contribution from its current account to its GDP growth, its current account position is constantly improving. Such a policy is nothing else than a beggar-thy-neighbour policy as it then drains demand from the country's trade partners.

3
The Real Balance Effect: Shortcomings

Why does wage restraint not increase domestic demand, as proclaimed in the SICCD models? In this chapter, I will argue that the real balance effect which is at the heart of the above models may not work as assumed. Falling prices do not necessarily and automatically increase aggregate domestic demand, as the real balance effect proclaims. It is not a coincidence that the real balance effect does not work: I will show that, for institutional and theoretical reasons, it *cannot* play a significant role in a world of modern central banking as we know it from the euro-zone, post-war Germany or the USA.

The reason for this is that in a modern monetary economy, basically all of the money in circulation is *endogenous inside money*. The term 'endogenous' refers to the fact that money is created only in an interaction between private agents, commercial banks and the central bank and that monetary authorities thus cannot increase or decrease the amount of money in circulation at will. 'Inside money' refers to the fact that the money stock cannot be seen as net wealth for the private sector.

With the nominal money stock not exogenously fixed, a change in prices does not necessarily change the real money stock. Instead, it is plausible that nominal money holdings move proportionally with price level changes. Consequently, it is not clear that the amount of credits granted or demanded for investment purposes changes with changing prices. With the money stock not being net wealth, a change in the price level does not change the private sector's net wealth. If private real wealth remains unchanged and incomes change proportionally to the price level, there is no reason why changing prices should influence real consumption demand.

This chapter will explore these ideas in greater detail. It is organised as follows. I will first quickly review the real balance effect in its two forms: the *Keynes effect* influencing investment demand and the *Pigou effect* influencing consumption demand (Section 3.1). Both effects play two central roles in macroeconomic models: explaining the both effects of monetary policy and how a monetary economy finds its equilibrium (by balancing aggregate demand and aggregate supply). In Sections 3.2–3.3 I will explore from both a theoretical as well as an empirical point of view whether these effects are a satisfactory representations for monetary policy.

Of course, assumptions about the working of an economy are commonplace (and necessary) in economics, and models are usually not criticised for allegedly 'unrealistic' assumptions. However, if a single assumption can be traced to be *central* for a certain conclusion, the conclusion is not evident on an empirical basis and the assumption has logical flaws, it might be time to explore economic models free from that assumption. I will show that this is precisely the case for the real balance effect. There thus is a strong case against building macroeconomic models centred around the real balance effect. Consequently, I will propose an alternative in Chapter 5.

These conclusions are not only of importance for the interaction of monetary policy and wage bargaining, as will be laid out in more detail in later chapters of this book. They also cast doubts on the ability of standard macroeconomic models such as standard (old) Keynesian IS-LM, the neo-classical synthesis (AS-AD) or the New Classical to represent real-world economic mechanisms, as these models also rely heavily on the real balance effect. This is not the main topic of this book, but might be of interest to some readers. The Appendix (p. 232) will therefore explain in detail what role the real balance effect plays for the conclusions of standard economic textbook models. More recent models, such as Clarida, Gali and Gertler (1999), and Romer (1999, 2000), as well as most of the models from Woodford (2003), are not open to the criticism voiced in this chapter, as there is no real balance effect in those contributions.

3.1 The real balance effect revisited

The 'real balance effect' is the way the money stock influences the economy in many (older) macroeconomic standard models. The argument is simple: either investment or consumption demand (or both) are a function of real money holdings in the economy.

Monetary policy increases the nominal money stock in circulation. These increased nominal money holdings translate into higher real money holdings as long as prices remain unchanged. The increased money stock then leads to more consumption or investment demand and thus to higher aggregate demand. Whether this additional aggregate demand translates into higher real output depends on assumptions concerning aggregate supply. If supply is fixed, the additional demand can translate only into higher prices. If spare capacities exist, the additional demand will also translate into higher real output.

The real balance effect also guarantees that aggregate demand and aggregate supply balance. If aggregate demand is below aggregate supply, prices begin to fall. With falling prices and a constant nominal money stock, the real money stock increases. As investment and/or consumption demand are assumed to be functions of the real money stock, this increases demand up to a level at which aggregate demand and aggregate supply balance again.

The Pigou effect

The variant of the real balance effect which influences consumption demand is called the *Pigou effect*[1] As Pigou (1943, p. 349) had argued, the Pigou effect assumes that consumption demand is a function of net private wealth while the money stock is assumed to be part of this net wealth. With higher real money balances, it is argued, net wealth is increased and people consume more. These higher real balances can come about by falling prices or by an increase in the nominal money stock in circulation.

The Keynes effect

The type of real balance effect that influences investment demand is called the *Keynes effect*. It focuses on the way that individuals allocate their savings between bonds and cash holdings and argues that higher real balances lead to lower interest rates, which in turn increase investment demand. The mechanism is as follows: when real balances are increased, individuals suddenly find themselves with a higher share of money in their portfolio than they would prefer, and they will try to rebalance their portfolios. Individuals will buy bonds, thus bidding up bond prices. With rising bond prices, the interest rate falls. This lower interest rate in turn makes investments more profitable, thus increasing investment demand.

As with the Pigou effect, higher real balances can come about either by a fall in the price level or by an exogenous increase of the nominal money stock. Either will lower interest rates and increase investment demand so that aggregate demand and aggregate supply balance.[2]

The real balance effect in the interaction models

The real balance effect is of central importance for the models presented in Chapter 2. In SICCD models, it is the real balances that guarantee that aggregate demand increases, as unions exercise wage restraint. In these models, wage restraint leads to lower prices in the goods market. With an exogenously given nominal money stock, these lower prices lead to higher real balances, which in turn lead to higher aggregate demand.[3] Only via the real balance effect does wage restraint here have any effect on real output.

Barro–Gordon, and thus the models building on their approach, also rely on a monetary policy transmission via the real balance effect, even if implicitly. Given a simple quantity equation

$$Mv = P\bar{y} \qquad\qquad (3.1)$$

with M as the money stock, v as the velocity of money, P as the price level and $\bar{y}$ as the level of output determined in the labour market, the central bank can control the price level by simply setting the corresponding money supply. But, as it shown in the Appendix (p. 232), a causation from an exogenous increase in the money supply to higher demand requires a real balance effect to work.

3.2   Money: net wealth?

My first line of criticism targets the Pigou effect. In criticising the Pigou effect, one has to distinguish two lines of attack. First, one has to question whether the Pigou effect can work *in principle*. This is the case only if money can be seen as net wealth. Pigou had argued that an increase in real money balances increased individuals' wealth, thus inducing them to save less and spend more. This mechanism obviously could not work if an increase in money holdings did not increase the individuals' net wealth. This first line of criticism is important in order to determine whether the effects of monetary policy or the effects of a fall in the price level can be adequately modelled using the Pigou effect. If money were not net wealth, an increase in the money supply would not (directly) lead to higher consumption.

The second line of criticism asks whether the Pigou effect – if it exists in principle – can ensure that falling prices lead to a substantial increase in aggregate demand. In the SICCD setting, this question is important since the increase in aggregate demand comes about with lower wages and lower prices. For textbook macro-models this would translate into the question of whether the Pigou effect is able to stabilise the economy in the wake of a negative aggregate demand shock, thus assuring that demand never falls short of supply.[4] The problem here is that the falling price level which is at the heart of the Pigou effect might depress aggregate demand via other channels: as Fisher (1933) pointed out, firms' real debt burdens increase during a deflation, thus depressing investment. Even Patinkin (1948) – who in his own models relies heavily on the Pigou effect – is sceptical when it comes to its real-world relevance. During the Great Depression, he points out, the real value of net private balances rose by 46 per cent from 1929 to 1932, but real income (and thus real demand) fell by 40 per cent. In Patinkin (1987, p. 100), he writes:

> [T]he question remains whether [the real balance effect] is strong enough to offset the adverse expectations generated by a price decline, including those generated by a wave of bankruptcies that might well be caused by a severe decline. In brief, the question remains whether the real balance effect is strong enough to assure the stability of the system: to ensure that automatic market forces will restore the economy to a full-employment equilibrium position after an inital shock of a decrease in aggregate demand.

In the following subsections I will examine both questions: first, whether the Pigou effect exists in principle and draws a good picture of the monetary transmission mechanism and, second, whether it will be able to guarantee equality of aggregate supply and demand.

Can the Pigou effect adequately model monetary policy?

The case of commodity money

For commodity money, the question whether money is net wealth and the Pigou effect in principle possible can easily be positively answered.[5] *Commodity money* is defined as a special commodity which has been set aside from the mass of commodities to perform the role of money[6] (Green 1987). The commodity in use (e.g. wheat, precious metals, etc.) has a utility besides its utility as money. If the commodity were not used as money any longer, individuals could use their holdings in a different way. Wheat can be consumed, metals can be formed into tools or jewellery, yielding utility. Thus, if the stock of the commodity used as money increases, the economy as a whole becomes wealthier. Commodity money has an intrinsic worth (Marquis 1996, p. 27). In the example of gold being used as money, the individuals who have mined (or found) some additional gold are actually richer without anybody else in the economy being worse off. If consumption is now a function of real wealth, one could expect the now enriched individuals to spend more on consumption – precisely what the Pigou effect predicts. Consequently, an increase in the money supply in a commodity-money system can be modelled using the Pigou effect. Similarly, a fall in domestic prices relative to the commodity put aside as money increases the real value of the individuals' money holdings, and thus their net wealth.

At first sight, one could think that the same argument should hold for a system in which money is emitted only in exchange for a special commodity. If, for example, the central bank backs all of the domestic currency by gold or another commodity, the (narrow) money supply can increase only when economic agents exchange gold for currency. Here, it is already harder to argue that such an increase in the money supply can be modelled with the Pigou effect. In fact, it is the acquisition of gold which makes the economy richer, not the exchange of gold for paper money.

An analogous case can be made for currency boards. In a currency board system, domestic currency is emitted only if economic agents exchange a specific foreign currency at the central bank,[7] thus all domestic currency is backed by foreign currency. Here, too, the economy becomes richer the moment it earns foreign currency (e.g. by exporting goods), not the moment foreign currency is exchanged into domestic currency.

However, these objections can be easily put aside. If the currency board system or the gold convertibility is completely credible, gold – or, respectively, foreign currency – is a perfect substitute for domestic money. Consequently, one could define money not as the stock of domestic money in circulation but as the amount of gold or foreign currency in either the central bank's balance sheet or in the hands of the general public. For this aggregate, a Pigou effect then could show up: just as in the case of a pure commodity money system, a rise in the price of gold or foreign currency relative to domestic output makes the economy richer.

The case of credit

In modern monetary economies the story gets more complicated. Besides currency, there are a lot of close substitutes which function to a varying degree as money. Even if – let's say a bank account deposit – is not legal tender, bank transfers are widely accepted as means of payment. Consequently, most economists look at broader monetary aggregates than currency in order to monitor monetary developments. The ECB is particularly putting weight on the broad monetary aggregate M3[8] within its monetary policy strategy (ECB 1999b, p. 53f).

The extension of broader monetary aggregates such as M2 and M3 can happen without the stock of outstanding currency being increased, the banking system has only to decide to expand its balance sheet.[9] If a financial institute grants a loan to some private sector agent and increases the amount in the agent's bank account accordingly, broad monetary aggregates grow.

Tables 3.1–3.4 demonstrate this process: Table 3.1 shows the economy's balance sheets, aggregated for the private non-banking sector, the financial institutions, the central bank and the government.

The private non-banking sector holds currency, deposits at commercial banks, real assets (real estate, machinery, stocks, etc.) and government bonds. On the liability side, the private non-banks have only bank credits. On the asset side, financial institutions have currency in their vaults, deposits at the central bank and loans to the private non-banking sector and the government. On their liability side, we find deposits by non-banks, credits from the central bank and deposits by foreigners. The central bank holds gold, foreign assets, loans to the government and loans to commercial banks as assets. On the liability side of the central bank's balance, we find outstanding currency and deposits from commercial banks. The government has liabilities in form of government bonds in the hands of private non-banks, loans from commercial banks and loans from the central bank.

If we consolidate the central bank's balance sheet and the commercial banks' balance sheet, we get a consolidated balance sheet for the financial sector (Table 3.2).[10] As we see, the broad monetary aggregate[11] consists basically of currency outside the financial sector and deposits. As counterparts we find gold, foreign assets, loans to the government and loans to the private sector.

Now consider a new credit by a commercial bank to one of its customers (Tables 3.3 and 3.4). The bank books the amount lent (in this case fifteen monetary units) to the client's bank account. Consequently, the private non-banks' deposits increase. At the same time, the private non-banks' liabilities to the banking sector also increase. If we consolidated the financial sector balance sheet again, broad money supply has increased (Table 3.4).

What is important for the discussion of the Pigou effect is the fact that the private sector's net wealth has not changed. While private

Table 3.1   The economy's balance sheets

Private non-banks (PNB)		**Financial institutions (MFI)**	
Assets	*Liabilities*	*Assets*	*Liabilities*
Currency 60	Bank credits 150 Cr_{MFI}^{PNB}	Currency in 10 Vault	Deposits 115 D_{PNB}^{MFI}
Deposits 115 D_{PNB}^{MFI}	Private 190 net wealth NW^P	Deposits at 20 CB D_{MFI}^{CB}	Credits from 70 CB Cr_{CB}^{MFI}
Real assets 100		Loans 150 to PNB Cr_{MFI}^{PNB}	Deposits by 5 foreigners
D_F^{MFI}			
Government 65 bonds B		Loans to 10 government Cr_{MFI}^G	

Central bank (CB)		**Government (G)**	
Assets	*Liabilities*	*Assets*	*Liabilities*
Gold 5	Currency 70 outstanding	Government 100 assets	Government 65 bonds B
Foreign- 10 assets FA	Deposits 20 from MFIs D_{MFI}^{CB}		Credit from 5 CB Cr_{CB}^C
Government 5 loans Cr_{CB}^G			Credit 10 from MFIs Cr_{MFI}^G
Loans 70 to MFIs Cr_{CB}^{MFI}			Net 20 government wealth

Table 3.2   Consolidated balance sheet of the monetary sector

Financial sector (MFIs and CB)			
Gold	5	Currency outside monetary sector	60
Foreign assets	10	Deposits	115
Government debt	15	Deposits by foreigners	5
Loans to private non-banks	150		
Assets of monetary sector	180	Broad monetary aggregate	180

Table 3.3 The economy's balance sheets after credit expansion

Private non-banks (PNB)		Financial institutions (MFI)	
Assets	*Liabilities*	*Assets*	*Liabilities*
Currency 60	Bank credits **165** Cr_{MFI}^{PNB}	Currency in vault 10	Deposits **130** D_{PNB}^{MFI}
Deposits 130 D_{PNB}^{MFI}	Private 190 net wealth NW^P	Deposits at CB D_{MFI}^{CB} 20	Credits from CB Cr_{CB}^{MFI} 70
Real assets 100		Loans 165 Cr_{MFI}^{PNB}	Deposits by 5 foreigners D_F^{MFI}
Government 65 bonds B		Loans to 10 government Cr_{MFI}^{G}	

Central bank (CB)		Government (G)	
Assets	*Liabilities*	*Assets*	*Liabilities*
Gold 5	Currency 70 outstanding	Government 100 assets	Government 65 bonds B
Foreign assets 10 FA	Deposits 20 from MFIs D_{MFI}^{CB}		Credit from 5 CB Cr_{CB}^{G}
Government 5 loans Cr_{CB}^{G}			Credit 10 from MFIs Cr_{MFI}^{G}
Loans 70 to MFIs Cr_{CB}^{MFI}			Net 20 government wealth

Table 3.4 Consolidated balance sheet of the monetary sector after credit expansion

Financial sector (MFIs and CB)			
Gold	5	Currency outside monetary sector	60
Foreign assets	10	Deposits	**130**
Government debt	15	Deposits by foreigners	5
Loans to private non-banks	**165**		
Assets of monetary sector	195	Broad monetary aggregate	195

non-banks now hold more money in their bank accounts, they also face higher liabilities. For this kind of money, which has as counterpart a liability of the private sector, Gurley and Shaw (1960) have coined the term *inside money*. As inside money is not net wealth for the private sector, there can be no Pigou effect for the part of the money stock which consists of inside money. Of course, people who have larger deposits in their bank accounts are richer in real terms as long as the general price level does not change, but if this larger deposit goes hand in hand with an equally larger debt of some other agent, the private sector as a whole is not wealthier.

Consequently, only the part of the money supply which is *outside money* can bring about the Pigou effect. The exact size of this outside part of the money supply cannot be determined by regarding monetary aggregates, but it can be by analysing the asset side of the financial sector. Figure 3.1 shows the relationship between monetary aggregates and inside/outside money.[12] While the extent of each monetary aggregate is determined by deposits' maturities, the inside/outside characteristic is

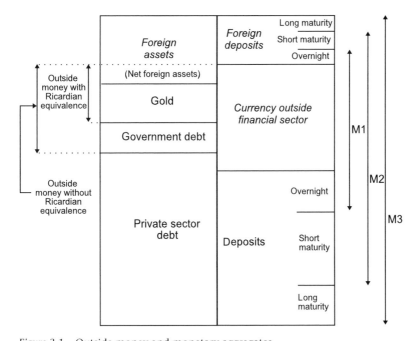

Figure 3.1   Outside money and monetary aggregates

solely determined by the net wealth character of an asset. By aggregating the private non-banks' and the financial sector's balance sheets, we see that the private sector's net wealth consists of real assets, central bank gold, net foreign assets and possibly (if one believes that Ricardian equivalence does not hold) government debt (see Table 3.5).[13]

Only if monetary policy were to increase one of these elements of private sector's net wealth could the Pigou effect adequately model monetary policy. This is not the case: the ECB increases neither the economy's gold nor the private sector's net foreign asset position in conducting monetary policy.[14]

Do central bank purchases of government bonds make the private sector richer?

At first, one might suspect that monetary policy could change the stock of government debt. Do central banks not buy government papers in exchange for currency? Against this notion there are two arguments – one empirical, the other theoretical. Empirically, the ECB hardly ever does buy government debt.[15] The ECB's standard procedure of conducting monetary policy is to lend money to the euro-area's financial institutions via the weekly main refinancing operations.[16] While the institutions have to deposit some security at the ECB, this does not have to be a government bond. Instead, the central bank accepts a wide range of private and public debt instruments (ECB 1998a, p. 40). And, more importantly, the financial institution remains a debtor to the ECB and owner of the security.

However, this institutional argument is only a weak one: The US Fed buys bonds from the general public (Marquis 1996, p. 129) just as the Bank of Japan does. Moreover, lately it has been widely proposed to use the large-scale purchase of government bonds to fight dangers of

Table 3.5   Net private wealth

Net private wealth			
Real assets	100	Net private wealth	190
Net foreign assets	5		
(foreign assets – deposits			
by foreigners)			
Gold	5		
Government debt	80		
	190		190

deflation.[17] Institutional structures might thus change and the ECB shift to purchases of government bonds. But even if the ECB conducted monetary policy by buying government bonds from the general public, heavy doubts about the Pigou effect would remain. As Table 3.6[18] shows, a central bank purchase of government bonds from the non-bank private sector against currency (in this case, ten monetary units) does not alter the net wealth position of the private sector. On the private sector's asset side, government bonds are swapped against currency, while the central bank's assets and liabilities increase by the same amount. If we aggregate private wealth from Table 3.6, we get the original net private wealth of Table 3.5. Monetary policy has not changed net wealth.

Only if the private sector considered government debt not as net wealth but money backed by government debt (at least partly) as net wealth could there be a Pigou effect. While it is quite easy and common to argue that government debt is *not* net wealth for the private sector as Barro (1974, 1989) does (*Ricardian equivalence*), it is somewhat harder to explain why private agents would consider money backed by government debt as net wealth while they believe that government debt itself is not net wealth.

To my knowledge, the only plausible attempt to this end has been made by Tobin (1998, p. 266).[19] Tobin argues that even in a world in which government debt is not net wealth and Ricardian equivalence holds, money can have a positive net value for the economy. With government debt in the hand of the public being swapped for non-interest-bearing currency at a rate corresponding to the real economy's growth rate (thus being non-inflationary), the government saves interest payment on this part of its debt.[20] As the government has to pay less interest, current and future tax obligations are lower and the economy thus better off. However, this explanation is only superficially satisfying. Interest payments are always at the same time the income of some private agent. As a government bond is bought against currency, the bond's former owner's income is reduced (Table 3.6). The sum of this income reduction equals exactly the sum of interest saved.[21]

Nevertheless, there is the possibility of a small wealth effect if one combines Tobin's argument with the fact that money is yielding utility to its holder in the form of transaction services, saved time or security through keeping part of the individual's wealth highly liquid. Following Sidrauski (1967), real money holdings are included in the individual's utility function along with consumption.

Table 3.6   The central bank buys government bonds against currency

Private non-banks (PNB)		Financial institutions (MFI)	
Assets	*Liabilities*	*Assets*	*Liabilities*
Currency 70	Bank credits 150 Cr_{MFI}^{PNB}	Currency in 10 vault	Deposits 115 D_{PNB}^{MFI}
Deposits 115 D_{PNB}^{MFI}	Private 190 net wealth NW^P	Deposits at 20 CB D_{MFI}^{CB}	Credits from 70 CB Cr_{CB}^{MFI}
Real assets 100		Loans 150 Cr_{MFI}^{PNB}	Deposits by 5 foreigners D_F^{MFI}
Government 55 bonds B		Loans to 10 government Cr_{MFI}^G	

Central bank (CB)		Government (G)	
Assets	*Liabilities*	*Assets*	*Liabilities*
Gold 5	Currency 80 outstanding	Government 100 assets	Government 65 bonds B
Foreign 10 assets FA	Deposits 20 from MFIs D_{MFI}^{CB}		Credit from 5 CB Cr_{CB}^G
Government 5 loans Cr_{CB}^G			Credit 10 from MFIs Cr_{MFI}^G
Loans 70 to MFIs Cr_{CB}^{MFI}			Net 20 government wealth
Government bonds 10			

If government bonds are now purchased against currency, real money holdings and individual utility increase. Using the results from microeconomic theory, one can estimate the extent (and the monetary equivalent) of this utility increase. As in the individual's optimum, marginal utility from an additional unit of consumption must equal marginal utility from the corresponding additional money holding, an increase in money holdings increases utility by the same amount that is forgone by selling an interest-bearing government bond against currency. This amount equals precisely the actual rate of interest. Thus, a central bank purchase of a government bond increases the agent's utility stream by the equivalent of the interest forgone while it decreases the agent's consumption possibilities by this same amount. These effects would cancel each other out if it were not for the government saving interest payments and thus needing fewer tax receipts. With present and/or future tax obligation falling by the same amount, the economy is in fact richer after the purchase.

I will illustrate this argument in a simple two-period framework. The representative individual's utility depends on first- and second-period consumption c_1 and c_2 and on real money holdings *per capita* m:

$$U = U(c_1, c_2, m) \tag{3.2}$$

The individual maximises her utility given her budget constraint given (exogenous) income y_1 and y_2, interest rate r for which she can invest money, interest b paid in period 2 on government bonds she owns and tax obligation t to be paid in period 2. Income from period 1 to period 2 can be stored either in non-interest-bearing money holdings m or in interest-bearing capital k. Budget constraints are (for the moment we assume constant prices and a price level of 1):

$$y_1 = c_1 + m + k \tag{3.3}$$
$$m + (1 + r)k + y_2 + b - t = c_2 \tag{3.4}$$

Maximising (3.2) subject to (3.3) and (3.4) yields the following optimality conditions:

$$\frac{\partial U}{\partial m} + \frac{\partial U}{\partial c_2} = \frac{\partial U}{\partial c_1} \tag{3.5}$$

$$\frac{\partial U}{\partial c_2}(1+r) = \frac{\partial U}{\partial c_1} \tag{3.6}$$

Substituting (3.6) in (3.5), we get the marginal utility of a unit of money:

$$\frac{\partial U}{\partial m} = r\frac{\partial U}{\partial c_2} = \frac{r}{1+r}\frac{\partial U}{\partial c_1} \tag{3.7}$$

As marginal utility of one unit of consumption in period 1 equals the price of one unit of consumption in period 1, an additional marginal unit of money has the same effect as an income transfer of $\frac{r}{1+r}$ in period 1.[22]

Consequently, this increased utility leaves the possibility of something comparable to the Pigou effect. As long as prices do not change (and the real money holdings thus change), an additional unit of money stock yields a permanent stream of utility worth $\frac{r}{1+r}$ per period. While this is not exactly an increase in wealth, but more similar to an increase in permanent income, effects on consumption can be expected.

However, one should ask whether these effects are of such a magnitude that they have any significant influence on macroeconomic variables. In the euro-area, base money[23] amounted to about €700 billion at the end of 2000. If monetary policy now increased this stock of money by buying government bonds worth €70 billion (a 10 per cent increase of the money stock) at an interest rate of 5 per cent, this would equal an increase of permanent income of roughly €3.3 billion. Even if individuals exhibit a marginal propensity to consume of 1, this impulse would amount only to 0.05 per cent of the euro-area's GDP (roughly €6,200 billion). Such small changes in GDP are almost completely negligible and are obviously not sufficient on which to base the monetary policy transmission mechanism of macroeconomic models.

Monetising a budget deficit

Another possibility for the existence of the Pigou effect turns up in a world in which Ricardian equivalence does not hold. In a world in which the government finances its budget deficit by borrowing directly from the central bank, private net wealth will increase. The central bank will print money and pay the private sector. Tables 3.7 and 3.8 show the effects of the government borrowing twenty monetary units from the central bank and paying the private sector with them.[24] As long as an increase in government debt (and an equivalent increase of bonds in the hands of the public) actually made the private sector richer (and Ricardian equivalence thus fails), higher private net wealth would lead to higher consumption demand. The Pigou effect would occur. However, one should note that it is not *monetary* policy that changes net wealth. If the government were financing its budget deficit by borrowing from the private sector, government debt and thus private net wealth would similarly increase. Thus it is a *sustained budget deficit* (and not monetary policy in a narrow sense) which increases private net wealth in a non-Ricardian world.

In addition, since we want to see whether the Pigou effect is suitable for showing how monetary policy works in the euro-area, one has to recall that financing budget deficits by printing money is not the way

Table 3.7 The economy's balance sheets with government financing a budget deficit by borrowing from the central bank

Private non-banks (PNB)		Financial institutions (MFI)		
Assets	*Liabilities*	*Assets*		*Liabilities*
Currency 80	Bank credits 150 Cr_{MFI}^{PNB}	Currency in vault	10	Deposits 115 D_{PNB}^{MFI}
Deposits 115 D_{PNB}^{MFI}	Private 190 net wealth NW^P	Deposits at CB D_{MFI}^{CB}	20	Credits from 70 CB Cr_{CB}^{MFI}
Real assets 100		Loans 150 Cr_{MFI}^{PNB}		Deposits by 5 foreigners D_F^{MFI}
Government 65 bonds B		Loans to government Cr_{MFI}^{G}	10	

Central bank (CB)		Government (G)		
Assets	*Liabilities*	*Assets*		*Liabilities*
Gold 5	Currency 90 outstanding	Government assets	100	Government 65 bonds B
Foreign 10 assets FA	Deposits 20 from MFIs D_{MFI}^{CB}			Credit from 25 CB Cr_{CB}^{G}
Government 25 loans Cr_{CB}^{G}				Credit 10 from MFIs Cr_{MFI}^{G}
Loans 70 to MFIs Cr_{CB}^{MFI}				Net 0 government wealth

Table 3.8 Net private wealth with government financing a budget deficit by printing money

Net private wealth			
Real assets	100	Net private wealth	210
Net foreign assets (foreign assets – deposits by foreigners)	5		
Gold	5		
Government debt	100		
	210		210

monetary policy is conducted in developed economies.[25] The EU treaty prohibits central banks from financing budget deficits[26] and the US Fed is subject to similar legislation (Meulendyke 1998, p. 166). In conclusion, one can thus say that the Pigou effect is not adequate for modelling the transmission of monetary policy in economies such as the euro-area or the USA.

Can falling prices cause a significant rise in consumption?

These objections against modelling the effects of monetary policy using the Pigou effect do not keep the Pigou effect from being *in principle* able to balance aggregate demand and aggregate supply (or, in terms of the SICCD approach, to increase demand when wages and prices fall). The question still remains whether the magnitude of price change necessary to attain equilibrium is plausible.

As already argued on p. 57, only money which is of the 'outside' kind can show the Pigou effect. If we take another look at Figure 3.1, we see that only the part of money which is either backed by foreign currency, gold or (possibly) government debt can be seen as outside money.

Whether or not public debt is net wealth to the private sector has been discussed in great length under the term *Ricardian equivalence* following the seminal work of Barro (1974). Barro argues that since individuals have an interest in their offsprings' well-being, a chain of related individuals with a finite lifespan has in fact to be analysed as if it were one individual with an infinite horizon. If one includes the child's utility in the parent's utility function, a temporal shift in taxation does not change the individual's consumption behaviour. Instead, consumption patterns are sustained by changes in savings and bequests. As a government deficit financed by public debt today will force the government to raise taxes later in order to pay interest on the debt (or even pay back the debt), in this model there is no difference between tax and debt financing of government expenditure. Consequently, any attempt by the government to stabilise aggregate demand by running budget deficits in a downturn and budget surpluses in an upswing would be ineffective, as households would change their own consumption in a way that would upset fiscal stimulus.

In this last consequence, Ricardian equivalence is still highly disputed. Not only is empirical evidence found for as well as against Ricardian equivalence,[27] but theoretical points can also be made against it. Most common criticisms are that:[28]

1. In each generation, a number of households is childless or indifferent to the lots of their children. Deficit spending enables these households to consume more at the expense of later generations.
2. A postponement of taxes to later generations redistributes from families with many children to households with none or only a few children.
3. The motivation for bequest need not be the offsprings' utility. For example, as Bernheim, Shleifer and Summers (1985) argue, a bequest can be paid by the parents in order to make their children behave in a way the parents prefer. Thus, bequests are left no matter how many taxes future generations have to pay.
4. Even if they internalise their children's utility, some parents will find utility optimal at zero-bequest corners rather than at interior points. They would prefer negative bequests, but these are not within their options. These parents will consume more if their taxes are reduced and those of their heirs correspondingly increased (Tobin 1998, p. 268).
5. Owing to capital market imperfections, even during their lifetime, individuals might not be able to shift consumption as they wish. Earnings expected at age fifty usually cannot be spent at age twenty-five. Even in countries with sophisticated financial institutions and well-developed capital markets, opportunities for borrowing against future earnings from labour are limited – if only because of the problems of enforcing debt repayment (Becker 1993, p. 49).

   Thus, even in affluent societies, a large number of households are liquidity-constrained. Their horizons for consumption plans are shorter than their lifetimes, let alone the lifetimes of their lineal families (Buiter and Tobin 1981).

All of these arguments hint that Ricardian equivalence can at best be viewed as a baseline consideration. Changes in budget deficits probably do have some effects on aggregate demand. In all recent natural experiments, such as German reunification, Reagan's budget deficits in the early 1980s or the Maastricht restrictive fiscal policy in Europe in the mid-1990s, fiscal policy had effects one would expect for a world in which Ricardian equivalence does not hold. Moreover, as Bernheim (1987, p. 293ff) finds in an empirical cross-country comparison, increasing budget deficits do raise aggregate consumption.

However, this does not invalidate one basic Ricardian notion: society cannot enrich itself by increasing the debts of some citizens to others. Neither can it impoverish itself by internal debt. Deficit spending does not make the society richer. But by giving income to those who are subject to a liquidity constraint (because they are out of work) or would like to consume more but cannot borrow in the capital market, varying budget deficits can have effects on aggregate demand and thus aggregate activity.

The story is slightly different when one asks whether a fall in the general price level can increase aggregate demand by a substantial amount via the Pigou effect for money backed by government debt. A fall in the general price level makes government bonds more valuable in real terms. At the same time, the real interest obligations of the government increase. Even if the initial debt were not to be paid back, the overall government balance would deteriorate and the government would have either to increase taxes or to cut spending.[29] All taxpayers and all beneficiaries of government spending (that is, basically all citizens as they benefit from public goods provided) thus become poorer in real terms while holders of money backed by government debt and holders of government bonds become richer by the same amount.

In order for the Pigou effect to work, one would have to assume that those becoming richer by the fall in prices would increase their consumption by more than those becoming poorer reduce their consumption. However, individuals who have large money and/or bond holdings get richer when prices fall. As both money and government bonds are highly liquid assets, it is not very plausible that this group has been subject to liquidity constraint before prices began to fall. Or, to argue within the standard criticism of Ricardian equivalence, one can assume that those who plan on leaving a bequest for their children hold larger stocks of bonds than those who do not provide for their heirs. Thus, while those being in a corner solution or under liquidity constraints get poorer when the price level falls, individuals for whom one could assume Ricardian equivalence to hold get richer. Individuals finding themselves in a corner solution or under constraints have to cut back their consumption (that is, their overall consumption consists of indirect consumption paid by the government and direct consumption paid out of their pockets). In contrast, individuals for whom Ricardian equivalence holds will spread their net wealth increase not only over their own life span but also over that of their heirs. In consequence, the increase of current consumption by those getting richer can be expected to be smaller than the decrease of consumption by those getting poorer. The net effect – if there is any – of a falling price level on current aggregate consumption due to wealth effects must be assumed to be negative. Thus, the Pigou effect cannot be expected to work for the part of money which is backed by government debt.

That leaves us with the part of money backed by net foreign assets or gold for a possible Pigou effect. Because, with a positive net foreign asset position, a falling price level with constant nominal exchange rates[30] actually enriches the economy while the rest of the world is getting poorer, here a genuine Pigou effect can safely be assumed. The only question is: are price changes necessary to attain equilibrium within a plausible range of magnitude?

Let us first consider the case of a pure commodity money system or a pure currency board.[31] A fall in prices of all goods relative to the commodity used as money (or the currency used as backing in a currency board system) actually makes the holders of money wealthier in real consumption terms. The same would be true in a currency board system. The foreign assets held by the currency board increase in value measured in domestic terms when the general price level is falling.

The question remains whether it is plausible that such a change in the real value of currency has an effect large enough to balance any shocks of considerable size. Let's take a look at the currency board system of Estonia.[32] In 1999, Estonia had a GDP of roughly EEK 75 billion. Currency circulation backed by foreign reserves amounted to roughly EEK 12 billion – about 16 per cent of GDP. How much would prices then have to fall in order to increase GDP and employment by 1 per cent? one per cent of GDP equals roughly EEK 750 million. Even if the individuals were to spend all of their windfall gain in net wealth due to a fall in the general price level, a fall in the general price level by 6.25 per cent would be necessary in order to increase demand by that amount (or to offset a negative demand shock of that magnitude). Given that hardly any industrialised economy has experienced such a fall in the general price level since the Second World War and given the problems the Japanese economy experienced with only slight deflation, one can suspect that the negative impact of this fall in prices outweighs the positive real balance effects.

Theoretic considerations about consumption behaviour also hint that it is very unlikely that individuals will spend all of their windfall profits at once on additional consumption. In economic models with micro-foundation such as Ramsey's (1928) growth model with infinite horizons or Diamond's (1965) growth model with overlapping generations, individuals try to smooth consumption over their lifetime. This is also the essence of Friedman's (1953) permanent income hypothesis. As an increase in the individual's net wealth cannot be considered a permanent increase in income but is clearly a windfall profit,[33] it would be distributed over the rest of the individual's life horizon.

Given an interest rate of 5 per cent and a horizon of thirty years, a windfall of €1 would lead to an increase in yearly consumption of ¢7. With the marginal propensity to consume out of wealth being 0.07,[34] real balances would have to more than double in order to increase consumption demand by 1 per cent of GDP. This would imply a fall in the general price level by half – which can only be considered as a very severe deflation.

The story looks even less realistic if one takes a look at the euro-area. In January 2001, external assets of monetary financial institutions and the ESCB amounted to €2,439.5 billion while external liabilities amounted to €2,256.5 billion, leaving a net foreign position of the monetary system of €182.9 billion. Assuming that all assets are denominated in euro, even if consumers were to consume all of their windfall profits at once, a fall in the general price level by roughly 25 per cent would be needed to balance an external 1 per cent shock to aggregate demand.[35] Against the background of more realistic assumptions such as a marginal propensity to consume out of wealth of 0.07, real balances would have to increase by a factor of 6. This would be equivalent to a fall of prices by more than 80 per cent – a value beyond any consideration.

Thus, even though the Pigou effect could work for the part of the money supply which has foreign assets as its accounting counterpart, the magnitude of price change necessary for reaching equilibrium after a medium-size demand shock must lead to the conclusion that the Pigou effect cannot be seen as a stabilising mechanism working in the real world.

3.3   Exogenous money supply?

My second line of criticism targets the Keynes effect. Under this term it is argued that an exogenous increase in the money supply conducted by the monetary policy authorities leads to excess demand in the bond market and thus falling interest rates, which then translate into higher investment demand. In the case of a falling price level, it is argued that the *real* money supply is increasing. People face real balances which are too high, bond demand increases, interest rates fall and investment demand increases.

In order for this process to work, the central bank needs to be able to control the supply of that monetary aggregate which is important for investment. The possibility of an exogenous control of the appropriate aggregate is also central to the question of whether an automatic stabilisation via the Keynes effect is thinkable. Only if the *nominal* stock of this aggregate does not change endogenously in the same direction and magnitude as the price level can the Keynes effect work.

Monetary aggregates and investment

So, what is the relevant monetary aggregate which could reveal investment demand?[36] A firm can either invest out of its own resources or on credit. For credits, it can rely on direct or indirect credits. Direct credits would involve the sale of corporate bonds to the general public; indirect credits would involve financial intermediation (Duwendag *et al.* 1999, p. 107).

In the case of both direct and indirect credit, currency does not have to be involved. The direct credit can simply be granted by a transfer of some bank deposit to the borrowing firm's bank account while the creditor household takes a bond in its portfolio. This direct credit does not change standard monetary aggregates such as M1, M2 or M3, but rather the liquidity of the household's portfolio and the aggregate credit volume. In the case of indirect credit, however, broad monetary aggregates such as M3 might well change. As the bank grants a loan, it books the amount agreed to the company's account. At the same time, its liabilities against that company increase by the same amount. When the company now pays the producer of the capital good via a bank transfer, the amount of credit in the economy has increased without the amount of currency having changed.

In order to monitor investment demand, a broad monetary aggregate should therefore be considered. M3 seems to be an appropriate choice, though an even wider aggregate such as the level of nominal debt would be even better.[37] It should be noted that investment finance, and thus an increase in investment demand, can occur *without* an increase in M3 or L by the households' choice to substitute assets which are not included in those aggregates with assets which are. On the other hand, an increase in M3 or L is not a guarantee that a real investment will take place. An inflation of certain asset prices such as real estate prices could also lead to an increase in monetary aggregates without any additional direct real investment.

Endogeneity of credit money

Older textbooks of monetary economics or macroeconomics[38] explain the expansion of broader monetary aggregates by the use of mechanistic money multipliers. Monetary aggregates such as M1, M2 or M3 are thus given a constant multiple of base money MB, which is under the direct control of the monetary authority:

$$M_x = m_x MB \tag{3.8}$$

The exact magnitude of the multiplier m_x for the different aggregates is computed given mandatory reserve requirements, voluntary excess reserve holding by the banking sector and the ratio of deposits of different maturities (overnight, time or saving deposits) to currency held by the general public.

Deducting the money multiplier for M1 should make this process clear: M1 consists of currency Cur and demand deposits DD. From each new deposit at a commercial bank, the share res_{mand} has to be held with the central bank. In addition, the commercial banks decide to hold an additional share res_{exc} of deposits in reserves. Thus, for each euro deposited, the bank can lend out €1 − res_{exc} − res_{mand}. From this amount, the general public keeps a share of cur in currency, thus depositing €1 − res_{exc} − res_{mand} − cur again with a bank, which then can lend out a share of this money again. This process continues until all currency is held by the general public and economic agents do not wish to deposit any more currency with the banking sector. If we now take the monetary base as the sum of reserves Res and currency outstanding Cur:[39]

$$MB = Cur + Res \tag{3.9}$$

and M1 as the sum of currency and deposits:

$$M1 = Cur + DD \tag{3.10}$$

we get for the money multiplier m_1:

$$m_1 = \frac{M1}{MB} = \frac{Cur + DD}{Cur + Res} \tag{3.12}$$
$$= \frac{Cur/DD + 1}{Cur/DD + Res/DD} = \frac{1 + cur}{cur + res_{exc} + res_{mand}}$$

This multiplier shows by how much M1 *could* expand when base money is increased by one unit, given that banks decided to expand their balance sheets, firms and households decided to borrow more and economic agents wanted to keep the ratio between currency and bank deposits in their portfolios constant.

The problem with the multiplier approach, as it is taught in older textbooks,[40] is that it is often presented in a way that implies a causal link from an increase in base money to credit (and thereby M1, M2 or M3) expansion, neglecting almost completely the individual decision making process which leads to the results. A look at (3.12) underlines how important individual decisions are for the multiplier to work in the way depicted: while the mandatory reserve requirements can easily be assumed to be constant,[41] the ratio of both excess reserves and currency to deposits depends on the interaction of banks and private non-banking units. Only if firms and households decide to enter into debt commitments to finance spending and only if banks decide to take assets into their balance sheets, can credit expansion occur (Wray 1990, p. 89). If private agents are not willing to borrow because profit expectations are low or if banks are unwilling to expand their balance sheet, an exogenous increase in the monetary base – if it were possible[42] – would only lead to an increase in excess reserves (and thus to a change in res_{exc}, not to a credit expansion (Minsky 1986, p. 117). While the ratio of excess reserves is empirically more stable than the ratio of currency to deposits, it is already volatile enough to lead Tobin (1963) to conclude:

> This indicates a much looser linkage between reserves and deposits than is suggested by the textbook exposition of multiple expansion for a system which is always precisely and fully 'loaned up'.

It could be argued that the linkage between reserves and deposits is tight enough to allow the central bank to control not the exact, but at least the approximate amount of credit money. Since it is not profitable for commercial banks to hold ever-increasing reserves, one could argue that the central bank could just increase liquidity until the banks finally expand their balance sheets. Similarly, the central bank could restrict liquidity until excess reserves were driven to zero and banks could not expand credit supply any further.

Endogenous instability of money multipliers

There are two objections to this argument, one for the case of (intended) expanding of the money supply and one for the case of (intended) contracting of the money supply. For the supply of credit money to expand, the central bank needs the cooperation of commercial banks. If banks are especially risk averse, as in the case of a weak capital position of the banking sector or a very dark macroeconomic outlook, they might decide not to expand their balance sheet even if the monetary base was expanding.[43] Instead they would just sell off risky assets without handing out new loans. As the central bank was buying assets, interest rates would fall. With interest rates for deposits approaching zero, and risk-adjusted returns from additional credits still being negative, the commercial banks would not have any incentives to increase credit supply.

Similarly, the central bank might not be able to induce a contraction in the credit supply just by contracting the monetary base. When the central bank tries to keep the monetary base constant or growing at a slow pace while commercial banks still would strongly like to expand their balance sheets, the money multiplier might endogenously change. Because commercial banks might face constraints on the reserve side as the central bank restricts monetary base growth, interest rates rise. With interest rates on deposits rising, the general public will try to economise its cash holdings (for example by additional trips to the bank), thus leading to a decreasing *cur*. Furthermore, with reserves getting more expensive and harder to obtain, commercial banks have a higher incentive to innovate financial instruments in order to economise on reserves (Minsky 1957). For example, when US interest rates increased sharply in the late 1970s, investment firms began to offer retail money market mutual funds (MMMFs).[44] They acquired funds that were intended by their owners to be held in highly liquid, short-term assets and placed them in short-term investments that had been unavailable to most small-scale savers because of the high minimum denomination of the issue (Marquis 1996, p. 33). As the firms offering these MMMFs were not subject to the Fed's reserve requirements, the relationship between M1 and broader monetary aggregates as well as real activity became erratic. In order to counter this development, the US Fed repeatedly had to redefine the monetary aggregate used to control the economy.

Similar experiences in the UK led Goodhart (1984, p. 96) to formulate what is now known as *Goodhart's law*: any attempt by monetary authorities to exploit an empirically stable relationship between monetary aggregates and real variables will lead to a breakdown of this relationship as the public is trying to evade the control. In fact, this observation is more or less in line with Lucas' (1976) critique of the Phillips-curve, where Lucas warned that one should not draw policy conclusions from empirically observed stable relationships of economic variables without formulating an underlying structural model.[45]

Thus, findings of empirical stability of German money demand functions, such as many of the authors surveyed in Müller (1998, p. 195) and Schächter (1999) provide, might not prove structural stability. It might as well be just an additional indicator that the Bundesbank in fact never actually tried to closely control monetary aggregates, as Bernanke and Mihov (1997) also find in their empirical investigation of Bundesbank monetary policy. Instead of concluding that monetary targeting is feasible since money demand is stable – as monetarists frequently do – one would conclude that the money demand function was indeed stable *because* the Bundesbank in fact never tried to control monetary aggregates closely.

Endogeneity of the monetary base

The idea of the central bank closely controlling monetary aggregates via control of the monetary base has another drawback: since the central bank in reality has additional objectives other than just keeping the stock of money within its targeted range, central bank regimes are usually constructed in a way that even the monetary base becomes endogenous. As the Bundesbank (1995, p. 92) admits, a central bank has to rely on the cooperation of financial institutions and private non-banks in order to increase or decrease base money:

> Die Bundesbank kann weder die Expansion der Geldmenge in beliebiger Weise unmittelbar beschränken, indem sie überschießende Nachfrage der Banken nach Zentralbankguthaben einfach unbefriedigt lässt, noch ist sie in der Lage, eine zu schwache Nachfrage nach Zentralbankgeld durch die Schaffung von Überschußguthaben der Kreditinstitute so nahtlos auszugleichen, daß die Ausweitung der Geldmenge zu keinem Zeitpunkt hinter den gesteckten Zielen zurückbleibt. Vielmehr liegt es in der Natur des komplexen Geldschöpfungsprozesses, in dem Notenbank, Kreditinstitute und Nichtbanken zusammenwirken, daß die Bundesbank nur durch entsprechende Gestaltung der Zinskonditionen und sonstigen Bedingungen, zu denen sie laufend Zentralbankguthaben bereitstellt, mittelbar darauf hinwirken kann, daß die Geldmenge sich in dem angestrebten Rahmen entwickelt.[46]

First of all, the central bank has an imminent interest in stabilising the financial sector. In order to achieve the final goal of monetary policy – price stability or price stability and growth, depending on the legal background of the central bank – monetary impulses have to be channelled into the economy. As systemic risks systemically disturb micro-behaviour, which impinges upon money demand and money supply, monetary policy becomes more difficult to perform when systemic risk increases (Goodhart and Huang 1999). A robust banking system is thus a precondition for monetary policy to work effectively.[47]

In order for the banking system to be robust against bank runs, the system needs a *lender of last resort*. Commercial banks usually hold assets with long-term maturities while their liabilities are of shorter maturities. When there is an unexpected withdrawal of deposits, not only from one bank but from all banks, the system can run into liquidity problems. While still having sound balance sheets, banks can become illiquid. As rumours of possible illiquidity spread, the public is induced to withdraw its funds, thus aggravating the financial system's liquidity problems. As the central bank is the only institution which can provide infinite liquidity (by creating reserves), it is the natural candidate for fulfilling the role of the lender of last resort.

This role makes it necessary that the central bank does not refrain from providing banks that have sound balance sheets with the liquidity they need. This function of a lender of last resort is institutionalised in the euro system. MFIs which have access to the ECB's monetary policy operations can borrow unlimited funds from the marginal lending facility at an interest rate above that charged in the main refinancing operations. Only in the case of 'exceptional circumstances' may the ECB limit or suspend individual counterparties' access to the facility (ECB 1998a, p. 22). One additional institutional feature of the marginal lending facility makes the endogeneity of base money in the euro-area even more evident: at the end of the day, counterparties' intraday debit positions on their settlement account with the national central banks are automatically considered to be a request for recourse to the marginal lending facility.

Institutional features of the European System of Central Banks (ESCB) make it similarly hard for the ECB to keep the stock of base money from falling under a predefined level. Liquidity is mainly introduced into the system via the main financing operations. Within this system, reserves are distributed according to the MFIs' bids. If MFIs decide not to expand their balance sheets (or even to reduce their credit supply), they consequently need less liquidity and will bid for fewer reserves. In addition, MFIs can put excessive reserves into the ESCB's deposit facility, where interest is paid and through which the monetary base is in fact reduced. As the ECB had to learn during early 2001, when commercial banks which were counting on an imminent interest rate cut hardly bid for any liquidity, it needs the commercial banks' cooperation to increase (or even keep constant) the nominal money stock under the current regime.

Thus, the ECB has to be seen as a price setter instead of a quantity setter not only for credit money, where the final interest and credit conditions are set by the financial sector as a function of the refinancing conditions, but also for the monetary base.[48] In consequence, modelling monetary policy operations using the Keynes effect seems inappropriate.

Can the Keynes effect stabilise the economy?

These arguments for an endogeneity of credit and monetary aggregates also calls into question the notion of an increased demand following a falling price level via the Keynes effect. In the standard textbook models, with lower prices the real value of money available for credit in the economy increases. However, as the money stock is not exogenously fixed, and money is created by granting loans to commercial banks who then give credits to firms and households, one can assume that the money stock moves proportionally with the price level: as households and firms need the credits in order to conduct *real* investment or to consume more in *real* terms, they will demand accordingly less credit when prices are falling (Betz 2001b, pp. 58ff). In the case of those firms and households which are credit-constrained, it is the banking sector who will change their nominal credit volume with a changing price level. With all prices decreasing, future nominal household or firm earnings will also decrease. The banks will lower their nominal credit ceilings. The opposite is true for rising prices. As expected future nominal cash flows increase, credit ceilings are raised. As neither banks nor firms live under money illusion, the real credit constraint does not change when the price level changes.

Consequently, one can expect that credit demand as well as the credit supply will move in line with the general price level. As the central bank sets neither broad money aggregates nor base money directly, but accommodates the liquidity demanded by the financial sector given the current refinancing rate, money supply will also move in line with the price level as long as the central bank does not change the real refinancing rate. Thus, theoretically, one cannot expect the Keynes effect to stabilise the economy. Without Keynes and Pigou effects, the case for lower nominal wages in order to boost demand and employment becomes dubious, as it is no longer clear how lower prices (which are a consequence of lower nominal wages) should increase aggregate demand.

4
Monetary Policy Transmission in a World of Endogenous Money

In Chapter 3, I questioned whether monetary policy transmits to the economy via the real balance effect. This chapter covers the question of *how* monetary policy can have an influence on interest rates in the absence of a real balance effect (that is, in this case, a Keynes effect) and how a change in interest rates translates to the real economy. The aim of this chapter is to provide a rationale for modelling monetary policy as a simple change in the interest rate. However, this chapter will not cover the restrictions a central bank faces when changing the short-term interest rate, as these will be covered in detail in Chapter 6.

The chapter argues that monetary policy predominantly transmits to the real economy by influencing the long-term interest rate. I will claim that long-term interest rates depend via an augmented expectation hypothesis on the expected course of future short-term interest rates. The fact that empirical studies have not always found convincing evidence for the expectation hypothesis stems from the fact that market participants try to anticipate the central bank's actions, and long-term rates might thus react before the central bank actually changes money market rates. Owing to this mechanism, the way in which the central bank reacts (that is, the weight it gives to output or inflation stabilisation – or in short, its policy stance) is central to the way markets react to new economic information.

Changes in long-term interest rates translate to the real economy by influencing aggregate investment and consumption. Lower interest rates lead to a higher aggregate demand by increasing both aggregate investment and aggregate consumption. Investment is higher due to lower opportunity costs of real investment. Consumption can be expected to be higher, as lower interest rates imply a higher *per capita* productivity and thus higher real wages.

This chapter is structured as followed: Section 4.1 will explain how the central bank can influence the relevant long-term interest rate by changing its short-term rate. Sections 4.2 and 4.3 will briefly review how investment and consumption demand can be influenced by the interest rate. Section 4.4 will conclude with a short section about the relevance of each channel of monetary policy in the euro-zone.

4.1   The instrument: the short-term interest rate

If the central bank is not able to change private net wealth by printing money, how does monetary policy work? The answer lies in the process by which money *comes into existence*: since money is created when commercial banks borrow from the central bank, it is the interest rate that the central bank charges for lending money which gives it the power to influence the real economy.

How can it be that the short-term interest rate influences the real economy? Classical and neo-classical theory (Böhm-Bawerk, Mill, Ricardo and Smith)[1] claim that it is the long-term interest rate which influences investment, saving and consumption decisions. This long-term interest rate cannot be influenced by monetary policy, as it is determined by the marginal product of capital and the supply of savings (Bofinger 2001, pp. 283ff). Yet, the empirical evidence that short-term interest rates influence real activity is rather strong.[2] Many recent theoretical studies[3] consequently explain monetary policy transmission with changes in the rate of interest (the *interest rate channel*). This chapter will argue that a central bank *can* influence the long-term interest rate and that the way it chooses to change its short-term interest rate signals how it will use this instrument in the long run.

Influencing the long-term interest rate

The classical view does not take into account that, even over longer time periods, it is money which is lent, not real capital. This money is created when private agents borrow from their commercial banks, which in turn borrow from the central bank. While banks usually lend for the long term, they have to refinance at the central bank over short maturities. Single banks can refinance themselves in the money or capital market. However, the system as a whole has to refinance at the central bank, as only the central bank can create base money. As the ECB provides money primarily via its main refinancing operation, which has a maturity of two weeks (ECB 2001, pp. 65ff), the financial system as a whole has a short maturity on the liability side, while its assets are at least partly of a long maturity.

The price for short-term money borrowing can easily be shown to be under the control of the central bank: since refinancing at the ECB by a single bank has to be renewed every two weeks, at this point, the single bank has the choice whether to borrow from the central bank or from other banks in the money market which may have excessive funds. If the ECB's interest rate is below the interest rate in the money market, commercial banks will borrow from the central bank and sell excessive liquidity in the money market, thus extending the monetary base, until the money market interest rate equals the ECB's marginal refinancing rate. If the ECB's interest rate is above the interest rate in the money market, banks will borrow in the money market and not refinance at the central bank. As former refinancing operations mature, money is paid back to the central bank without equivalent new refinancing, contracting the monetary base until the interest rate in the money market equals the refinancing rate.[4]

A similar argument can be made for the US Fed. While the Fed does tend to conduct some outright purchases of government papers, it still heavily relies on repurchase agreements to fine-tune the short-term federal funds rate to the targeted level (Marquis 1996, pp. 248ff). As we know from general equilibrium theory, it is the marginal price of a par-ticular good or service that determines the price for all units traded. Consequently, it is the marginal interest rate with which banks have to calculate that determines the interest rate in the money market. If the Fed finds that the Fed funds rate is below its target rate, it will offer banks the chance to purchase some government paper now and resell a few days later, with the repurchase price reflecting an interest rate equal to the target rate. It fact, this operation parallels the ECB's repuchasing agreements: banks will now sell securities to the Fed under the repurchasing agreement and loan the acquired funds in the money market, thus bidding down the short-term interest rate until it equals the Fed's target rate. On the other hand, if the Fed funds rate is below the target rate, the Fed will sell banks government papers under a repurchase agreement, selling government papers from its portfolio and repurchasing them a few days later. As long as the implicit interest rate of this contract is above the actual Fed funds rate, the banks will borrow in the Fed funds market to profit from the repurchase agree-ment, thus bidding interest rates up to the target rate.[5]

In a world of perfect foresight, banks would know the future course of monetary policy and thus future short-term interest rates. As long as the banking system has sufficient capital to expand its balance sheets, interest rates on long-term credits to safe debtors running for T periods would be solely determined by short-term interest rates via a non-arbitrage condition, just as the *Pure Expectation Theory* predicts:[6]

$$(1+i_{0,T}) = \sqrt[T]{(1+i_{0,1})(1+i_{1,2})...(1+i_{T-1,T})} \tag{4.1}$$

$$= \prod_{t=1}^{T}(1+i_{t-1,t})^{\frac{1}{T}} \tag{4.2}$$

However, neither debtors nor commercial banks have perfect foresight. Assuming rational expectations[7] and risk neutrality, with the short-term interest for the first period $i_{0,1}$ known we would get:

$$(1+i_{0,T}) = \sqrt[T]{(1+i_{0,1})(1+E(i_{1,2}))...(1+E(i_{T-1,T}))} \tag{4.3}$$

$$= \prod_{t=1}^{T}(1+E(i_{t-1,t}))^{\frac{1}{T}} \tag{4.4}$$

assuming risk neutrality is not satisfying. That individuals are risk averse is quite a common conclusion from microeconomic reasoning. And as Stiglitz (1992) shows, given the enormous costs of bankruptcy for banks, it is rational for financial institutions to act in a risk-averse manner. Thus, the interest rate on a loan that cannot go bad would be determined not only by expected future short-term interest rates, but also by term premia $\varphi_{m,t,s}$ which are demanded when agreeing in period m to lend money from period t to period s ($m < t < s$). For forward interest rates $f_{m,t,s}$ agreed upon in period m to lend from period t to period s, we then get:

$$f_{m,t,s} = E_m(i_{t,s}) + \Phi_{m,t,s} \tag{4.5}$$

And thus for the interest rate on a long-term loan:

$$(1+i_{0,T}) = \prod_{t=1}^{T}(1+f_{0,t-1,t})^{\frac{1}{T}} \tag{4.6}$$

$$= \prod_{t=1}^{T}(1+E(i_{t-1,t})+\Phi_{0,t-1,t})^{\frac{1}{T}} \tag{4.7}$$

The term premia can thus be interpreted as a risk premium that the financial institution charges for the risk that short-term interest rates will fluctuate and the short-term refinancing conditions thus change. Since the risk premium can well be expected to be a function of expected and actual fluctuations in the short-term interest rate (its variance), it is only rational for monetary authorities to smooth interest rates, as has been found by Goodhart (1997) or Srour (2001): only by keeping the term premia low will they be able push relevant long-term interest rates down far enough in an emergency to prevent the economy from falling into deflation. Issing (1997) gives a further hint as to why central banks change interest rates only gradually which also fits into the theory presented here. According to Issing, smoothing interest rates diminishes a signal extraction problem. Financial market participants know that an interest rate change will not be reversed again quickly, so a change has a larger impact on expectations about the medium and long term, which in turn leads to a larger impact on long-term rates.

The explanation presented in this chapter also fits well with the fact that forward contracts are a bad predictor for future short-term rates and generally overstate the interest charged in the future. Moreover, deducing forward interest rates (and thus long-term interest rates) from the commercial banks' considerations has the advantage that one can easily explain why the term premium φ is empirically positive on average for all term lengths. When only arguing with individuals' saving and investment decisions, as Hicks (1946) does following Keynes (1930), it is hard to show why all term premia should be positive. When an individual is, for example, saving for his children's education, he might care about his investment return in ten years, but not about interest variations (and thus temporary capital gains or losses) in the meantime (Modigliani and Sutch 1966). At least in an ageing society with a capital-funded pension system, one should expect low or even negative term premia. With the commercial banks' refinancing process as an explanation for term premia, this objection does not hold: the bank has to care about interest rate changes throughout all of a credit's maturity.

This line of argument results in the normal form of the yield curve (Figure 4.1).[8] Yields increase rather strongly at the short end of the curve, while the difference between the long term (ten years) and very long term (thirty years) is generally rather low. This can be interpreted as the expectation that in the very long run the central bank will keep inflation low (and thus keep nominal interest rates around some historical average when we assume that real interest rates will hover around a certain average as well), but with the possibility that in the meantime transitory shocks might drive inflation and interest rates temporarily away from the long-run stationary state.

Only in a situation in which it is strongly expected that interest rates will fall in the imminent future (perhaps due to an economic downturn which the central bank then tries to offset), can it be anticipated that these expectations overcompensate the risk premium demanded by the banks. In this situation, we get the inverted yield curve.

Empirical puzzles

Empirical testing of the implications of the expectation hypothesis (EH) and of monetary policy's effects on the yield curve has produced a vast range of literature.[9] Most authors find that the EH in its crudest form does not seem to provide a satisfactory explanation for the real-world reaction to short- and long-term interest rates. First, there is disagreement over whether the relationship between short- and long-term interest rates is stable over time. While Hardouvelis (1994) finds that the term structure spread is stationary, both Hassler and Nautz (1998) and Nautz and Wolters (1998) claim, following Campbell and Shiller (1987), that there is no stable relationship between money market interest rates and interest rates with a maturity of several years. Moreover, the magnitude of the reaction of long-term rates to changes in overnight rates differs widely.[10] Although it is well established that

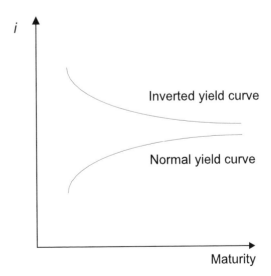

Figure 4.1   A normal and inverted yield curve

monetary policy *in general* has an influence on long-term interest rates in the direction expected from EH, there are well-known episodes in which long-term interest rates reacted in the opposite direction from what would have been expected from EH. For example, on a number of occasions in 1994 when the Fed announced an increase in its target rate, interest rates on long maturities fell (Ellingsen and Söderström 2001).

However, evaluating EH by testing whether a given shift in the short-term rate leads to a shift in the expected magnitude in long-term rates, poses several problems. First, if a central bank enters the picture which uses the short-term interest rate in order to control inflation and stabilise output, complications arise. As for the transmission to the real economy, it is the real rate, not the nominal rate which matters; market participants have to form expectations about both the future course of real interest rates and inflation and about the central bank's policy stance. They have to predict how the real economy will develop and how the central bank will react to these developments. In addition, they have to forecast how the monetary authority will react to transitory shocks. If the central bank places a higher weight on output stabilisation than on inflation stabilisation, an inflationary shock would be answered with a smaller reaction. Returning to the inflation target would take longer, while real interest rates might remain higher for a prolonged period (as there is no stabilisation recession caused by the central bank, and thus there will be no need to lower interest rates later on in order to stimulate a recovery).

Moreover, there might be information asymmetry between the central bank and market participants as to the state of the economy. This does not necessarily mean that the central bank has private knowledge about macroeconomic data.[11] In fact, very little macroeconomic data is private information. However, as Romer and Romer (2000) show, the Fed's inflation and output predictions are far better than those of commercial market participants.[12] Romer and Romer relate this finding to the vast resources which the central bank devotes to forecasting macroeconomic developments. Thus, a change in the short-term interest rate might signal some information which had been hidden from the private sector until then.

A monetary policy move which changes the short-term rate can therefore be classified as follows:[13]

1. *Affirmative policy action:* Interest rates are changed as an expected reaction to publicly known macroeconomic data.

2. *Data-revealing policy action:* Interest rates are changed as a reaction to the central bank's private information on the state of the economy, be it information about the state of the financial sector, judgements or forecasts of the state of the economy computed from publicly known macroeconomic data.

3. *Preference-revealing policy action:* Interest rates are changed as the weight the central bank gives to output stabilisation relative to inflation stablisation changes. A shift to a disinflation policy would be an extreme example of such a change.

To further complicate the picture, the risk premium charged by financial institutions does not need to be constant or stationary. If one assumes this risk premium to be a function of the single bank's balance position or the economy's state in the cycle, shifts in risk premia seem plausible. Nautz and Wolters (1998) show that the econometric evidence would be in line with non-stationary, shifting term premia.

Depending on the type of policy action, the effects on inflation and interest rate expectations as well as on long maturities' rates can be expected to differ greatly. Affirmative policy actions will not cause inflation or interest rate expectations to change. Ideally, they will have been completely priced in, and the long-term interest rate then remains unchanged. Almost all of the literature finds that only unanticipated changes in the short-term interest rate have significant effects on bond yields (Nautz and Wolters 1998, Kuttner 2001).

Data-revealing policy actions, on the other hand, demonstrate that there is some danger to output and/or inflation of which the private sector is not yet aware. In this case, interest rates on long maturities should move in the same direction as the policy instrument. If, for example, the central bank knows of an as-yet publicly undetected inflationary shock and raises the interest rates in reaction, it is only rational for market participants to increase their inflation expectation *and* their interest rate expectation, as the inflationary shock will bring about a reaction by the central bank.

Finally, a preference-revealing policy action will change inflation and output expectations. With a more inflation-averse central bank, the economy can be expected to have a lower inflation rate and fewer output stabilisation. Consequently, it is rational for individuals to lower their inflation expectations when the central bank tightens interest rates due to a preference shift. Here an increased short-term interest rate should be associated with a fall in nominal long-term rates (or a tilting yield curve) (Ellingsen and Söderström 2001).

That an affirmative policy action does not change long-term interest rates, however, does not mean that the central bank influences long-term interest rates only by data- or preference-revealing policy actions. Instead, for interest rates to come down in an economic slump, it is crucial that market participants expect the affirmative actions: as market participants see the real economy weakening and inflationary pressure vanishing, they will expect the central bank to lower interest rates some time in the future. Consequently, they will lend and borrow for longer terms for reduced rates. At the same time, when inflationary pressure is mounting, long-term interest rates will rise *because* the central bank is expected to act in the future.

But, and this is important, if market participants did not expect the central bank to act on economic conditions, the long-term interest rate would not react. Central to this assumption is the refusal of the standard Wicksellian notion of a natural rate of interest. In Wicksell's world, any monetary interest rate below the natural rate of interest would induce an accelerating increase of the rate of inflation, any deviation above the natural rate a spiral of falling inflation (and ultimately, increasing deflation). The model presented in Chapter 5 draws a different picture. It is shown there that in a world with strategically acting trade unions, there is no natural tendency for an accelerating inflation or deflation when the rate of interest changes. Instead, changes in the interest do change the price *level*, but there are multiple equilibria in the goods and financial markets. As long as unit labour costs (influenced by the nominal wages contracted by trade unions and employers) remain stable, in a relatively closed economy no permanently accelerating inflation or deflation will develop.

If there are multiple equilibria, the central bank can influence which point is chosen, given the restrictions from the financial markets, which will prohibit the central bank from choosing an interest rate so low that a depreciation of the domestic currency destroys its value and sets into motion an inflationary spiral. By setting its actual short-term rate of interest, it can signal which future course of monetary policy it will conduct.

We can put this argument into an imaginary experiment: If the ECB announced that short-term interest would remain at 6 per cent from now on (which in 2002 could safely be assumed to be above an inflationary level), and if it were credible that the ECB would stick to this promise, there would be little reason that the yield on two-year bonds should be different from 6 per cent. A higher or lower yield on two-year bonds would be quickly competed away, as commercial banks could borrow at 6 per cent from the ECB and have a free lunch if the yield on two-year bonds were higher. Similarly, no one would buy two-year bonds with yields below 6 per cent if she could permanently invest the same amount in the money market and get 6 per cent there.

Of course, a 6 per cent interest rate would have real consequences: many of the investments undertaken until then would suddenly be unprofitable. Firms would disinvest and aggregate demand would fall. The aggregate capital stock would shrink and employment would sharply contract. However, in the end, the economy would settle for a new price level and a new, lower level of output and employment. With strategically acting unions, there would be no reason for wages also to fall. As will be shown in Chapter 5, a fall in nominal wages would leave real wages unchanged and thus not increase employment. Consequently, unions would have no incentive to settle for lower nominal wages.

A central bank which does not react to macroeconomic data with an expected interest rate change would in fact signal a preference shift. Here, the long-term interest rate should change in the opposite direction, as it would be expected that the monetary authority would change its short-term instrument.

In reality, the private sector seldom knows exactly why a central bank changes its interest rates. In addition, real-world policy actions may even be a combination of those classified above. If the central bank behaves as expected, market participants will assume that the central bank decided on the basis of the same data as the private sector used to predict the central bank's moves. But if the central bank acts differently from what individuals expected, the question is: did monetary authorities have private information, or did their preference just shift? Different opinions, the wording of central bank statements and the degree to which a monetary policy innovation has been expected can explain why there is no stable relationship between short- and long-term interest rates.

Again, this all leaves monetary policy with plenty of room for influencing the interest rate. First, a policy stance which puts more weight on output stabilisation leads to automatic changes in the long-term rate when data show that the real economy is deteriorating. Secondly, if one assumes risk premia not to be constant, but to vary with the uncertainty surrounding the future course of monetary policy, a central bank can decrease the long-term interest rate by acting in a predictable way and explaining its policy moves so that the public does not confuse data- and preference-revealing policy actions.

4.2   Investment and the interest rate

But how does a change in the interest rate translate to the real economy? One possible demand component influenced by the central bank's monetary policy is *aggregate investment*.

The short run

The economic argument for a short-run effect of lower interest rates on investment is quite simple: the individual entrepreneur compares her return of a possible investment opportunity[14] to either her financing costs or her alternative yield were she to invest in financial assets. If the proposed return on real investment is higher than the opportunity costs, she will conduct the investment; otherwise, she will not.

This approach can be nicely transformed into a macroeconomic investment function using Tobin's (1969) q.[15] Originally, q is defined as the ratio of the market value of some investment or enterprise to its replacement value. With a market value above replacement value, there is an incentive to invest in new equipment. With a replacement value above market value, there is an incentive not to invest, as similar equipment can be bought more cheaply in the market. Thus, in the absence of monopoly power and risk, the equilibrium value for q is unity; with some monopoly power and risk averse entrepreneurs, $\bar{q}$ might well be above unity. In a static situation[16] we thus get the following investment function:

$$\frac{I}{K} = \phi(q) \quad \text{with} \quad \frac{\partial \phi}{\partial q} > 0, \, \phi(\bar{q}) = 0 \tag{4.8}$$

Under certain assumptions[17], q can also be written as the ratio of the return on real investment R to the return demanded from investors for holding real capital r^K. If real investment is seen as a perfect substitute for investment in the money market, Tobin's q can be written as the simple ratio of R to the real interest rate on monetary holdings r^M. Note that R and r^K in this formulation can be expressed in nominal or real terms; the only important thing is that both variables have the same dimension:

$$q = \frac{R}{r^M} \tag{4.9}$$

Though this final simplification has the disadvantage of ignoring not only the transmission via the financial sector, but also complications from the individual's portfolio allocation, it is still widely used (or implied) in macroeconomic models which describe a link between interest rate and investment demand (Bofinger 2001, pp. 82ff).

The appeal of this approach is that by including R, which describes the return on a real investment, actual demand conditions are also taken into account. With R being a function of aggregate excess demand, an interest rate cut which affects the amount of investment also increases the profitability of capital employed in the economy, since aggregate demand is increased. As long as there is excess demand, firms are able to make extra profits above what could be expected in long-run equilibrium.[18]

Fiscal policy (which is not analysed in depth in this book), on the other hand, would not have as large an impact on q.[19] While monetary policy changes both denominator and numerator of (4.9) so that the initial impulse on r^M is amplified by an increase of aggregate demand and thus the return on capital R, fiscal policy changes only aggregate demand and thus the numerator of (4.9). Moreover, in interaction with monetary policy, the effect of the initial fiscal impulse might even be dampened. If fiscal policy is running a deficit and the supply of bonds is increased, the central bank might find itself forced to raise interest rates as a reaction, and fiscal policy would also push up r^M. This would limit the impact on q or even be counterproductive if the increase in r^M overcompensates the increase in R. Consequently, expansionary fiscal policy might at best increase R, but it will not be able to *decrease r^M*.

However, even though the exact transmission is different, both fiscal and monetary policy are able to influence aggregate demand in ways that push up extra profits.[20] These extra profits (whether from an increase in government expenditure or monetary policy innovations) are not permanent, however. With q being larger than $\bar{q}$, capacities are increased (thus the higher investment demand I). With larger capacities, aggregate supply increases and extra profits are competed away with R approaching $\bar{q}r^M$ and q again approaching $\bar{q}$ (Collignon 2002a, Chapter 8).[21]

In the real world, this mechanism seems to be amplified by the *credit channel* (Bernanke and Gertler 1995). This credit channel works in two ways. The traditional way of viewing this channel was through the *bank lending channel* (Bernanke and Blinder 1988). As the central bank drains reserves (and hence deposits) from the banking system as it tightens monetary policy, so it was argued, the banks' access to loanable funds would be reduced. Consequently, commercial banks were restricted in their possible credit supply.

However, this view has several shortcomings – especially regarding the economy of EMU. First of all, reserve requirements have to be fulfilled only *ex post*. With the possibility of always accessing the standing marginal lending facility (albeit at an interest rate above the main financing rate), financial institutions change their credit supply *before* acquiring the necessary reserves. Thus credits come before deposits.[22] As the money supply has to be elastic if the ECB is to fulfil its function as lender of last resort (and is evidently elastic owing to the central bank's institutional setup), the banking sector as a whole is not reserve-constrained. Consequently, the banking channel in its traditional form is not a very plausible explanation of how monetary policy works in EMU.

The second way in which the credit channel might work on investment demand is the *balance sheet channel*. Here, it is argued that a borrower has to pay an external financing premium depending on her own financial position. As a tightening of monetary policy increases the interest the borrower has to pay, her financial position weakens and the premium she has to pay increases.[23] In addition, rising interest rates are typically associated with declining asset prices, which shrink the value of the borrower's collateral, further magnifying this effect.

Finally, increased extra profits might boost investment via the *cash flow effect*. If capital markets exhibit information asymmetries, and some firms are therefore credit-constrained even though they are profitable, the extra profits from increased aggregate demand might provide them with the liquidity necessary for conducting extra investment.

The long run

Falling interest rates can thus be associated with an increase in the investment demand and so with an increase in aggregate demand. When the adjustment process towards $\bar{q}$ has finished, however, it is not *a priori* clear what happens to aggregate demand. Only if aggregate demand has permanently increased can the larger capital stock be sustained. If aggregate demand fell to its initial level, profits on the now higher aggregate capital stock would not be high enough to sustain the achieved yield on capital R. With R falling below r^M, q would fall below unity, thus leading to disinvestment.

Whether a change in the equilibrium long-term interest rate has any permanent influence on aggregate investment depends on the assumptions one makes about the nature of capital and whether one assumes the existence of a neo-classical macroeconomic production function.[24]

If one follows the Cambridge (US) position (the neo-classical approach) in the debate (which is also followed by most mainstream economic textbooks), the argument is quite simple. Output per unit of effective labour is a function of capital stock per unit of labour k with diminishing marginal returns to capital:

$$y = y(k), \frac{\partial y}{\partial k} > 0, \frac{\partial^2 y}{\partial k^2} < 0 \qquad (4.10)$$

In equilibrium, the real interest rate r must equal the marginal productivity of capital. When assuming the special, simplified case of a Cobb–Douglas production function, one can calculate the equilibrium capital stock k^* as a function of the equilibrium real rate of interest r^*:

$$y = k^\alpha, 0 < \alpha < 1 \qquad (4.11)$$

$$\Rightarrow k^* = \left(\frac{\alpha}{r^*}\right)^{\frac{1}{1-\alpha}} \qquad (4.12)$$

If additionally depreciation is assumed as a constant share δ of the capital stock, equilibrium real investment demand j^* would be a decreasing function of the equilibrium real rate of interest:

$$j^*(r^*) = \delta k^*(r^*) = \delta\left(\frac{\alpha}{r^*}\right)^{\frac{1}{1-\alpha}} \qquad (4.13)$$

Thus, a lower equilibrium interest rate would permanently increase aggregate demand, as a higher capital stock would need more investment to be sustained. In a world in which aggregate employment is determined by aggregate demand, this would permanently lead to higher employment.

4.3 Consumption and the interest rate

While this interpretation is consistent with the standard neo-classical capital theory, it is not satisfactory for those who have opted for the Cambridge (UK) side in the capital controversy. As Sraffa (1960) has shown, the capital intensity of production is not monotonous in the interest rate. Instead, one can easily construct examples in which 'double-switching' can be observed: At a high interest rate, a production process *A* with low capital intensity is preferred over process *B* with high capital intensity. When the interest rate falls, *B* then becomes more favourable than *A*, but with a further falling interest rate, *A* again is more profitable than *B*.

Moreover, even if one accepts a neo-classical production function as (4.10) and a world in which aggregate demand determines aggregate output, it is still not clear whether a fall in interest rates could lead to higher output *equilibrium*. As in equilibrium, aggregate demand and aggregate supply have to match, without any changes in exports, government and private consumption; additional investment demand from additional depreciation would have to match the additional production due to higher capital inputs.

If additional production were larger than additional demand, companies could not sell their product for what they expected to earn. Companies would be cutting back capacities until the capital stock had fallen to a lower level again. If, on the other hand, production were smaller than additional demand created, the excess demand would drive up prices, which would lead to more investment, additional demand again – and an explosive path.

Substitution between present and future consumption

The solution for both problems lies in relating consumption to the *interest rate*. In the standard short-run approach, it is argued that the interest rate is the relative price of consumption today in units of future consumption. With interest rates rising, current consumption becomes more expensive relative to future consumption, thus inducing economic agents to consume less today and save more for the future.

While this line of argument has sound micro-foundations, it has one problem: empirically, studies such as Mankiw (1981), Hansen and Singleton (1983), Hall (1988) or Campbell and Mankiw (1989) were not able to find a significant effect of variations in interest rates on consumption. So, the ECB (2000a) concludes that the effect of interest rates on substitution between consumption and saving is too small to be a reliable transmission channel of monetary policy.

Still, there are other ways in which changes in the interest rate might affect consumption. The balance sheet effect at work at the corporate level might also constrain households. As McCarthy and Peach (2002) show, an increase in interest rates has a significant negative effect on house prices. Decreased net wealth of the individuals not only dampens their desire to consume (as one would conclude from the permanent income hypothesis), but it might also make it harder for them to obtain new credits (e.g. for the purchase of durable consumer goods). Thus, aggregate consumption might fall.

Liquidity and distributional considerations

For those households which are heavily indebted or have a mortgage on a house,[25] changes in the interest rate will change current disposable income. Of course, this would only be a redistribution between debtors and lenders. But if it is the lenders who have a higher marginal propensity to consume or are credit-constrained, this would have a negative effect on aggregate consumption. Though this effect might not be as large in the euro-zone as in the UK, as a smaller part of mortgage loans is indexed, the share remains large enough to make a measurable contribution (Barran, Coudert and Mojon 1997).

Alternatively, one could argue that interest incomes are received by different households than are wage incomes. As recipients of capital income generally have higher incomes than those receiving labour incomes, one could assume households with capital incomes to have a lower propensity to consume.[26] A redistribution from individuals living from capital incomes to those living on wages would thus increase the overall propensity to consume, thereby boosting aggregate demand.[27]

Consumption and unemployment

In a Keynesian world in which there is involuntary unemployment and in which employment is determined by aggregate demand, interest rate changes affect aggregate consumption via the multiplier effect: a change in the interest rates changes aggregate investment, which in turn leads to a change in unemployment. Higher unemployment reduces aggregate consumption as the income of those being unemployed is reduced. On the other hand, lower unemployment increases aggregate consumption as some of the formerly unemployed now earn wages which they can spend on consumption. As lower interest rates usually come with higher investment demand, the lower the interest rate, the higher also is aggregate consumption due to this employment effect. Chapter 5 depicts a Keynesian world in which this mechanism is at work.

Long-run productivity

Besides these short-run effects, there might be further long-run effects from interest rates on consumption. For establishing a negative long-run correlation between consumption and interest rates, one has first to remember the components which make up a standard Keynesian consumption function. Consumption is defined as autonomous consumption C_0 and consumption as a share of current income:

$$C = C_0 + cY \qquad (4.14)$$

What is important here is to remember that 'autonomous' does not mean that this part of consumption is independent from income. It is merely independent from *current* income. Instead, one can safely assume that C_0 is a function of lifetime income. As is the essence of Friedman's (1953) permanent income hypothesis, individuals try to smooth their consumption over their lifespan. Thus, an increase in the individual's permanent income might well translate into a proportional increase in consumption.[28]

Figure 4.2 shows that, at least for the rich countries, this proposition empirically seems to be a better approximation than Keynes' (1936, p. 97) assumption that the gap between income and consumption would widen when real income increased. If we look at the data from the Penn World Table (Heston and Summers 1995) for countries with a BIP of more than US$10,000 per head (basically the industrialised world), we cannot find a significant negative relationship between a country's *per capita* income and its consumption share. This does not

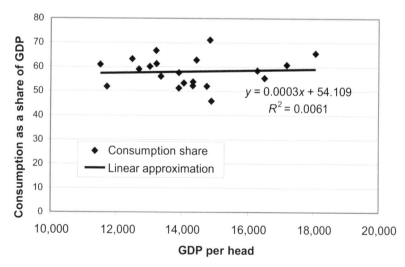

Figure 4.2   Consumption share and GDP, 1990 (US$)
Source: Penn World Table, Heston and Summers (1995).

mean that affluent individuals in a given economy have the same propensity to consume as the low-income individuals. If the average income in an economy is one of the indicators from which economic agents form their expectations about their lifetime income, lower-income households still would consume a larger share of their income. However, as the whole economy gets richer, there is no reason to expect a falling consumption share.

Permanent income can be expected to be influenced by the interest rate. If labour is paid its marginal product, wages are a function of labour productivity. There are two mechanisms by which a lower interest rate can translate into higher consumption via labour productivity: First, in a world with a neo-classical production function, a lower interest rate leads to a higher per *capita capital* stock and thus to higher labour productivity. This increased labour productivity would lead to higher real wages and thus higher consumption demand.

Second, a lower interest rate might influence total factor productivity (TFP). With the emergence of New Growth Theory (NGT), it has become evident that labour productivity is not some exogenous parameter. Instead, it is influenced not only by economies of scale (*learning-by-doing* in its intertemporal form), but also by intended accumulation of knowledge, such as investments in human capital (e.g. training) and research and development (R & D).[29]

As lower interest rates bring about investments with longer amortisation periods – and both investment in human capital and basic R & D are investments with long horizons – lower interest rates can be expected to funnel investment into these activities (Schelkle 2001, p. 218). This in turn would lead to higher productivity growth and thus to higher lifetime income of the individuals in an economy. Consequently, one could also expect autonomous consumption and thus aggregate demand to increase permanently. This mechanism will even work in a world in which it is not clear whether a lower interest rate really leads to a higher capital stock per worker.

4.4   Notes on the exchange rate channel

Besides monetary policy effects on investment and consumption, models of monetary policy transmission usually also include an exchange rate channel.[30] With a loosening of monetary policy, most macroeconomic models suggest a depreciation of the domestic currency. This depreciation exerts a widespread influence on the economy – both directly and via the financial markets. It causes an increase in exports, partly compensated by an increase in the import volume of goods for which demand is not very price elastic (e.g. crude oil). At the same time, for an economy with a positive net foreign asset position, it increases private wealth in domestic currency and thus leads to an increase in consumption. For a country with a negative net foreign asset position, the effect is less obvious: here, the net wealth decreases with a depreciation of the domestic currency, thus depressing consumption. Moreover, if firms are indebted in foreign currency, a depreciation weakens their financial position, thus dampening investment.

But even for countries with a positive net foreign asset position, an exchange rate shift can bring about a permanent and stable increase of aggregate demand only if we assume that a current account can permanently be in disequilibrium. However, in the long run, this assumption is dubious. Any increase in net exports would lead to a decrease in another country's net exports. As long as the trade balance was in equilibrium before a cut in domestic interest rates, it will show a surplus after the depreciation.[31] If this surplus persists (and net interest payments were zero in the beginning), the foreign country accumulates debt. Even if we do not take into account a period of repayment, this accumulating debt increases the interest payments the country in question has to make.[32] So even with a permanently changed trade balance and the resulting export demand, the current account surplus would continue to widen.

If we assume that the current account would return to equilibrium at some time in the distant future (that is, net exports plus net interest payments adding up to 0), the domestic currency would have to appreciate again over the long run – either merely in real terms through a rising domestic price level or also in nominal terms through a change in the exchange rate. Exports would consequently fall again. As the foreign asset position would then have improved, interest flows into the homeland would also be bigger. Net exports would thus have to fall below the initial level to reach a balanced current account again. Higher net exports now would inevitably lead to *lower* equilibrium net exports in the future.[33] Consequently, *permanently* changing aggregate demand by depreciation is not a viable option.

Moreover, even for the short-run tuning of aggregate demand, the exchange rate channel seems a dubious choice: empirically, the link between the exchange rate and monetary policy action is not stable, or at least dominated by other factors. No recognised economic model has yet been developed to explain in a satisfactory manner the large swings in the euro/dollar exchange rate during the first years of existence of the euro-zone in 2001, the Fed lowered short-term interest rates[34] from 6.5 per cent in late 2000 to 1.75 per cent at the end of the year – the lowest level since the 1950s. At the same time, the ECB cut interest rates from 4.75 to 3.25 per cent. The interest rate differential between the two economic regions thus first narrowed and then even switched sign. As given by standard theory, this should have brought about a sharp appreciation of the euro. Instead, however, the euro further depreciated, from US$0.95 to US$0.89. A sharp turn in the euro/dollar rate came only in 2003, after both central banks lowered their respective interest rates by an additional 0.75 per centage points, bringing the euro back to almost US$1.30.

There thus seems much anecdotal evidence that short-run behaviour cannot be explained well by fundamentals, but more by market sentiment. Unfortunately, the research on this area dubbed *behavioural finance* is only in its infancy. However, the first theoretical models underlining the importance of noise traders or limited arbitrage possibilities in financial markets are promising.[35]

4.5 Transmission in the euro-zone: empirical evidence

The ECB has conducted some extensive research on the transmission of monetary policy to the real economy of the euro-zone. Within its 'Monetary Transmission Network', a series of working papers was published in which the transmission mechanism was empirically tested not only on a euro-zone basis, but also for individual countries.

Using synthetic data for the euro-zone from 1980 to 1998 within a VAR framework, Peersman and Smets (2001) find that monetary policy has a significant effect on output in the euro-area. Decomposing the effect into changes in investment and consumption, they find that investment reacts far more strongly than consumption and that its reaction pattern is close to that of GDP. Angeloni *et al.* (2002) report similar findings.

Mojon, Smets and Vermeulen (2001) provide similar results for the individual countries of the euro-zone using original data. Using firm-level panel data, robust evidence emerges for a significant influence of changes in the user cost of capital on investment demand, as well as of a significant influence of sales on investment demand, for both a European panel of firm data as well as for national data sets.[36] Which is broadly consistent with Tobin's *q* theory of investment as presented in this chapter.

Additionally, the studies provide evidence that a credit channel is at work in the euro-zone. Though Chatelain *et al.* (2001) find evidence for a significantly different reaction of small and large firms only for Italy and not for Germany, France and Spain, companion papers hint that a correlation between other indicators for balance sheet quality and investment demand does exist. Von Kalckreuth (2001) finds for Germany that firms with a bad credit rating seem to be credit-constrained. As cash flows vary with interest payments, this constraint becomes more severe in times of monetary contraction. For France, firms belonging to the equipment goods sector, firms with a lower rating and firms with a high share of trade credit in the balance sheet are also more sensitive to cash flow (Chatelain and Tiomo 2001). For Italy, firms with a high share of intangible assets over total assets, an indication of the extent of asymmetric information, respond more to cash flow and stock of liquidity available (Gaiotti and Generale 2001).

It can thus be concluded that monetary policy in the euro-zone transmits directly to investment and consumption demand as described in this chapter. The most important channel of transmission seems to be via the cost of capital, while there might be a relevant, but limited credit channel effect. The GDP component most important for this transmission seems to be investment.

5
Output and Prices in a World Without the Real Balance Effect

As has been shown in Chapter 4, one can conclude that monetary policy in the euro-area works primarily through the interest rate channel on aggregate investment. By changing the short-term interest rate, the ECB changes yields on other financial instruments, which in turn change the interest rate that firms have to pay for financing their investment. Depending on the demand conditions they face, they will decide which of their potential investment projects looks sufficiently promising and will conduct the investments necessary for these projects. The lower the interest rates, the more projects promise profit, given certain fixed demand conditions, thus the higher the aggregate investment.

Moreover, just as monetary policy does not transmit by exogenously changing the money supply, changes in the real money stock induced by changes in the price level also do not influence aggregate demand. Falling prices – which would increase the real value of a given outstanding money stock – do not by themselves lead to higher aggregate demand. Since the money stock in circulation is not net wealth to the economy, changes in the price level do not alter the net wealth position and thus do not change aggregate real consumption. And as the money stock is a consequence of credits demanded and loans granted, a change in the price level which leaves the real profitability of firms unchanged also leaves investment demand unchanged.

This chapter will present a variation of a standard macroeconomic model of monopolistic competition which includes these features (Section 5.1). A model of monopolistic competition is chosen not only since much of the recent literature uses such macroeconomic models, but also since monopolistic competition is probably the best approximation of reality that economists have so far.

By solving the model, it is demonstrated that the overall nominal wage level of an economy does not influence output, employment or profits. Instead, it is the *interest rate* which determines these variables, together with other parameters such as the technologically given share of labour in the production function or the degree of monopolisation. All of these parameters also enter into the price function. In addition, it can be shown that the price level is proportional to the nominal wage level in the economy.

Sections 5.2–5.3 examine how large and small wage setters in an economy as depicted in the model would behave, and what consequence the model's properties have on the economic policy responsibilities with regard to price stability, employment and output. It is found that the central bank's task is to keep the nominal wage level from drifting upwards. This has to be done by threatening to induce pain in wage bargainers by using the interest rate to push down employment and output. As wage setting in the euro-zone seems to work to a large extent as wage setting relative to a core EMU wage, which in turn is heavily influenced by the German wage level,[1] the ECB's task would thereby be to target German wages. Wage setters are not able to influence aggregate employment, but have to rely on the central bank to react benignly to their wage setting behaviour. Appendixes 1–3 consider further aspects of the model and give computational details.

5.1   Equilibrium in a baseline model

The model used in this chapter builds on the formulation of Blanchard and Kiyotaki (1987) and Blanchard and Fischer (1989, Chapter 8) as also used by SICCD models. The derivation of the demand function that a single firm faces for its products remains essentially the same as in Blanchard and Fischer (1989, Chapter 8) or in the preceding work of Dixit and Stiglitz (1977). Instead of having worker-producers who directly provide the economy with their products, as in the early Blanchard contributions, a profit-maximising firm is modelled following Coricelli, Cukierman and Dalmazzo (2000). Consequently, there is not only a price for the single product sold (which the worker-producer would receive), but also an explicit nominal wage paid to workers employed by the single firms.

What is different from these models, however, is the introduction of a capital stock and a different formulation of aggregate demand. While in the standard models of monopolistic competition only labour enters into the production function as input, the single firm in my model chooses both capital and labour employed. What is also different is, of course, the aggregate demand function. While in the original formulations, aggregate demand depends on real balances $\frac{M}{P}$ in the economy, the model presented here does not incorporate this chain of causation. Monetary policy thus does not work by changing the money supply M, but by setting the rate of interest.[2] This rate of interest then leads firms to change their decision about capital input, which leads to a higher capital stock on the supply side and to higher investment demand on the demand side.[3]

The single firms' decisions

The economy is composed of n monopolistically competitive firms, each producing a good i given a simple Cobb–Douglas production function. Labour N_i and capital K_i are the two input factors of firm i. In addition, some technological level A also enters the production function as Hick-neutral technological progress:

$$y_i = AN_i^\alpha K^{1-\alpha}{}_i, \; 0 < \alpha < 1 \tag{5.1}$$

Each firm faces a (real) demand y_i^D for its output,[4] being a function of the price of its good P_i, the price level P, the number of goods n which are produced and thus enter into the individuals' CES utility function, the (absolute value of the) elasticity of demand facing the individual firm η (which is also the constant elasticity of substitution in the CES utility function)[5] and the aggregate nominal demand Y^D, which will be elaborated in more detail later:

$$y_i^D = \frac{1}{n}\left(\frac{P_i}{P}\right)^{-\eta} \frac{Y^D}{P} \tag{5.2}$$

As is standard in models of monopolistic competition, for a stable equilibrium to exist, $\eta > 1$ must hold (Blanchard and Fischer 1989, p. 377). The aggregate price level is given by:

$$P = \left(\sum_{j=1}^{n} \frac{1}{n} P_j^{(1-\eta)}\right)^{\frac{1}{1-\eta}} = \left(\frac{1}{n} \sum_{j=1}^{n} P_j^{(1-\eta)}\right)^{\frac{1}{1-\eta}} \tag{5.3}$$

For the long-run equilibrium, each firm chooses its capital stock and its employment per unit of output so that unit costs uc_i are minimised given the capital costs (interest rate i^K that it has to pay on the nominal capital employed[6] plus the technical rate of depreciation δ[7]) and the wage W_i the single firm has to pay:

$$\min_{K_i, N_i} uc_i = W_i\left(\frac{N_i}{y_i}\right) + P(\delta + i^K)\left(\frac{K_i}{y_i}\right) \tag{5.4}$$

Using (5.1) as a constraint, (5.4) yields capital and labour employed in equilibrium per unit of output produced:[8]

$$\frac{K_i^*}{y_i} = \frac{1}{A}\left(\frac{W_i}{P}\right)^\alpha \frac{(1-\alpha)^\alpha}{(\delta + i^K)^\alpha \alpha^\alpha} \tag{5.5}$$

$$\frac{N_i^*}{y_i} = \frac{1}{A}\left(\frac{P}{W_i}\right)^{1-\alpha} \frac{(\delta + i^K)^{1-\alpha} \alpha^{1-\alpha}}{(1-\alpha)^{1-\alpha}} \tag{5.6}$$

Equilibrium unit costs uc_i^* are given by:

$$uc_i^* = W_i\left(\frac{N_i^*}{y_i}\right) + P(\delta + i^K)\left(\frac{K_i^*}{y_i}\right) \tag{5.7}$$

$$= W_i\frac{1}{A}\left(\frac{P}{W_i}\right)^{1-\alpha} \frac{(\delta + i^K)^{1-\alpha} \alpha^{1-\alpha}}{(1-\alpha)^{1-\alpha}}$$

$$+ P\frac{1}{A}\left(\frac{W_i}{P}\right)^\alpha \frac{(\delta + i^K)^{1-\alpha}(1-\alpha)^\alpha}{\alpha^\alpha} \tag{5.8}$$

$$= \frac{1}{A}P^{1-\alpha}W_i^\alpha \frac{(\delta + i)^{1-\alpha}}{\alpha^\alpha (1-\alpha)^{1-\alpha}} \tag{5.9}$$

Given the unit costs in this cost-minimum equilibrium, the single firm in a second stage maximises its profits Π_i by choosing the price for its product P_i given the general price level and the demand function it faces. The firm then produces as much as is demanded for the price it asks:

$$\max_{P_i} \Pi_i = [P_i - uc_i^*]y_i^D \tag{5.10}$$

$$= [P_i - uc_i^*]\frac{1}{n}\left(\frac{P_i}{P}\right)^{-\eta} \frac{Y^D}{P} \tag{5.11}$$

Maximising yields:

$$P_i = \frac{-\eta}{(1-\eta)} uc_i^* \qquad (5.12)$$

When all firms are faced with the same wage level W and the same technological conditions (expressed in a similar total factor productivity A and similar weight of labour in the Cobb–Douglas production function α), all prices P_i are necessarily identical. We can thus solve for all prices and the general equilibrium price level P^* by substituting (5.6) and (5.5) as unit costs (5.7) into (5.12):[9]

$$P^* = P_1 = \ldots = P_n = A^{-\frac{1}{\alpha}} \left(\frac{-\eta}{1-\eta} \right)^{\frac{1}{\alpha}} \frac{(\delta + i^K)^{\frac{1-\alpha}{\alpha}}}{\alpha(1-\eta)^{\frac{1-\alpha}{\alpha}}} W \qquad (5.13)$$

The price level is thus proportional to the nominal wage level. The assumption of a uniform wage level is not as restrictive as it seems at first sight: a uniform wage level would either be the result of a monopoly trade union bargaining for wages in the whole economy or of a completely flexible (that is, atomistic and friction-free) labour market in which free movement of labour would guarantee that wages in a single firm did not deviate from the market wage W.[10]

With all prices being identical, (5.2) simplifies to:

$$y_i^D = \frac{1}{n} \frac{Y_D}{P} \qquad (5.14)$$

Equilibrium capital K_i^* and labour N_i^* employed in each firm are given by multiplying capital (5.5) and labour (5.6) per unit of output by the firm's actual production (5.14):

$$K_i^* = \frac{1}{nA} \left(\frac{W}{P} \right)^\alpha \frac{(1-\alpha)^\alpha}{(\delta + i^K)^\alpha \alpha^\alpha} \cdot \frac{Y^D}{P} \qquad (5.15)$$

$$N_i^* = \frac{1}{nA} \left(\frac{P}{W} \right)^{1-\alpha} \frac{(\delta + i^K)^{1-\alpha} \alpha^{1-\alpha}}{(1-\alpha)^{1-\alpha}} \frac{Y^D}{P} \qquad (5.16)$$

These results are not very startling yet: as is standard also in neo-classical models, the higher the real wages, the more capital and the less labour is employed per unit of output. The higher the rate of interest, the less capital and the more labour is employed per unit of output. The results also embody Keynes' (1936, p. 135) notion of marginal efficiency of capital: the firm employs an additional unit of capital if the proceeds from selling the additional production are at least equal to the cost of employing the additional unit of capital.[11]

Macroeconomic aggregates

Aggregating the firms' capital stocks and employment and substituting (5.13), the aggregate equilibrium capital stock K^* and aggregate equilibrium employment level N^* are thus:

$$K^* = \frac{1}{A}\left(\frac{W}{P}\right)^{\alpha} \frac{(1-\alpha)^{\alpha}}{(\delta+i)^{\alpha}\alpha^{\alpha}} \frac{Y^D}{P} \tag{5.17}$$

$$= \left(\frac{1-\eta}{-\eta}\right)\frac{1-\alpha}{\delta+i^K} \frac{Y^D}{P} \tag{5.18}$$

$$N^* = \frac{1}{A}\left(\frac{P}{W}\right)^{1-\alpha} \frac{(\delta+i^K)^{1-\alpha}\alpha^{1-\alpha}}{(1-\alpha)^{1-\alpha}} \frac{Y^D}{P} \tag{5.19}$$

$$= \left(\frac{-\eta}{1-\eta}\right)^{\frac{1-\alpha}{\alpha}} \frac{(\delta+i^K)^{\frac{1-\alpha}{\alpha}}}{A^{\frac{1}{\alpha}}(1-\alpha)^{\frac{1-\alpha}{\alpha}}} \frac{Y^D}{P} \tag{5.20}$$

What is interesting here is that the nominal wage disappears from both capital stock and labour employed. The reason is that the price level (5.13) is itself proportional to the nominal wage level W, thus leaving the real wage independent from the nominal wage.

So far, this result also holds when we use an aggregate demand function with real money supply M/P as an argument. In this case (and with an exogenously set M), unions could actually increase employment by lowering their wage demands. Lower wages would translate into lower prices via (5.13) and higher real balances. As higher real balances then would lead to higher demand, employment and output would be higher than before. The direct link proclaimed in the SICCD models from lower nominal wage demands to higher output when the central bank is not active, would still be intact.

However, as I have shown in Chapter 3, a significant real balance effect cannot be expected to work in the real world. Instead, one should include both income flows from wages and profits and investments derived from the firms' individual decisions in the aggregate demand function. The part of consumption that depends on income[12] is modelled as a constant share c of the wage bill.[13] Investment demand is derived from the fact that firms maximise their profits by varying labour and capital input and thus production of their product. Given the demand conditions, firms will aim for some equilibrium capital stock. For given demand conditions and given nominal wages, firms will employ more capital the lower the interest rate i^K. As soon as they have attained this capital stock, they will invest only precisely the amount necessary to replace depleted capital stock. In equilibrium, investment demand is thus precisely equal to the depreciation on the capital stock employed.[14] In situations in which the equilibrium is not yet reached, there is also some net investment bridging a share ξ between the actual capital stock K and the desired equilibrium capital stock K^*.[15] Real capital demand is thus a function of the interest rate i^K which is set by the central bank. As capital is a real variable, to deduct nominal demand we have to multiply investment demand by the price level P.[16] Finally, we will allow for one further autonomous[17] real demand component y_0^D, which could either be government demand or autonomous consumption demand:

$$Y^D = cNW + \xi P(K^* - K) + \delta PK + Py_0^D \qquad (5.21)$$

For the equilibrium case $K = K^*$, this simplifies to:

$$Y^D = cNW + \delta PK^* + Py_0^D \qquad (5.22)$$

Substituting (5.21) for (5.20) yields an equilibrium aggregate real output for the whole economy as well as an equilibrium aggregate employment which is independent from the nominal wage level:

$$y^* = \frac{-\eta}{-\eta + (\eta - 1)(c\alpha + \dfrac{\delta(1-\alpha)}{(\delta + i^K)})} y_0^D \qquad (5.23)$$

$$N^* = \left(\frac{-\eta}{1-\eta}\right)^{\frac{1-\alpha}{\alpha}} \frac{-\eta(\delta + i^K)^{\frac{1-\alpha}{\alpha}}}{A^{\frac{1}{\alpha}}(1-\alpha)^{\frac{1-\alpha}{\alpha}}\left[-\eta + (\eta - 1)\left(c\alpha + \dfrac{\delta(1-\alpha)}{(\delta + i^K)}\right)\right]} y_0^D \qquad (5.24)$$

Both output and employment are proportional to autonomous demand. However, the respective multipliers differ both in form and in the way they depend on other parameters. While output clearly increases with lower interest rates, the employment effect of a change in interest rates is ambiguous due to the fact that a substitution between capital and labour takes place depending on the level of nominal interest rates i^K. This mechanism will be covered in greater detail on p. 108.

Dividing aggregate output (5.23) by labour employed (5.24), we get for labour productivity λ:

$$\lambda = A^{\frac{1}{\alpha}} \left(\frac{1-\eta}{-\eta} \right)^{\frac{1-\alpha}{\alpha}} \frac{(1-\alpha)^{\frac{1-\alpha}{\alpha}}}{(\delta + i^K)^{\frac{1-\alpha}{\alpha}}} \tag{5.25}$$

These three terms can be interpreted as follows: the first term represents the technological progress component. With increasing TFP, labour productivity increases by its share in the production function. The second term is a competition term. The larger the degree of monopoly power of the single firm (and thus the smaller η),[18] the larger the mark-up of goods over labour costs. As the prices of capital goods move with the prices of all goods, this larger mark-up leads to higher prices of capital relative to labour. The more expensive the capital, the less is used in the production process relative to the labour input. Consequently, the higher the monopoly power, the less capital-intensively will goods be produced and thus the lower the labour productivity will be. Finally, the last term is a capital employment term: the higher the cost of capital, the smaller the capital stock employed and the less productive each unit of labour.

The real wage per unit of labour employed is given by:

$$\varpi = \frac{W}{P} = \alpha A^{\frac{1}{\alpha}} \left(\frac{1-\eta}{-\eta} \right)^{\frac{1}{\alpha}} \frac{(1-\alpha)^{\frac{1-\alpha}{\alpha}}}{(\delta + i^K)^{\frac{1-\alpha}{\alpha}}} \tag{5.26}$$

$$= \alpha \left(\frac{1-\eta}{-\eta} \right) \lambda \tag{5.27}$$

Thus, as can be expected, the real wage depends on the productivity of labour λ. However, it also depends on the weight labour has in the production function and on the degree of monopolisation in the economy. If firms have high monopoly power (and η is thus low), workers receive a smaller share of their labour productivity in wages.

Real profits per unit of production are given by:

$$\frac{\Pi^*}{Py} = 1 - \frac{1-\eta}{-\eta} \left(\alpha + \delta \frac{1-\alpha}{\delta + i^K} \right) \tag{5.28}$$

And aggregate real profits (including both capital rent and entrepreneurs' profits) by:

$$\Pi^* = \left(1 - \frac{1-\eta}{-\eta}\left(\alpha + \delta\,\frac{1-\alpha}{\delta + i^K}\right)\right)\frac{-\eta}{-\eta + (\eta - 1)\left(c\alpha + \dfrac{\delta\,(1-\alpha)}{(\delta + i^K)}\right)}\,y_0^D \qquad (5.29)$$

Interpretation

These results, which are again summarised in Table 5.1, are quite interesting. First, it has to be noted that *the price level (5.13) is proportional to the wage level*. In addition, the price level is a positive function of the nominal interest rate. *The higher the interest rates, the higher are also prices.* This conclusion might at first be startling (as higher interest rates are used by central banks to fight inflation), but is only a result of the fact that higher interest rates in this model translate into higher capital costs for the single firm.[19] Moreover, it has to be remembered that the price level just deduced is an equilibrium price level. In the short run, changes in interest rates can be expected to cause the opposite effect than in the long-run equilibrium as is shown on page 30. Additionally, the higher the elasticity of substitution between different products, the lower the price level. As the elasticity of substitution can be interpreted as the inverse degree of the firms' monopoly power (Blanchard and Giavazzi 2000, p. 10ff.), this is easily explainable: the higher the degree of monopoly power, the higher monopoly profits and the higher thus the mark-up over wage and capital costs.

Second, *output and employment are not functions of the nominal wage level*.[20] Variations in the wage level therefore do not have any influence on the level of output or employment. Instead, both output and employment are functions of the parameters concerning the technological production function, the technological progress and the elasticity of substitution of the single goods (which can be interpreted as some measure of monopoly power), the interest rate, the rate of depreciation and autonomous demand. Employment is proportional to output and, in addition to being a function of output, itself a function of the degree of monopolisation as well as the capital costs. The higher the capital costs, the more labour is used to produce a single unit of output and the less capital is used. Thus, with higher interest rates, production becomes more labour-intensive. Similarly, the higher the degree of monopoly power, the less efficient the production that takes place. Consequently, employment per unit produced is a positive function of η.

However, this increased employment per unit produced stands in contrast to the fact that overall output is reduced when interest rates are higher as well as when there is a higher degree of monopoly power. Higher interest rates translate into a lower aggregate capital stock and thus lower investment demand. A higher degree of monopolisation lowers real wages and thus the workers' consumption demand.

In this world, *unemployment could persist even if there were a completely competitive labour market:* as it is the nominal wage level which is contracted in the labour market, excess unemployment in a setting with a completely flexible wage market would put downward pressure only on nominal wages and prices, but would not lead to a return to some (however defined) full employment equilibrium.

Third, *real wages and real profits are independent of nominal wages.* Instead, they are – as prices – a function of the technological parameters A, δ and α, the monopoly power η and the interest rate. For the real wage and the profit per unit of production, the influence is as expected: a higher weight of labour in the production function increases real wages and decreases real profits per unit of production. A higher degree of monopoly power increases profits per unit and decreases real wages. Higher interest rates translate into lower real wages and higher unit profits. For aggregate profits, things get more complicated. As a higher monopoly power leads to less demand via the demand multiplier in (5.23), the effect of higher unit profits is countered by a volume effect which dampens aggregate production. However, the overall effect of higher monopoly power on aggregate profits remains positive.

Fourth, as the interest rate influences the amount of capital employed, *both supply and demand of goods rise with lower interest rates:* with a larger capital stock per worker, productivity and output per head are higher. At the same time, a higher capital stock needs higher equilibrium (gross) investments to sustain and thus increases aggregate demand. Lower interest rates thus lead to higher output in this setting (Table 5.1).

The fact that some kind of substitution between labour and capital takes place at the firm level leads to somewhat ambiguous results as to how changes in the interest rate translate into changes in employment, as two effects with different signs appear. On the one hand, lower interest rates lead to a substitution of labour for capital at the firm level. At the same time, demand increases as real wages increase and the equilibrium capital stock per unit of output gets bigger, thus leading to a higher investment demand. At low interest rates, the demand effect is larger than the substitution effect. At very high interest rates, on the other hand, the capital stock is already very low.

Table 5.1 Macroeconomic variables in the baseline model

Real output (5.23):

$$y^* = \frac{-\eta}{-\eta + (\eta - 1)\left(c\alpha + \frac{\delta(1-\alpha)}{(\delta + i^K)}\right)} y_0^D$$

Employment (5.24):

$$N^* = \frac{1}{A}\left(\frac{P}{W}\right)^{1-\alpha} \frac{(\delta + i^K)^{1-\alpha} \alpha^{1-\alpha}}{(1-\alpha)^{1-\alpha}} y^*$$

$$= \left(\frac{-\eta}{1-\eta}\right)^{\frac{1-\alpha}{\alpha}} \frac{-\eta(\delta + i^K)^{\frac{1-\alpha}{\alpha}}}{A^{\frac{1}{\alpha}}(1-\alpha)^{\frac{1-\alpha}{\alpha}}\left[-\eta + (\eta - 1)\left(c\alpha + \frac{\delta(1-\alpha)}{(\delta + i^K)}\right)\right]} y_0^D$$

Price level (5.13):

$$P^* = A^{-\frac{1}{\alpha}}\left(\frac{-\eta}{1-\eta}\right)^{\frac{1}{\alpha}} \frac{(\delta + {}_i K)^{\frac{1-\alpha}{\alpha}}}{\alpha(1-\alpha)^{\frac{1-\alpha}{\alpha}}} W$$

Productivity (5.25):

$$\lambda = A^{\frac{1}{\alpha}}\left(\frac{1-\eta}{-\eta}\right)^{\frac{1-\alpha}{\alpha}} \frac{(1-\alpha)^{\frac{1-\alpha}{\alpha}}}{(\delta + i^K)^{\frac{1-\alpha}{\alpha}}}$$

Real wage (5.27):

$$\varpi = \alpha\left(\frac{1-\eta}{-\eta}\right)\lambda$$

Aggregate real profits (5.29):

$$\frac{\Pi^*}{P^*} = \left(1 - \frac{1-\eta}{-\eta}\left(\alpha + \delta\frac{1-\alpha}{\delta + i^K}\right)\right)y^*$$

Variables used

A	Technological progress	λ	Labour productivity
α	Capital coefficient in Cobb–Douglas production function	N^*	Aggregate employment
		Π^*	Aggregate (nominal) profits
c	Consumption share	ω	Real wage
η	Elasticity of substitution between different goods	P^*	Equilibrium price level
		W	Nominal wage level
δ	Technological rate of depreciation	y^*	Real aggregate output
i^K	Interest rate to be paid by firms	y_0^D	Autonomous demand

A variation here does not bring much variation in the demand for investment goods to replace depreciated capital. Here, the substitution effect is bigger than the income effect; lower interest rates here would lead to lower employment.

Differentiating (5.24) with respect to the interest rate i^K and solving shows that the employment effect of lower interest rates is positive as long as

$$i^K < \frac{\delta((\eta - 1)c\alpha - 1)}{\eta - \eta c\alpha + c\alpha} \tag{5.30}$$

holds. Unfortunately, the interpretation of this term is not trivial. Partial differentiation shows that the right-hand term is a positive function in α, c, η and δ. This can be explained, as with an increase in any of these parameters; the amount by which an additional unit of capital employed increases aggregate demand also increases: with less monopoly power, real wages are higher, and consumption thus increases more strongly when employment rises. The same is valid for α: with a higher weight of labour in the production function, the effect of an increase in aggregate demand on the real wage bill and thus on aggregate consumption is higher. For c and δ the argument is that higher parameter values lead to a higher increase in aggregate demand for any given increase in the capital stock.

However, for a wide range of plausible parameter values, the interest rates observed in the real world are clearly in the range in which an increase in interest rates would lead to a fall in employment: assuming that η is in the range of 20, α around 0.7,[21] δ around 0.2, interest rate increases up to roughly 20 per cent would lead to a decrease in equilibrium employment. For the rest of this work, I will thus assume that the parameters are in a range such that a cut in interest rates actually also leads to an increase in employment.

The conclusions that employment and output are independent of the general wage level would explain why unit labour cost increases below inflation and target inflation in Italy, France or Germany during some of the 1990s did not lead to significant increases in employment. In a closed economy as depicted in this model, cutting nominal wages does not create employment, as aggregate demand falls with falling costs and firms are not able to demand the same prices for their products as they used to before the change in wages.

This is a conclusion completely at odds with macroeconomic text-book models. While it is usually not disputed that a cut in wages also diminishes the workers' consumption demand, real money balances suffice in standard models to increase aggregate demand when wages are falling. Lower wages and prices then lead to an increase in private wealth, which translates either into higher consumption demand (via the Pigou effect) or into higher investment demand (via the Keynes effect).

In the model presented here, real balance effects do not exist. A cut in nominal wages thus dampens nominal demand directly and proportionally. As all firms are faced with both lower costs and a shifted nominal demand curve, they cut their prices until their profit maximum is reached. In this new equilibrium, real variables have not changed. Only prices have adjusted.

5.2 The labour market and wage dynamics

So far, we have not analysed wage setting in detail. In Section 5.1, it was stated that in both a highly competitive labour market and in a labour market with a centralised wage setting, the wage level W would be uniform across firms. As long as one is interested only in real wages, output and employment, this approach is justified, as nominal wages do not influence any of the real variables. However, as we know from (5.13), the development of nominal wages is central for inflation dynamics. To understand inflation, we consequently need to analyse how nominal wages are set in the labour market. To this end, this section will now first look at a situation in which a perfect neo-classical labour market exists. In a second step, I will show how a setting with a single large, strategically acting wage setter changes the picture. Finally, I will look at a setting in which one large and one small wage bargaining area exist.

Theoretical considerations: a neo-classical labour market

In a standard neo-classical or textbook atomistic labour market, there is a natural rate of unemployment, or more precisely the non-accelerating inflation rate of unemployment (NAIRU). Whenever actual unemployment rises above the NAIRU, labour supply is greater than demand for labour. Consequently, nominal wage increases start to decline. When actual unemployment falls below the NAIRU, excess demand for labour triggers rising nominal wage increases (Blanchard and Fischer 1989, p. 544, or Romer 1996, p. 225ff.). Figure 5.1 illustrates this concept. Unemployment below U_{NAIRU} leads to accelerating wage increases, unemployment below U_{NAIRU} to decelerating wage increases.[22]

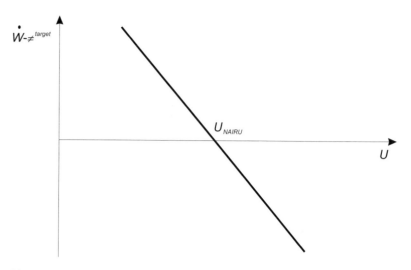

Figure 5.1   Wage increases and unemployment in an atomistic labour market

Adding such a labour market to the model presented in this chapter would not change any of the conclusions from Section 5.1. However, such a labour market would introduce significant instability to the system. As falling nominal wages do not help to solve the lack of effective demand, any shortfall in demand would finally turn into a deflationary spiral. Such a system would not show any tendency to stabilise itself; instead, economic policy would have to assume an active role and keep aggregate demand exactly at the point unemployment equaled the NAIRU.

It is interesting to note that in such a system increased rigidities in the labour market can exert a stabilising influence. The quicker the overall wage level reacts to deviations of aggregate demand from the level at which unemployment equals the NAIRU, the easier the system might experience high inflation or deflation. However, the speed with which wages adjust depends critically on labour market rigidities: the less frequent wage readjustments, for example, the smaller the danger of the system spiralling into deflation or inflation.

A monopoly union

The picture changes completely when there is a monopoly trade union setting wages for the whole economy. In standard theory, there would still be a single-point NAIRU with a monopoly union. By pushing for higher nominal wages, the union could influence real wages and unemployment (Burda and Wyplosz 1997, p. 150). The case of why a union cares about its members' real wages is clearcut: real wages translate into union members' higher personal incomes and thus higher utility.

There are several reasons why a union might also care about unemployment. First, in countries with developed unemployment or welfare systems, there are costs associated with higher unemployment. If these costs are financed by either general or payroll taxes, unions have an interest in keeping them low. Second, as Blanchard and Summers (1987) note, a decline in employment might also lead to a drop in union membership. Union leaders should fear such a development as they would lose power and revenue. Third, higher unemployment increases the union members' fear of becoming unemployed themselves. This fear lowers their respective utility, and they can be expected to push their leaders to care about unemployment as well. A rational monopoly union would thus take into account whether its wage demands increase unemployment and choose its optimum level of unemployment and real wages. According to standard theory, the union would use its monopoly power to push for somewhat higher wages than in the atomistic labour market case, accepting unemployment above the NAIRU in an atomistic labour market. However, if aggregate demand caused unemployment to rise above that threshold, it would be rational for the union to take back its wage demands to get unemployment back to that optimum. If increased aggregate demand pushed unemployment below that point, the union would increase wage demands to find its optimum.

In this chapter's model, however, the wage level set by centralised wage bargaining W does not influence employment or the real wage. In contrast to the argument in the SICCD models (see chapter 2), there is thus no reason for unions to restrain their wage demands in order to increase employment. Similarly, there is no reason for unions to push for generally higher nominal wages to improve their real wage position. The monopoly union should thus be completely indifferent to the nominal wage level. As long as wage bargaining structures (and thus the union's monopoly to bargain for wages) remain stable, there are multiple equilibria of stable wage inflation and unemployment: price stability is thus compatible with a wide range of unemployment.

This does not necessarily mean that stable prices are compatible with every level of unemployment. From a certain unemployment rate downwards, there might be real shortages in the labour market. A single firm looking for workers might just offer them higher wages or non-monetary benefits in order to lure them into its factories. The rate of wage increases would accelerate.

Similarly, from a certain rate of unemployment upwards, it could be difficult to uphold union monopoly power. As will be shown on p. 103, a small union bargaining wages for a single firm or even a small group of firms is able to increase employment in its constituency at the expense of the rest of the economy by cutting its nominal wage. If unemployment becomes too pressing, there is a danger that the unemployed will try to price themselves back into the market by way of this mechanism, monopolised wage bargaining breaks down. From a certain point of unemployment upwards, wage increases would thus decelerate.

Figure 5.2 illustrates this argument: In the range between U_1 and U_2, there are multiple equilibria for stable wage inflation. If unemployment falls below U_1, labour market shortages lead to rising nominal wage pressure. If unemployment rises above U_2, centralised wage setting structures might endogenously break up. However, as nominal wages do not change anything in aggregate employment, this change in bargaining structures would not help at all in lowering unemployment. For the rest of this chapter, the logic of an economy hovering in the range between U_1 and U_2 will be analysed.

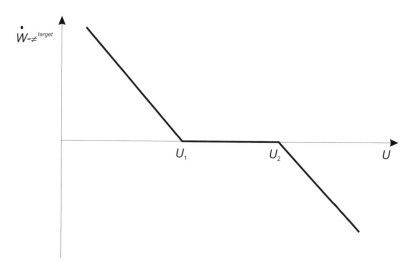

Figure 5.2   Wage increases and unemployment in a world with a large wage setter

In a setting of highly coordinated wage bargaining, unions can be expected to behave similarly to monopoly unions. With the union setting the wage contract closely followed by the rest of the economy – which knows that changes in the nominal wage level translate neither into real wage increases (for their members nor for the other unions' members) nor into changes in employment – this single union will behave as the monopoly union.

The case of a small country in EMU

The union's maximisation problem looks different if a single union sets wages for only a small part of the economy. In this case, a single union *can* influence its members' real wages and employment by setting its nominal wage to be different from the wage level paid in the rest of the economy.

We assume that the big union sets the wage level W_{-m} for most of the economy as a Stackelberg leader. The small union then follows by setting wages W_m for $m < n$ of the firms in the economy. For the rest of this chapter, variables with the index m denote variables for firms 1 ... m, variables with the index $-m$ denote variables for firms $m + 1$ ... n.

In the context of EMU, this small union would represent a small country such as the Netherlands or Ireland. When setting wages, the small union has to take into account the firms' unit cost minimisation and profit maximisation problems from (5.4) and (5.11). Solving for the firms' products price P_m, output y_m^D, employment N_m and profits (including interest costs) Π_m, we get:[23]

$$P_m = \left(\frac{n-m}{n} \left(\frac{W_{-m}}{W_m} \right)^{\alpha(1-\eta)} + \frac{m}{n} \right)^{\frac{1-\alpha}{\alpha(1-\eta)}}$$

$$\cdot \frac{1}{A^{\frac{1}{\alpha}}} \left(\frac{-\eta}{1-\eta} \right)^{\frac{1}{\alpha}} \frac{(\delta + i^K)^{\frac{1-\alpha}{\alpha}}}{\alpha(1-\alpha)^{\frac{1-\alpha}{\alpha}}} W_m \qquad (5.31)$$

$$= \left(\frac{n-m}{n} \left(\frac{W_{-m}}{W_m} \right)^{\alpha(1-\eta)} + \frac{m}{n} \right)^{\frac{-1}{1-\eta}} P \qquad (5.32)$$

$$y_m^D = \left(\frac{n-m}{n} \left(\frac{W_{-m}}{W_m} \right)^{\alpha(1-\eta)} + \frac{m}{n} \right)^{\frac{\eta}{1-\eta}} \frac{mY^D}{nP} \qquad (5.33)$$

$$N_m^* = \left(\frac{n-m}{n} \left(\frac{W_{-m}}{W_m} \right)^{\alpha(1-\eta)} + \frac{m}{n} \right)^{\frac{1-\alpha+\eta\alpha}{\alpha(1-\eta)}}$$

$$\cdot \left(\frac{-\eta}{1-\eta} \right)^{\frac{1-\alpha}{\alpha}} \frac{1}{A^{\frac{1}{\alpha}}} \frac{(\delta + i^K)^{\frac{1-\alpha}{\alpha}}}{(1-\alpha)^{\frac{1-\alpha}{\alpha}}} \frac{m}{n} \frac{Y^D}{P} \tag{5.34}$$

$$= \frac{m}{n} \left[\frac{n-m}{n} \left(\frac{W_{-m}}{W_m} \right)^{\alpha(1-\eta)} + \frac{m}{n} \right]^{\frac{1-\alpha+\eta\alpha}{\alpha(1-\eta)}} N^* \tag{5.35}$$

$$K_m^* = \frac{1}{A} \left(\frac{W_i}{P} \right)^{\alpha} \frac{(1-\alpha)^{\alpha}}{(\delta + i^K)^{\alpha} \alpha^{\alpha}} \left(\frac{P_i}{P} \right)^{-\eta} \frac{m}{n} \cdot \frac{Y^D}{P}$$

$$\frac{\Pi_m}{P} = \frac{1-\eta}{-\eta} \left[\frac{n-m}{n} \left(\frac{W_{-m}}{W_m} \right)^{\alpha(1-\eta)} + \frac{m}{n} \right]^{-1} \frac{m}{n} \cdot \frac{Y^D}{P} \tag{5.36}$$

Faced with the wage level W_m, the firms covered by the large union's wage bargaining also maximise their profits by choosing their prices and capital and labour input, given the competition by the firms 1 ... m and given their own cost structure. For the prices asked by those firms we get P_{-m}, for employment in those firms N_{-m}:

$$P_{-m} = \left[\frac{n-m}{n} + \frac{m}{n} \left(\frac{W_m}{W_{-m}} \right)^{\alpha(1-\eta)} \right]^{\frac{1-\alpha}{\alpha(1-\eta)}}$$

$$\cdot \frac{1}{A^{\frac{1}{\alpha}}} \left(\frac{-\eta}{1-\eta} \right)^{\frac{1}{\alpha}} \frac{(\delta + i^K)^{\frac{1-\alpha}{\alpha}}}{\alpha(1-\alpha)^{\frac{1-\alpha}{\alpha}}} W_{-m} \tag{5.37}$$

$$N_{-m}^* = \left[\frac{n-m}{n} + \frac{m}{n} \left(\frac{W_m}{W_{-m}} \right)^{\alpha(1-\eta)} \right]^{\frac{1-\alpha+\eta\alpha}{\alpha(1-\eta)}}$$

$$\cdot \left(\frac{-\eta}{1-\eta} \right)^{\frac{1-\alpha}{\alpha}} \frac{1}{A^{\frac{1}{\alpha}}} \frac{(\delta + i^K)^{\frac{1-\alpha}{\alpha}}}{(1-\alpha)^{\frac{1-\alpha}{\alpha}}} \frac{n-m}{n} \frac{Y^D}{P} \tag{5.38}$$

$$\frac{\Pi_{-m}}{P} = \frac{1-\eta}{-\eta} \left[\frac{n-m}{n} + \frac{m}{n} \left(\frac{W_m}{W_{-m}} \right)^{\alpha(1-\eta)} \right]^{-1} \frac{n-m}{n} \cdot \frac{Y^D}{P} \tag{5.39}$$

As the price for goods produced in firms 1 ... m is now different from the price for the goods produced in firms $m + 1$ ... n, the aggregate price level has changed as well. Using (5.3) gives us for the aggregate price level in the case of wage differentiation P_{Wd}^*:

$$P^*_{Wd} = \left(\frac{n-m}{n} \left(\frac{W_{-m}}{W_m} \right)^{\alpha(1-\eta)} + \frac{m}{n} \right)^{\frac{1}{\alpha(1-\eta)}}$$

$$\cdot \frac{1}{A^{\frac{1}{\alpha}}} \left(\frac{-\eta}{1-\eta} \right)^{\frac{1}{\alpha}} \frac{(\delta + i^K)^{\frac{1-\alpha}{\alpha}}}{\alpha(1-\alpha)^{\frac{1-\alpha}{\alpha}}} W_m \qquad (5.40)$$

$$= \left(\frac{n-m}{n} \left(\frac{W_{-m}}{W_m} \right)^{\alpha(1-\eta)} + \frac{m}{n} \right)^{\frac{1}{\alpha(1-\eta)}} P^* \qquad (5.41)$$

Table 5.2 again summarises the main results, substituting the terms

$\left(\frac{n-m}{n} \left(\frac{W_{-m}}{W_m} \right)^{\alpha(1-\eta)} + \frac{m}{n} \right)$ and $\left(\frac{n-m}{n} + \frac{m}{n} \left(\frac{W_{-m}}{W_m} \right)^{\alpha(1-\eta)} \right)$ by h_m and h_{-m} to

make the interpretation of the results more simple. To that end, note that the small union term h_m increases with W_m and decreases with W_{-m}, while the large union term h_{-m} decreases with W_m and increases with W_{-m}.

The results thereby obtained are quite interesting. The selling price of products made in firms 1 ... m, the real production and the employment in these firms are thus all functions of the wage W_m relative to the wages in the rest of the economy W_{-m}. Confronted with a lower nominal wage than the (monopolistic) competitors ($W_m < W_{-m}$), the firms 1 ... m will be able to offer their goods for a lower price than the competitors charge for their products. Consequently, *firms 1 ... m are able to reap a larger share of aggregate demand and are able to sell more of their products.*

At the same time, as labour in firms 1 ... m is now cheaper relative to capital employed, those firms will also produce in a more labour-inten-sive way. *At the firm level, a substitution of labour for capital takes place.* The single firm not only produces more, but uses more capital input per unit of production. Thus *employment in those firms reacts even more strongly than the firm's production and sales to a change in the firm's wage level,* as can be seen as $h_m^{\eta/1-\eta}$ enters the employment function (5.39) instead of $h_m^{\frac{1-\alpha-\alpha\eta}{\alpha(1-\eta)}}$ in the output function (5.33).

The reaction in the rest of the economy is just the opposite. With lower wages and prices in firms 1 ... m, the aggregate price level is lower than in the case in which everyone pays a wage equivalent to W_{-m}. Consequently, the real wage in firms $m + 1$ ... n is also higher than in the baseline case. Here, a substitution between labour and capital towards a more capital-intensive production takes place. At the same

Table 5.2 Prices, output, employment and profits when a small union sets wages for m firms in the economy

---

Price of goods 1...m (5.32):

$$P_m = h_m^{\frac{-1}{1-\eta}} P$$

Real output of firms 1...m (5.33):

$$y_m = h_m^{\frac{\eta}{1-\eta}} \frac{m}{n} y^*$$

Employment in firms 1...m (5.35):

$$N_m = h_m^{\frac{1-\alpha+\eta\alpha}{\alpha(1-\eta)}} N^*$$

Real profits in firms 1...m (5.36):

$$\frac{\Pi_j}{P} = \frac{1-\eta}{-\eta} h_m^{-1} \frac{m}{n} \cdot \frac{Y^D}{P}$$

Employment in firms 1...m (5.39):

$$N_{-m} = h_{-m}^{\frac{1-\alpha+\eta\alpha}{\alpha(1-\eta)}} N^*$$

Aggregate price level (5.41):

$$P_{Wd} = h_m^{\frac{1}{\alpha(1-\eta)}} P^*$$

With h_m and h_{-m} defined as:

$$h_m = \left(\frac{n-m}{n} \left(\frac{W_{-m}}{W_m} \right)^{\alpha(1-\eta)} + \frac{m}{n} \right)$$

$$h_{-m} = \left(\frac{n-m}{n} + \frac{m}{n} \left(\frac{W_{-m}}{W_m} \right)^{\alpha(1-\eta)} \right)$$

$$\frac{\partial h_m}{\partial W_m} > 0, \frac{\partial h_m}{\partial W_{-m}} < 0, \frac{\partial h_{-m}}{\partial W_m} < 0, \frac{\partial h_{-m}}{\partial W_{-m}} > 0$$

Variables used:

α	Capital coefficient in production function
η	Elasticity of substitution between different goods
m	Number of firms paying wage W_m
n	Number of firms/goods in the economy
N^*	Aggregate employment in monopoly union case
N_m	Employment in firms 1 ... m
N_{-m}	Employment in the rest of the economy
Π_j	Nominal profits in firm j
P_{Wd}	Aggregate price level with wage differentiation
P_m	Price for goods 1 ... m
W_m	Nominal wages paid in firms 1 ... m
W_{-m}	Nominal wages paid in the rest of the economy
y_m	Real output in firms 1 ... m

time, demand for products from firms $m + 1 \ldots n$ falls, as they are more expensive relative to goods $1 \ldots n$ than before. Output in firms $m + 1 \ldots n$ thus decreases with increasing output in firms $1 \ldots m$.

Finally, profits in firms $1 \ldots m$ increase when the wage for those firms falls. However, as production becomes more labour-intensive and labour thus becomes less productive, the firm's profit does not react quite as strongly as the firm's output.

As would be expected in standard neo-classical theory, a lower nominal wage in firms $1 \ldots m$ leads to higher profits, higher output and higher employment in these firms. The difference between the model presented here and standard neo-classical models is that in this chapter's model, these results hold only for a single firm. Moreover, *the expansion of employment in firms $1 \ldots m$ comes at the expense of decreasing employment, output and profits in the rest of the economy.*

In principle, one could think that this strategy still might lead to an increased aggregate real output. However, as can be shown, real aggregate demand $\dfrac{Y^D}{P}$ is independent from both W_m and W_{-m} even for the case that $W_m \neq W_{-m}$, so that aggregate real output also remains unchanged.[24] Thus, lowering wages in the firms $1 \ldots m$ relative to the wage level paid in the rest of the economy is nothing more than a beggar-thy-neighbour policy by real devaluation. In the aggregate, nothing is won by such a strategy, only firms $1 \ldots m$ fare better at the expense of the firms $m + 1 \ldots n$.

Turning to wage bargaining, it is now plausible that employers in firms $1 \ldots m$ would have an incentive to keep wages as low as possible. The case for workers in those firms and the unions representing them is less clearcut. As the general price level changes less than proportionally with falling wages in firms $1 \ldots m$, real wages in those firms are a direct function of nominal wages W_m. Consequently, workers in those firms will not necessarily be too happy about a wage cut. On the other hand, they might have higher job security when employment in their firms is increased. In order to find out what the small union bargaining for workers working in firms $1 \ldots m$ makes of this trade-off between wages and employment, we need to define the union's utility.

As is standard in the theory of trade unions' behaviour as surveyed by Oswald (1982), we assume that both the real wage and the employment's deviation from some employment target $\bar{N}_m$ in the single union's constituency enter with weights γm_1 and γ_{m2} ($\gamma_{m1} + \gamma_{m2} = 1$; $\gamma_{m1}, \gamma_{m2} > 0$) into the union's utility function. Instead of opting for a unemployment entering the utility function in a quadratic form as is standard in the theory of trade unions' behaviour, I have chosen an absolute term as it allows the function to be solved more easily.[25]

$$U^{union} = \gamma_{m1} \frac{W_m}{P} - \gamma_{m2} \mid N_m - \bar{N}_m \mid \tag{5.42}$$

For the sake of simplicity of exposition, we assume that firms $1 \ldots m$ cover only a very small part of the economy, so that the small union does not have to take its own wages' effects on the aggregate price level into account.[26] Formally, this translates into $\frac{m}{n} \to 0$. Thus, (5.40) and (5.34) translate to:

$$P = A^{-\frac{1}{\alpha}} \left(\frac{-\eta}{1-\eta} \right)^{\frac{1}{\alpha}} \frac{(\delta + i^K)^{\frac{1-\alpha}{\alpha}}}{\alpha(1-\alpha)^{\frac{1-\alpha}{\alpha}}} W_{-m} \tag{5.43}$$

$$N_m^* = \alpha_j \left(\frac{-\eta}{1-\eta} \right)^{\frac{1-\alpha}{\alpha}} \frac{(\delta + i^K)^{\frac{1-\alpha}{\alpha}}}{A^{\frac{1}{\alpha}} (1-\alpha)^{\frac{1-\alpha}{\alpha}}} \left(\frac{W_{-m}}{m} \right)^{1-\alpha+\eta\alpha} \frac{Y^D}{P} \tag{5.44}$$

We now substitute (5.44) into (5.42) and maximise:

$$\max_{W_m} = \gamma_{m1} \frac{W_m}{P} - \gamma_{m2} \left| \frac{m}{n} \left(\frac{-\eta}{1-\eta} \right)^{\frac{1-\alpha}{\alpha}} \frac{(\delta + i^K)^{\frac{1-\alpha}{\alpha}}}{A^{\frac{1}{\alpha}} (1-\alpha)^{\frac{1-\alpha}{\alpha}}} \left(\frac{W_{-m}}{W_m} \right)^{1-\alpha+\eta\alpha} \frac{Y^D}{P} - \bar{N}_m \right| \tag{5.45}$$

As a result, for reasonably low values[27] of γ_{m1}, we get a local maximum at the point at which the actual employment equals the union's target level of employment $N_m = \bar{N}_m$. The wage $W_m^{\bar{N}}$ which would bring firms $1 \ldots m$ to that point is a function of the wage paid in the rest of the economy W_{-m} and the deviation of the employment in firms $1 \ldots m$ from the union's employment target if its wage were equal to the general wage level $\frac{m}{n} N^*$:

$$W_m^{\bar{N}} = W_{-m} \left(\frac{\frac{m}{n} N^*}{N_m} \right)^{\frac{1}{1-\alpha+\eta\alpha}} \tag{5.46}$$

However, if this point exists as a maximum, it is only a local maximum. Examining the limit behaviour of (5.45) shows that with increasing W_m, U^{union} first falls, but then starts to increase again without any limit. Taking this function at face value, a union would always choose a point of a very high real wage even if employment then drops virtually to 0. This functional behaviour is inherent to the union's utility function as used in most of the literature on trade unions:[28] while employment for the union can drop only to 0, and the burden of unemployment thus asymptotically approaches $\gamma_{m2}\bar{N}_m$, benefits from higher real wages are constantly (linearly) rising.[29]

In order nevertheless to use a utility function as (5.42) in a meaningful way in the model presented here, I limit the range over which the union can choose its wage to 0 to W_{mmax}, while W_{mmax} would be a function of the union's relative bargaining power *vis-à-vis* the employers: in contrast to the case of a uniform wage level in Section 5.1, in which aggregate profits are independent from the wage level paid, for the small single firm m, profits (5.36) are in fact a (negative) function of the wage paid in that firm. Thus, employers in firms 1 ... m have a strong incentive to keep wages low. The more powerful the small union is *vis-à-vis* its employers, the higher the maximum wage it can extract from them. As it is the relative wage which determines the competitiveness and the amount of real profits, I define the maximum wage negotiable under a given institutional setting as a multiple of the wage level in the rest of the economy $b_m > 0$:

$$W_{mmax} = b_m W_{-m} \tag{5.47}$$

Now the union's utility function has two local maxima: one at the point at which employment equals target employment $\bar{N}_m$ (a high-employment/low-real wage solution) and one at the maximum wage point W_{mmax} (a low-employment/high-real wage point). The union thus has two options from which to choose: the high-employment/low-real wage point or the low-employment/high-real wage point. Which of the two solutions is chosen depends on the weight the union contributes to unemployment and the real wage in its constituency. Using (5.47), we get the condition under which the union chooses the low-employment/high-real wage point:

$$\gamma_{m1} > \frac{\gamma_{m2}}{b_m} \frac{P}{W_{-m}} \left| \alpha_i \left(\frac{-\eta}{1-\eta} \right)^{\frac{1-\alpha}{\alpha}} \frac{(\delta + i^K)^{\frac{1-\alpha}{\alpha}}}{A^{\frac{1}{\alpha}}(1-\alpha)^{\frac{1-\alpha}{\alpha}}} \left(\frac{1}{b_m} \right)^{1-\alpha+\eta\alpha} \frac{Y^D}{P} - \bar{N}_m \right| \tag{5.48}$$

The larger the weight a union attributes to its members' real wages γ_{m1} and the larger the union's bargaining power b_m, the more likely it is that it will choose the low-employment point. The intuition is simple:

a union which focuses on its members' real wage position cares less about unemployment and is therefore more likely to opt for the low-employment outcome. The greater the union's bargaining power, the higher is the real wage it can attain, and the higher thus the promised reward for pushing for higher nominal wages.

Possible union utilities as a function of the wage paid in the union's constituency W_m (and the resulting employment in its constituency) are illustrated in Figures 5.3 and 5.4. At the left of $W_m^{\bar{N}}$, there is no unemployment. Consequently, the union's utility is rising with rising (real) wages.[30] To the right of $W_m^{\bar{N}}$, unemployment increases above the union's employment target with rising wages. At first, the union's utility also falls. From a certain point onwards, however, the positive effect of rising real wages overcompensates for the effect of further falling employment, as employment has fallen to such a low level that it only slowly deteriorates further.

In Figure 5.3, the two local maxima are marked *A* and *B*. Point *A* represents the high-employment/low-real wage point, at which employment exactly equals the union's employment target $W_m^{\bar{N}}$. In Figure 5.3, the parameters are chosen in such a way that the union's employment target is above the employment it would experience were it to choose the same wage as is paid in the rest of the economy W_{-m}. Consequently, *A* lies to the left of W_{-m} and $W_m^{\bar{N}}$ is smaller than W_{-m}.

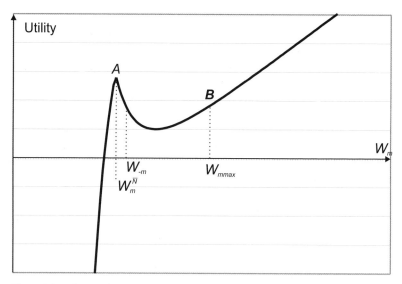

Figure 5.3   The single union's utility function

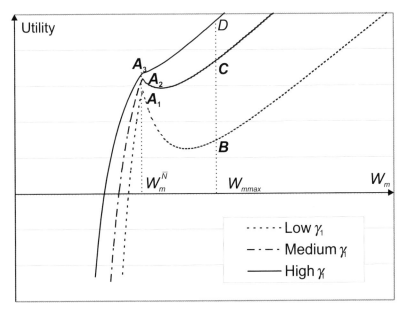

Figure 5.4 The single union's utility function with different weights for unemployment

Point B represents the low-employment/high-real wage point. As this point lies to the right of W_{-m}, unemployment there is higher than it would be for the wage in the small constituency W_m equalling the wage in the rest of the economy W_{-m}. As the union's move towards higher real wages is restricted by its bargaining power, point B lies exactly at the highest nominal wage the union can extract from its employers ($W_m = W_{mmax}$).

Figure 5.3 shows a situation in which the union's utility in the high-employment/low-real wage (point A) lies below the utility in the low-employment/high-real wage point (in mathematical terms U^{union} ($W_m^{\bar{N}}$) > U^{union} (W_{mmax})). In this example, the union's bargaining power is not sufficient to reach a wage which would provide it with a utility higher than in the situation in which employment in its constituency equals its employment target. The union in this case will thus go for the low-real wage/high-employment outcome (point A).

Figure 5.4 shows how this outcome changes with the different priorities that the union gives to real wages and to its employment target. With an increasing weight for the real wage in the utility function, the utility curve becomes steeper to the right of $W_m^{\bar{N}}$. Consequently, a lower (real) wage is needed to compensate for the unemployment connected with this wage. From a certain γ_{m1} onwards, utility in W_{mmax} is higher than in $W_m^{\bar{N}}$. In Figure 5.4 this case is illustrated with the graph described as 'medium γ_1': Utility at point C is higher than at point A_2. The union would then choose the low-employment/high-real wage solution (point C) over the high-employment/low-real wage solution (point A_2).

With a very high weight of the real wage in the union's utility function γ_1, the point $W_m^{\bar{N}}$ even ceases to be a meaningful local maximum, as then all points with higher wages yield a higher union utility. This case is illustrated with the graph described as 'high γ_1' in Figure 5.4. As in the case of a medium γ_1, the union in question will then without a doubt go for the high-real wage/low-employment outcome D and ignore the corresponding high employment solution A_1.

Differences in the institutional parameters b_m, γ_{m1} and γ_{m2} could help explain why small countries in EMU behave differently from each other. In the context of EMU, the solution with $W_m = W_{mmax} > W_{-m}$ might provide an explanation for why some small countries, notably Portugal and Greece, did not get involved in *beggar-thy-neighbour* policies as the Netherlands and Ireland did. The Netherlands and Ireland in this model would have γs and b_m of a magnitude such that (5.48) does not hold. Their unions' utility function would have a shape like that of the low-γ_1-curve in Figure 5.4. As their utility is higher in the high-employment/low-real wage point A_1 than in the low-employment/high-real wage point B, wage bargainers in these countries would settle for the high-employment/low-real wage point A_1. In Greece and Portugal, on the other hand, the union's utility would have a shape like that of the medium γ_1 or the high γ_1-curves. As in these cases, utility in the low-employment/high-real wage situation (points C and D, respectively) lies above utility in the high-employment/low-real wage situation A_2 and A_3, and the wage setters would not engage in a beggar-thy-neighbour policy, but push for higher wages.

One might ask why the large union setting W_{-m} as a Stackelberg leader does not try to counteract the foreseeable attempts to beggar-thy-neighbour by the small union setting W_m. The answer is quite simple: as long as the wage setting process does not change structurally (i.e. sequence of wage setting in the different sectors), the large union cannot do anything about the small union's actions, as the small union always sets its wage level *relative* to the large union. Lowering W_{-m} preemptively would lead only to falling prices, but would not hinder the beggar-thy-neighbour strategy of the small union, which would only lower its own nominal wages further.

These results cast a sad shadow on the future of EMU. If union structures do not converge, there will be some small countries which systematically strive for a lower-real wage/higher-employment solution by beggaring their neighbours and others who will constantly have a problem with an overvalued real exchange rate and high unemployment.

5.3 The central bank

Now having an economic system in which the price level is determined mainly by the nominal wage level, we have to ask where the central bank comes in. If we take a look at the price equation (5.13), we see that very few parameters are actually within the control of the central bank. The degree of monopoly power η, technological parameters A, α and δ are clearly not within the monetary authority's realm of influence. Only the interest rate i^K can be assumed to be under the direct control of the central bank. The way by which the central bank thus influences the price level is a very indirect one: by changing the interest rate, it influences aggregate demand and the firms' capital costs so that their price setting behaviour comes close to what the central bank desires.

Prices in equilibrium

As can be seen from (5.13), to keep the equilibrium price level stable when there is no technological progress, it is crucial that the nominal wage level remains stable. Thus, in a world such as the one modelled in this work, it is the wage level which the central bank has to monitor closely. If there are strategically acting wage bargainers, the central bank has to influence their behaviour by its monetary policy.

If we take into account some measure of technological progress as expressed in a change in A, we can deduce a wage rule for a given target rate of equilibrium price level change (target inflation) π^{target}. The rate of inflation is defined as a change of the price level relative to the price level:

$$\frac{dP^*}{P^*} = \pi^{target} \tag{5.49}$$

Completely differentiating the equilibrium price level (5.13) while keeping the interest rate, the share of labour in the production function and the degree of monopolisation all constant yields:

$$dP^*|_{d\eta=di^K=d\alpha=0} = -\frac{1}{\alpha}A^{-\frac{1+\alpha}{\alpha}}\left(\frac{-\eta}{1-\eta}\right)^{\frac{1}{\alpha}}\frac{(\delta+i^K)^{\frac{1-\alpha}{\alpha}}}{\alpha(1-\alpha)^{\frac{1-\alpha}{\alpha}}}dA + \frac{P^*}{W}dW \qquad (5.50)$$

Dividing (5.50) by the equilibrium price level (5.13) yields:

$$\frac{dP^*}{P^*} = -\frac{1}{\alpha}\cdot\frac{1}{A}dA + \frac{dW}{W} \qquad (5.51)$$

Substituting (5.49) into (5.51) and solving for $\frac{dW}{W}$ yields:

$$\frac{dW}{W} = \pi^{target} + \frac{1}{\alpha}\cdot\frac{1}{A}dA \qquad (5.52)$$

Also differentiating labour productivity (5.25) while keeping interest rates, the degree of monopolisation and labour's share in the production function all constant yields:

$$d\lambda|_{d\eta=di^K=d\alpha=0} = \frac{1}{\alpha}A^{\frac{1-\alpha}{\alpha}}\left(\frac{1-\eta}{-\eta}\right)^{\frac{1-\alpha}{\alpha}}\left(\frac{(1-\alpha)^{\frac{1-\alpha}{\alpha}}}{(\delta+i^K)^{\frac{1-\alpha}{\alpha}}}dA\right) \qquad (5.53)$$

For the growth rate of labour productivity as a function of changes in the level of technological progress A, dividing by λ yields:

$$\frac{d\lambda}{\lambda} = \frac{1}{\alpha}\cdot\frac{1}{A}dA \qquad (5.54)$$

Using (5.54) and (5.52) yields a wage rule that will keep the steady-state inflation rate exactly at the central bank's target rate of inflation:

$$\frac{dW}{W} = \pi^{target} + \frac{d\lambda}{\lambda} \qquad (5.55)$$

Thus, the central bank has to induce wage bargainers to have their wages increased by the trend growth of labour productivity (due to technological progress) plus the central bank's target rate of inflation. As we can see from (5.55), this would translate into a unit labour cost growth exactly at the target rate of inflation: unit labour costs are defined as the wage level divided by labour productivity. Thus the growth rate of unit labour costs equals the rate of wage increases minus the rate of productivity increases.

At first sight, the rule (5.55) shows similarities with the Meinhold rule-of-thumb which economists close to unions regularly use as a macroeconomic guideline.[31] The Meinhold rule states that nominal wage increases should equal the rate of productivity growth plus inflation. However, what is important here is that in the rule presented in this chapter, it is the *target* rate of inflation which figures in the rule, not the *actual* rate of inflation. If the actual rate figured in the rule, changes in inflation would become permanent, as they would translate into a corresponding change of unit labour costs in the following periods.

It is important to note that the rule above is describing a stable *trend*. λ from (5.55) has to be interpreted as a trend in productivity growth, not the actual observed productivity increase. In a downturn when firms hoard labour while demand and output plunges, labour productivity will fall due to cyclical reasons. In an upturn when production increases, labour productivity surges. However, as wages are set only infrequently and new contracts come into effect only with some delays, it seems impractical to try to follow these cyclical movements of labour productivity with wage adjustments. Instead, it seems sensible to follow trend productivity.

The central bank consequently has to keep the nominal wage level (in a situation without technological progress) or the rate of change of the nominal wage level (in a situation with technological progress) under control. This is a direct consequence of the fact that the price level (5.13) is proportional to the nominal wage level, and the rate of inflation (5.51) in the absence of technological process thus proportional to the trend change in wages.

Because wages are set by wage bargainers, the central bank can control them only indirectly. It must signal credibly to unions and employers that wage contracts which are not compatible with price stability (however defined) will be punished by an increase in interest rates, which in turn will lead to lower output, lower profits and higher unemployment. Because unions dislike unemployment, the central bank can accomplish this by credibly threatening to decrease output and increase unemployment via (5.23) if unions were to push forward wage demands which were incompatible with low rates of inflation.

At least for a monopoly union, this threat can be expected to work reasonably well: when prices and quantities react instantaneously to new cost and demand conditions, as is the case in this chapter's model,[32] the monopoly union does not have anything to lose if it relinquishes excessive wage demands. As real wages do not react to nominal wage increases, there are no costs for the union in restraining wage demands. Nevertheless, it has a lot to lose if it does not obey the central bank's demands: higher unemployment at given real wages would undoubtedly lower its utility.

Real-world monopoly unions

However, reality might exhibit some deviation from this theoretical model. As it is well known in modern macroeconomic theory, reality often shows some degree of price stickiness (Blinder *et al.* 1998). Some models, such as Fischer (1977) or Taylor (1980),[33] simply assume that not all prices will be reset in any given period. Price changes in these models just take time. Alternatively, price stickiness can be deduced from *menu costs* associated with price changes (Akerlof and Yellen 1985; Mankiw 1985). Only when equilibrium prices depart far enough from current prices will firms change their prices. As soon as such price rigidities enter the world so far presented in this chapter, even a monopoly union will be inclined to push for higher nominal wages: until prices have adjusted to their new equilibrium, higher nominal wages will for a transition period translate directly into higher real wages. Similarly, a monopoly union will then resist wage cuts: even if real wages reach their equilibrium value again after an adjustment period, during adjustment, real wages will be below their equilibrium value.

Moreover, increasing nominal wages could be interpreted as an attempt to improve the relative income situation of employed workers relative to recipients of different nominally fixed incomes, such as welfare recipients. If those incomes are not linked to the price level or the aggregate wage level, an increase in nominal wages would increase the overall price level. While the workers' real wage position would not be changed, the welfare recipients' real income would shrink, thereby improving the workers' relative income position.

Finally, nominal wage increases might bring political gains for union leaders, just as accepting nominal wage cuts might come with political costs. While it is nowadays common sense that economic models and especially economic policy advice must not base their conclusions on any kind of money illusions, it is quite sensible to assume that union members will perceive a cut in their money wages as a loss in income (which in fact is a kind of money illusion), even if real wages recover to their original position in the medium and long run. As I will argue on p. 209, it is questionable whether the assumption of rational expectation in its most rigid form is a good approximation for unions' behaviour. Union members will seldom have the macroeconomic model of this chapter in their head when they judge their union leader's performance. If they believed in the standard neo-classical model, they would perceive an increase in nominal wages as a bargaining gain of real wage increases – and would blame the subsequent price increases on the central bank.

However, all of these arguments point to spurious or only temporary utility gains for the monopoly union, whereas the central bank could credibly threaten to decrease the monopoly union's utility substantially and permanently by using its interest rate to dampen output and employment. Consequently, while the central bank might need to use its interest rate from time to time in order to show that it is really willing to incur real costs in the economy in order to keep wage demands non-inflationary, overall the central bank should be able to deter inflationary wage demands.

Observations on the euro-zone

But what does the fact that some small unions set their wages relative to the rest of the economy's wages mean for EMU? It translates into the central bank's imperative to keep the wage level in the core of EMU stable, as wages in small peripheral countries are set in relation to the core wage level (see (5.47) and (5.46)). With a stable core wage level W_{-m}, peripheral countries might deviate from the wage trend in the overall union, but the trend of wages and prices set there will still follow the wage trend set by the core of EMU. The central bank would thus have to target the large unions' wage developments and would have to signal to them that it would not tolerate wage developments above what would be compatible with price stability, as the smaller unions' wage targets are a function of the general wage level. The general wage level, however, is predominantly influenced by the large unions (or the monopoly union).

For the euro-zone as a whole, it is not yet clear how the coordination of wage setting between the different unions will take place – or which union (or bloc of unions) will assume the role of wage leader. In fact, the period since the beginning of EMU is still too short to empirically determine for certain the pattern of wage interaction between the single trade unions within EMU.

However, the hypothesis of Soskice–Iversen (1998) seems to be bolstered by evidence that wage bargaining in core Europe is taking the shape of a Stackelberg game: the Netherlands, Belgium, Austria, Italy and France are relating their wage increases to unit labour cost changes in Germany after German wage contracts are known. This setting is of course not a formalised one. Instead, in the core countries of the euro-zone, wages are set as a function of relative competitiveness (Soskice and Hancké 2002, p. 18ff.), that is relative unit labour cost developments *vis-à-vis* trade partners. As Germany, as the largest economy of EMU, is a very important trading partner for all of the EMU countries, German wage contracts become a central parameter for wage setting in EMU. Via this mechanism, wage bargaining outcomes in the euro-area seem to be coordinated, even though there is no implicit or explicit coordination in the process itself other than taking into account the other countries' wage contracts' effects on competitiveness.[34] The result was that the German union federation[35] found itself in the position to set the anchor wages in EMU (or the wage W_{-m} in this model) around which the other countries set their wages.

Recent empirical observations do not contradict this picture. Pichelmann (2001) reports a convergence of unit labour cost developments within the euro-zone with the standard deviation of unit labour cost growth rates across EU-11 countries sharply falling in the late 1990s. Pichelmann also reports a further fall in the standard deviation among countries of the DM-bloc (Austria, Germany, Belgium, the Netherlands and Luxembourg) which experienced a high degree of convergence during the early 1990s. However, it is not yet clear whether this is a trend towards a more uniform wage setting in EMU or only a consequence of the fall and convergence in inflation expectation and the stabilisation of exchange rates.

If the Soskice–Hancké hypothesis turns out to be correct and the setting stable,[36] one could easily translate the EMU setting into this chapter's model. Germany would thus represent the large union that is important for the general wage trend. Consequently, it would be German wage inflation that the ECB would have to target with its monetary policy. Similarly, it would be the German trade unions that the ECB would have to address primarily with its monetary policy threats.

While the signalling game between German wage setters and the Bundesbank worked reasonably well,[37] it is unclear whether the interaction between German unions, their employers' federations and the ECB will work comparably. First of all, the purpose of being a wage anchor for other unions in different European countries whose wage developments then jointly determine European inflation might be far harder to comprehend from the German unions' perspective than their former influence on German inflation. Second, it would be politically difficult for the ECB to admit that it targets German wages. Since the ECB is a European institution and there has already been much quarrelling over the bank's geographic location and the nationality of its first governor, it is very unlikely that it would publicly announce such a step. With no clear public indications of what the ECB is really targeting, German unions might be tempted to go for inflationary wage increases to reap some short-term political gains.

Finally, if euro-area inflation stems from small unions in countries other than Germany pushing for a high-real wage/high-unemployment solution, the ECB would possibly have to tighten monetary policy and push for German wage *deflation* in order to get euro-area inflation under control. Such a situation might come about when in some smaller countries parameters shift so that they might switch from a low-real wage/high-employment to a high-real wage/low-employment point. During times of steady-state wage growth and inflation, such a danger will not exist, as both the low-employment/high-real wage points as well as the high-employment/low-real wage points are defined for wages (and thus prices) in relation to the general wage level W.

Differences between European and US monetary policy

This mechanism of controlling inflation is quite different from controlling inflation in a system with an atomistic labour market, as has been described on p. 109. While in a neo-classical atomistic labour market, the focus needs to be on keeping employment exactly at the point U_{NAIRU} where inflation is stable, the focus in a system with large, strategically acting wage bargainers is to deter inflationary wage demands by these unions.

Yet it is not clear which of the two setups (atomistic labour market vs. a large wage setter) is economically more efficient. The atomistic labour market by itself does not guarantee that unemployment will stay at the rate which is compatible with stable inflation. If a shock which pushes unemployment below U_{NAIRU} hits the economy, wages and prices will begin to fall, but there is no natural tendency to a new equilibrium. As nominal wages fall, the equilibrium real wage level (5.27) nevertheless stays constant. So also do output (5.23) and employment (5.24). Only when the central bank reacts strongly enough can this economy be prevented from drifting into a deflationary spiral. A system with an atomistic labour market might thus be more prone to the consequences of policy mistakes.

However, if one idealises the US labour market as rather 'atomistic' while the euro-zone labour market is dominated by strategically acting unions, these differences in labour markets might offer a rationale for why the US Fed has a different mandate from the ECB. While the US Fed is supposed to target both high growth and low inflation, the ECB's sole official target is to achieve 'price stability'.[38] One could now argue that in a setting with an atomistic labour market, a central bank might have to act more quickly for precautionary reasons to keep unemployment from falling below U_{NAIRU}, as an unemployment rate below that point leads to falling prices and might lead to a deflationary spiral. In a setting with a large wage setter, on the other hand, the economy-wide wage contract acts as an anchor for the price level so that the central bank does not have to care as much about keeping unemployment at a certain level.

Of course, the USA definitely does not have an atomistic textbook labour market as described above. A wide range of rules and institutions, such as minimum wage legislation or the fact that contracts are usually not frequently renegotiated and wages thus show some downward stickiness, helps to bring some additional stability. Nevertheless, the US labour market is without a doubt closer to the atomistic model than is the euro-zone's. Placing a larger weight on the central bank's output stabilisation might thus be just the necessary condition for this setup to be stable.

Price dynamics

So far, we have looked at the development of equilibrium prices. However, it is not only the trend in equilibrium prices that the central bank has to worry about. While disequilibrium price changes are in principle of minor significance, because the price level will return to its equilibrium level, there might be additional reasons why a central bank might feel itself forced to control disequilibrium price changes. Especially if a central bank does not yet have a reputation as a stability-oriented central bank (as one could argue for the young ECB), it might be tempted to care more about disequilibrium price changes: observers in general might focus on the headline inflation and might not discern whether a price change is a disequilibrium or an equilibrium phenomenon. They might conclude from temporary price hikes that the central bank *per se* is not inflation averse.

Such a spike might thus also be important for the equilibrium price level. If wage setting is at least partly backward-looking, a disequilibrium price change might induce unions to try to regain lost real wages, and in so doing shift the equilibrium price level higher.

Temporary deviations from equilibrium in the model presented in this chapter come about when aggregate demand changes by a shift of parameters, a change in autonomous aggregate demand or changes in the interest rate. As goods market deregulation (which would change structural parameters such as η) is not the topic of this work, I will focus on shifts in the autonomous aggregate demand and interest rates.

If real aggregate demand changes to $\frac{Y^D}{P} + \epsilon$ (e.g. by a shift in fiscal policy), firms are suddenly confronted with a different demand function for their own products. Assuming that the capital stock is fixed in the short run to $\bar{K}_i$, but will be changed only over time to meet the desired equilibrium capital stock, production can be changed only by changes in labour employed. The single firm's production function thus is:

$$y_i = A N_i^\alpha \bar{K}_i^{1-\alpha} \quad 0 < \alpha < 1 \tag{5.56}$$

The firm maximises its profit by setting its price P_i and producing the goods thus demanded given its capital stock $\bar{K}_i = K_i^*$, but varying employment N_i:

$$\max_{P_i} \Pi_i = P_i y_i^D - W \frac{\left(y_i^D\right)^{\frac{1}{\alpha}}}{A^{\frac{1}{\alpha}} (K_i^*)^{\frac{1-\alpha}{\alpha}}} + i^K P K_i^* \tag{5.57}$$

Solving and assuming the symmetrical case of all firms reacting to the changes in aggregate demand conditions yields for aggregate employment and the general price level:

$$N^{Diseq} = \frac{(y^D + \epsilon)^{\frac{1}{\alpha}}}{(y^D)^{\frac{1-\alpha}{\alpha}}} N^* \tag{5.58}$$

$$P^{Diseq} = P_i$$

$$= A^{-\frac{1}{\alpha}} \left(\frac{-\eta}{1-\eta}\right)^{\frac{1}{\alpha}} (\delta + i^K)^{\frac{1-\alpha}{\alpha}}$$

$$\frac{1}{\alpha(1-\alpha)^{\frac{1-\alpha}{\alpha}}} \left(\frac{y^D + \epsilon}{y^D}\right)^{\frac{1-\alpha}{\alpha}} W \tag{5.59}$$

$$= P^* \left(\frac{y^D + \epsilon}{y^D}\right)^{\frac{1-\alpha}{\alpha}} \tag{5.60}$$

An increased aggregate demand is thus satisfied by the firms, but only at higher prices, which translate into an upward shift in aggregate prices.[39] Thus, nominal and real output as well as prices are higher due to the positive demand shock.

If this aggregate demand shock is assumed to be more than transitory, the initial effect is further amplified by the firms' desire to adjust their capital stock to the now permanently changed aggregate demand. While producing with a sub-optimal combination of capital and labour per unit of production maximises profits in the short run (in which the capital stock cannot be changed), it does not in the long run. In the long run, firms would thus try to adjust their capital stock to the new equilibrium level K^{**}:

$$K^{**} = \frac{y^D + \epsilon}{y^D} K^* \tag{5.61}$$

The gap between the former equilibrium capital stock K^* and the new equilibrium capital stock K^{**} puts additional pressure on prices as it further changes aggregate demand in the same direction as the initial shock ϵ (see (5.21)). As during this time of disequilibrium, nominal wages remain constant, real wages fall with increasing prices. Over time, prices will adjust back to the old equilibrium – if ϵ is transitory, because the original cause for the price shift disappears. If ϵ is not transitory, then firms adjust their capital stock so as to produce with their original (relative) combination of labour and capital again, causing unit costs and consequently the price level to move back to equilibrium, albeit at a higher level of employment and production.

As real wages are falling during a transitory period after a positive demand shock, unions might be inclined to *increase their nominal wage demands to secure their real wage position*. This is a danger for price stability (or a stable rate of inflation), as shifts in the nominal wage level triggered by disequilibrium price changes also change the *equilibrium price level*. If unions do not fully understand the economic mechanisms and think that the temporary price hike is indeed permanent, they might be reluctant to keep still and will push for higher wages. A central bank which cannot be sure about the unions' behaviour, might prefer to act to offset the shock ε. Even if the central bank does not decide to offset the shock right away, it will have to monitor wage developments especially carefully in times of demand shocks and will have to be keen on making clear that it would punish any deviation from stability-oriented wage demands.

Figure 5.5 illustrates this argument for the case of a positive equilibrium rate of inflation (e.g. the target rate of inflation π^{target}). The thick solid line represents the logarithm of the equilibrium price level, given a steady-state rate of inflation (and thus unit labour cost increases) of 2 per cent. The thin solid line shows the actual price level. The dotted line shows the rate of inflation. In period 10 the economy is hit by a shock pushing up the actual price level by 4 per cent. While in the following periods the disequilibrium price hike disappears again, and the price level returns to its old trend,[40] a spike in inflation is noticed in period 10. Observers who only see P and the rate of inflation in period 10 do not know whether the shift is due to a permanent shift in the equilibrium price level or only to some transitory component. Moreover, with fixed nominal contracts, the union's real wage position in period 10 is weakened and only gradually returns to its initial level with the actual price level approaching the equilibrium price level again.

The mechanism by which the central bank keeps the price level from rising during a positive transitory shock[41] would thus be as follows: the central bank would increase interest rates so that the desired equilibrium capital stock would fall. Since the new equilibrium capital stock

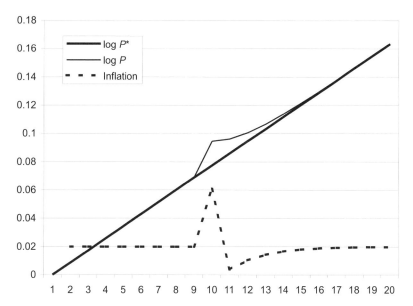

Figure 5.5   Actual and equilibrium log price level when a transitory shock hits the economy

would now be below the old equilibrium capital stock, firms would want to disinvest; investment demand would fall. This dampened investment demand would ideally offset precisely the additional demand from the shock. As soon as the shock faded away, the central bank could lower interest rates again, so that once again additional investment demand would offset the diminished shock. Ideally, in the end, the economy would find itself in the same position as in the initial situation, with employment, output and price level as before.

In the case of a permanent shock, things are not that easy. Of course the central bank could increase interest rates so as to offset the demand shock. However, it would then increase the *equilibrium* price level. The movement to this price level would be gradual and less pronounced than the initial price hike following the demand shock, but it would be permanent. If, on the other hand, the central bank could make the permanent shock work through the system, without unions pushing for nominal wage increases to compensate the transitory deterioration in their real wage position, it would in the end increase output, employment and the capital stock permanently without altering the price level.

The path to a low-interest rate situation

Price dynamics might also pose a problem when the central bank desires to reach a lower interest rate to increase equilibrium output and employment. Though a cut in interest rates lowers the equilibrium price level (5.13), it comes with some short-run risks to price stability: as a lower interest rate means a higher equilibrium capital stock (see (5.18)), investment demand will increase during the transition period by the share ξ of the gap between the old and the new equilibrium capital stocks. Just as with the exogenous demand shock ϵ, this will translate into higher output and demand as well as higher prices during the transition period.

In the long run, when the capital stock has adjusted, prices will actually fall to the new (lower) level. Equilibrium capital stock and equilibrium output will then be higher than in the original situation.[42] As long as unions are aggressive or simply not willing to accept the transitory real wage losses during the adjustment period, however, interest rate cuts might spark an upward trend in wages and consequently in the equilibrium price level. For a risk averse central bank, it might thus be rational not to try to go for lower interest rates, as they come with the risk of igniting a price–wage spiral.

The price dynamics following a cut in interest rates when wages do not react are shown in Figure 5.6:[43] It is assumed that technological progress *A* grows at a steady rate so that labour productivity grows by roughly 1.5 per cent. Moreover, it is assumed that wages grow at a rate of 2.5 per cent. In period 5, the central bank cuts its interest rate. Consequently, the equilibrium price level falls as firms are now confronted with lower capital costs. However, because with lower capital costs the equilibrium capital stock also increases, aggregate demand thrives. The extra demand thus created pushes the actual price level upwards, causing a higher rate of inflation. Then, when capacities are increased and the extra profits from the extra demand disappear again, prices converge to the new, by then lower, price level. During this later adjustment period, the rate of inflation undershoots the trend growth rate in unit labour costs.

However, as long as unions keep their wage demands under control and the wage level does not change in reaction to a lower interest rate, the real economy does not place any obstacles in the way of the central bank as it strives for such a high-employment, low-interest rate solution. Nevertheless, the central bank still faces restrictions from financial markets. These will be covered in Chapter 6.

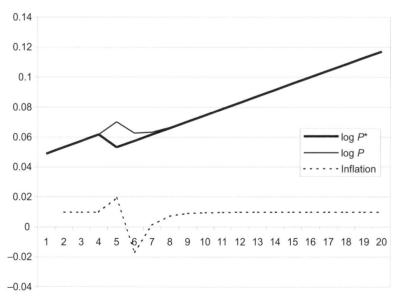

Figure 5.6 Actual and equilibrium log price level when interest rates are lowered

Appendix 5.1:   Basic Setup

The wage level W is uniform across all firms.

The firms' maximisation problem

Minimising unit cost uc_i by choosing the optimum combination of capital K_i/y_i and labour N_i/y_i per unit of production under the constraint of (5.1) yields (5.5) and (5.6). Given this combination of labour and capital inputs, firm i maximises its profit by choosing its sales price P_i:

$$\max_{P_i} \Pi = [P_i - uc_i] y_i^D \tag{A1.1}$$

$$= [P_i - uc_i] \frac{1}{n} \left(\frac{P_i}{P} \right)^{-\eta} \frac{Y^D}{P} \tag{A1.2}$$

$$\frac{\partial \Pi}{\partial P_i} = \frac{1}{n} P_i^{-\eta} \frac{1}{P^{-\eta}} \frac{Y^D}{P} - \frac{1}{n} \eta [P_i - uc_i] P_i^{-\eta - 1} \frac{1}{P^{-\eta}} \frac{Y^D}{P} \tag{A1.3}$$

$$= \frac{1}{n} \frac{1}{P^{-\eta}} \frac{Y^D}{P} [P_i^{-\eta} - \eta P_i^{-\eta-1}(-P_i - uc_i)] = 0 \tag{A1.4}$$

$$\Leftrightarrow P_i^{-\eta} - \eta P_i^{-\eta-1}(P_i - uc_i) = 0 \tag{A1.5}$$

$$\Leftrightarrow (1-\eta) P_i^{-\eta} + \eta P_i^{-\eta-1} uc_i = 0 \tag{A1.6}$$

$$\Leftrightarrow P_i = \frac{-\eta}{1-\eta} uc_i \tag{A1.7}$$

$$= \frac{-\eta}{1-\eta} \frac{1}{A} P^{1-\alpha} W^\alpha (\delta + i)^{1-\alpha} \left(\frac{\alpha^{1-\alpha}}{(1-\alpha)^{1-\alpha}} + \frac{(1-\alpha)^\alpha}{\alpha^\alpha} \right) \tag{A1.8}$$

For the symmetric case of $P = P_i$ this becomes:

$$P_i^\alpha = \frac{-\eta}{1-\eta} \frac{1}{A} W^\alpha (\delta+i)^{1-\alpha} \left(\frac{\alpha^{1-\alpha}}{(1-\alpha)^{1-\alpha}} + \frac{(1-\alpha)^\alpha}{\alpha^\alpha} \right) \tag{A1.9}$$

$$\Leftrightarrow P_i = A^{-\frac{1}{\alpha}} \left(\frac{-\eta}{1-\eta} \right)^{\frac{1}{\alpha}} (\delta+i)^{\frac{1-\alpha}{\alpha}} \frac{1}{\alpha(1-\alpha)^{\frac{1-\alpha}{\alpha}}} W \tag{A1.10}$$

Aggregate demand and output I: only workers consume

Assuming that all of the firms' profits and all interest incomes are saved, we get for nominal aggregate demand Y^D, aggregate real demand y^D and output y:

$$Y^D = cN^* W + \delta PK^* + P y_0^D \tag{A1.11}$$

$$= cW \left(\frac{-\eta}{1-\eta} \right) \frac{(\delta + i^K)^{\frac{1-\alpha}{\alpha}}}{A^{\frac{1}{\alpha}} (1-\alpha)^{\frac{1-\alpha}{\alpha}}} \frac{Y^D}{P} + \delta P \left(\frac{1-\eta}{\eta} \right) \frac{1-\alpha}{\delta + i^K} \frac{Y^D}{P} + P y_0^D \tag{A1.12}$$

$$\Leftrightarrow Y^D = \frac{-\eta}{-\eta + (\eta - 1)\left(c\alpha + \frac{\delta(1-\alpha)}{(\delta + i)}\right)} P y_0^D \qquad (A1.13)$$

$$\Leftrightarrow y^D = y^* = \frac{-\eta}{-\eta + (\eta - 1)\left(c\alpha + \frac{\delta(1-\alpha)}{(\delta + i)}\right)} y_0^D \qquad (A1.14)$$

Using (A1.14) and (5.20) yields total aggregate employment:

$$N^* = \left(\frac{-\eta}{1-\eta}\right)^{\frac{1-\alpha}{\alpha}} \frac{-\eta(\delta + i^K)^{\frac{1-\alpha}{\alpha}}}{A^{\frac{1}{\alpha}}(1-\alpha)^{\frac{1-\alpha}{\alpha}}\left(-\eta - (1-\eta)\left[c\alpha + \delta\frac{1-\alpha}{\delta + i^K}\right]\right)} y_0^D \qquad (A1.15)$$

Differentiating with respect to i^K yields:

$$\frac{\partial N^*}{\partial i^K} = \left(\left(\frac{-\eta}{1-\eta}\right)^{\frac{1-\alpha}{\alpha}} \eta(\delta + i^K)^{\frac{1-\alpha}{\alpha}}(1-\alpha)\right)$$

$$\left(\frac{\delta(1-\eta)}{A^{\frac{1}{\alpha}}(\delta + i^K)^2(1-\alpha)^{\frac{1-\alpha}{\alpha}}\left(-\eta - (1-\eta)\left[c\alpha + \delta\frac{1-\alpha}{\delta + i^K}\right]\right)^2}\right.$$

$$\left. - \frac{1}{\alpha(\delta + i^K)A^{\frac{1}{\alpha}}(1-\alpha)^{\frac{1-\alpha}{\alpha}}\left(-\eta - (1-\eta)\left[c\alpha + \delta\frac{1-\alpha}{\delta + i^K}\right]\right)}\right) \qquad (A1.16)$$

which can be shown to be positive for positive i^K which fulfil

$$i^K < \frac{\delta((\eta - 1)c\alpha - 1)}{\eta - \eta c\alpha + c\alpha} \qquad (A1.17)$$

Thus, in this range, an interest rate cut leads to increased employment.

Aggregate demand and output II: entrepreneurs consume

By subtracting the firm's wage costs and capital depreciation from its revenue, we get the profit for each firm (including interest payments):

$$\Pi_i = P_i y_i^D - W N_i^* - \delta K_i^* \qquad (A1.18)$$

$$= \frac{1}{n} P_i \frac{Y^D}{P} - \frac{1}{n} W \left(\frac{-\eta}{1-\eta}\right)^{\frac{1-\alpha}{\alpha}} \frac{(\delta + i^K)^{\frac{1-\alpha}{\alpha}}}{A^{\frac{1}{\alpha}}(1-\alpha)^{\frac{1-\alpha}{\alpha}}} \frac{Y^D}{P} -$$

$$\frac{1}{n} \delta \frac{1-\eta}{-\eta} \left(\frac{(1-\alpha)}{(\delta + i^K)}\right) \frac{Y^D}{P} \qquad (A1.19)$$

$$\Leftrightarrow \frac{\Pi_i}{P} = \frac{1}{n}\left[1 - \frac{1-\eta}{-\eta}\left(\alpha + \delta\frac{1-\alpha}{\delta + i^K}\right)\right] \frac{Y^D}{P} \qquad (A1.20)$$

Aggregating for the whole economy yields for aggregate profits (including interest costs):

$$\Pi = \sum \Pi_i = \sum \frac{1}{n}\left[1 - \frac{1-\eta}{-\eta}\left(\alpha + \delta\,\frac{1-\alpha}{\delta + i^K}\right)\right]Y^D \qquad \text{(A1.21)}$$

$$\left[1 - \frac{1-\eta}{-\eta}\left(\alpha + \delta\,\frac{1-\alpha}{\delta + i^K}\right)\right]Y^D \qquad \text{(A1.22)}$$

Assuming that capital owners and entrepreneurs consume a share c_Π of their income yields for aggregate demand Y^{D+} and output y^{**}:

$$Y^{D+} = cN^* W + c_\Pi\left(1 - \frac{1-\eta}{-\eta}\left(\alpha + \delta\,\frac{1-\alpha}{\delta + i^K}\right)\right)Y^{D+}$$
$$+ \delta PK^* + Py_0^D \qquad \text{(A1.23)}$$

$$= cW\left(\frac{-\eta}{1-\eta}\right)\frac{(\delta + i^K)^{\frac{1-\alpha}{\alpha}}}{A^{\frac{1}{\alpha}}(1-\alpha)^{\frac{1-\alpha}{\alpha}}}\frac{Y^{D+}}{P} +$$
$$c_\Pi\left(1 - \alpha\,\frac{1-\alpha}{-\eta}\right)Y^{D+}$$
$$+ (1 - c_\Pi) - \delta P\left(\frac{1-\eta}{-\eta}\right)\frac{1-\alpha}{\delta + i^K}\frac{Y^{D+}}{P} + Py_0^D \qquad \text{(A1.24)}$$

$$\Leftrightarrow \frac{\left(-\eta - (1-\eta)\left[c\alpha + (1-c_\Pi)\delta\,\frac{1-\alpha}{\delta + i^K}\right] - c_\Pi(-\eta - \alpha + \alpha\eta)\right)}{-\eta}Y^{D+} = Py_0^D \quad \text{(A1.25)}$$

$$y^{*+} = \frac{-\eta}{\left(-\eta - (1-\eta)\left[c\alpha + (1-c_\Pi)\delta\,\frac{1-\alpha}{\delta + i^K}\right] - c_\Pi(-\eta - \alpha + \alpha\eta)\right)}y_0^D \qquad \text{(A1.26)}$$

Thus, only the multiplier changes. The basic notion that changes in the nominal wage do not lead to changes in real output remains intact.

Return on capital

Using (5.83), we can compute a real product yield per unit of capital employed:

$$R = \frac{\Pi_{real}}{K^*} = \left(1 - \frac{1-\eta}{-\eta}\left(\alpha + \delta\,\frac{1-\alpha}{\delta + i^K}\right)\right)\frac{y^*}{K^*} \qquad \text{(A1.27)}$$

$$= \left(1 - \frac{1-\eta}{-\eta}\left(\alpha + \delta\,\frac{1-\alpha}{\delta + i^K}\right)\right)\left(\frac{-\eta}{1-\eta}\right)\left(\frac{\delta + i^K}{(1-\alpha)}\right) \qquad \text{(A1.28)}$$

$$= \left(\frac{-\eta}{1-\eta} - \alpha\right)\left(\frac{\delta + i^K}{(1-\alpha)}\right) - \delta \qquad \text{(A1.29)}$$

Appendix 5.2 A Small Union *vis-à-vis* A Large Union

A small number m of the economy's n firms pays a different wage W_m than the rest of the economy, which pays wage W_{-m}. A small union bargains for workers in firms 1 … m and sets wages after a large union has set wages for the rest of the economy.

The firms' maximisation problem

The firms' maximisation is the same as in (A1.1). Thus each firm's price is again:

$$P_i = \frac{-\eta}{1-\eta} uc_i \tag{A2.1}$$

However, unit costs are different across firms if some of them pay a different wage W_m than the rest of the economy, which pays W_{-m}, leading to a different price P_m than P_{-m}. Unit labour costs in firms 1 … m are given by

$$uc_m = \frac{1}{A} P^{1-\alpha} W_m^\alpha \frac{(\delta+i)^{1-\alpha}}{\alpha^\alpha (1-\alpha)^{1-\alpha}} \tag{A2.2}$$

while the overall price level is given by

$$P = \left(\frac{n-m}{n} P_{-m}^{1-n} + \frac{m}{n} P_m^{1-n} \right)^{\frac{1}{1-\eta}} \tag{A2.3}$$

The price of products from those firms paying the wage W_m is then:

$$P_m = \frac{-\eta}{1-\eta} \frac{1}{A} \left(\frac{n-m}{n} P_{-m}^{1-\eta} + \frac{m}{n} P_{-m}^{1-\eta} \right)^{\frac{1-\alpha}{1-\eta}} W_m^\alpha \frac{(\delta+i^K)^{1-\alpha}}{\alpha^\alpha (1-\alpha)^{1-\alpha}} \tag{A2.4}$$

and for the rest of the economy:

$$P_{-m} = \frac{-\eta}{1-\eta} \frac{1}{A} \left(\frac{n-m}{n} P_{-m}^{1-\eta} + \frac{m}{n} P_m^{1-\eta} \right)^{\frac{1-\alpha}{1-\eta}} W_{-m}^\alpha \frac{(\delta+i^K)^{1-\alpha}}{\alpha^\alpha (1-\alpha)^{1-\alpha}} \tag{A2.5}$$

Dividing (A2.4) by (A2.5) yields:

$$\frac{P_m}{P_{-m}} = \left(\frac{W_m}{W_{-m}} \right)^\alpha \tag{A2.6}$$

Solving for P_{-m} yields

$$P_{-m} = \left(\frac{W_{-m}}{W_m}\right)^\alpha P_m \tag{A2.7}$$

Substituting in (A2.4) yields:

$$P_m = \frac{-\eta}{1-\eta} \frac{1}{A} \left[\frac{n-m}{n} P_m^{1-\eta} \left(\frac{W_{-m}}{W_m}\right)^{\alpha(1-\eta)} + \frac{m}{n} P_m^{1-\eta}\right]^{\frac{1-\alpha}{1-\eta}}$$

$$W_m^\alpha \frac{(\delta + i^K)^{1-\alpha}}{\alpha^\alpha (1-\alpha)^{1-\alpha}} \tag{A2.8}$$

$$= \frac{-\eta}{1-\eta} \frac{1}{A} \left[\frac{n-m}{n} \left(\frac{W_{-m}}{W_m}\right)^{\alpha(1-\eta)} + \frac{m}{n}\right]^{\frac{1-\alpha}{1-\eta}} P_m^{1-\alpha}$$

$$W_m^\alpha \frac{(\delta + i^K)^{1-\alpha}}{\alpha^\alpha (1-\alpha)^{1-\alpha}} \tag{A2.9}$$

$$P_m^\alpha = \frac{-\eta}{1-\eta} \frac{1}{A} \left[\frac{n-m}{n} \left(\frac{W_{-m}}{W_m}\right)^{\alpha(1-\eta)} + \frac{m}{n}\right]^{\frac{1-\alpha}{1-\eta}} W_m^\alpha \frac{(\delta + i^K)^{1-\alpha}}{\alpha^\alpha (1-\alpha)^{1-\alpha}} \tag{A2.10}$$

From which we get for the price P_m:

$$P_m = \left[\frac{n-m}{n}\left(\frac{W_{-m}}{W_m}\right)^{\alpha(1-\eta)} + \frac{m}{n}\right]^{\frac{1-\alpha}{\alpha(1-\eta)}} \frac{1}{A^{\frac{1}{\alpha}}} \left(\frac{-\eta}{1-\eta}\right)^{\frac{1}{\alpha}} \frac{(\delta + i^K)^{\frac{1-\alpha}{\alpha}}}{\alpha(1-\alpha)^{\frac{1-\alpha}{\alpha}}} W_m \tag{A2.11}$$

Employment, output and profits

For computing output and employment in the two bargaining sectors of the economy, it is handy first to compute $\frac{P}{W_m}$ and $\frac{P}{P_m}$:

$$P = \left[\frac{n-m}{n}\left(\frac{W_{-m}}{W_m}\right)^{\alpha(1-\eta)} + \frac{m}{n}\right]^{\frac{1}{1-\eta}} P_m \tag{A2.12}$$

$$= \left[\frac{n-m}{n}\left(\frac{W_{-m}}{W_m}\right)^{\alpha(1-\eta)} + \frac{m}{n}\right]^{\frac{1}{\alpha(1-\eta)}}$$

$$\frac{1}{A^{\frac{1}{\alpha}}} \left(\frac{-\eta}{1-\eta}\right)^{\frac{1}{\alpha}} \frac{(\delta + i^K)^{\frac{1-\alpha}{\alpha}}}{\alpha(1-\alpha)^{\frac{1-\alpha}{\alpha}}} W_m \tag{A2.13}$$

$$\frac{P}{W_m} = \left(\frac{n-m}{n} \left(\frac{W_{-m}}{W_m} \right)^{\alpha(1-\eta)} + \frac{m}{n} \right)^{\frac{1}{\alpha(1-\eta)}} \frac{1}{A^{\frac{1}{\alpha}}} \left(\frac{-\eta}{1-\eta} \right)^{\frac{1}{\alpha}} \frac{(\delta + i^K)^{\frac{1-\alpha}{\alpha}}}{\alpha(1-\alpha)^{\frac{1-\alpha}{\alpha}}} \quad \text{(A2.14)}$$

$$\frac{P}{P_m} = \left(\frac{n-m}{n} \left(\frac{W_{-m}}{W_m} \right)^{\alpha(1-\eta)} + \frac{m}{n} \right)^{\frac{1}{1-\eta}} \quad \text{(A2.15)}$$

We know from (5.6) and (5.2) that employment in a single firm which has a price and wage different from the rest of the economy is:

$$N_m^{\star} = \frac{m}{n} \cdot \frac{1}{A} \left(\frac{P}{W_m} \right)^{1-\alpha} \frac{(\delta + i^K)^{1-\alpha} \alpha^{1-\alpha}}{(1-\alpha)^{1-\alpha}} \left(\frac{P_m}{P} \right)^{-\eta} \frac{Y^D}{P} \quad \text{(A2.16)}$$

Using (A2.15), (A2.14) and (A2.16) we get:

$$N_m^{\star} = \left(\frac{n-m}{n} \left(\frac{W_{-m}}{W_m} \right)^{\alpha(1-\eta)} + \frac{m}{n} \right)^{\frac{1-\alpha+\eta\alpha}{\alpha(1-\eta)}}$$
$$\cdot \left(\frac{-\eta}{1-\eta} \right)^{\frac{1-\alpha}{\alpha}} \frac{1}{A^{\frac{1}{\alpha}}} \frac{(\delta + i^K)^{\frac{1-\alpha}{\alpha}}}{(1-\alpha)^{\frac{1-\alpha}{\alpha}}} \frac{m}{n} \frac{Y^D}{P} \quad \text{(A2.17)}$$

The rest of the economy has an employment of:

$$N_{-m}^{\star} = \frac{m}{n} \cdot \frac{1}{A} \left(\frac{P}{W_{-m}} \right)^{1-\alpha} \frac{(\delta + i^K)^{1-\alpha} \alpha^{1-\alpha}}{(1-\alpha)^{1-\alpha}} \left(\frac{P_{-m}}{P} \right)^{-\eta} \frac{Y^D}{P} \quad \text{(A2.18)}$$

From (A2.6) and (A2.12) we get:

$$\frac{P}{P_{-m}} = \left(\frac{n-m}{n} \left(\frac{W_{-m}}{W_m} \right)^{\alpha(1-\eta)} + \frac{m}{n} \right)^{\frac{1}{1-\eta}} \left(\frac{W_m}{W_{-m}} \right)^{\alpha} \quad \text{(A2.19)}$$

With

$$\frac{P}{W_{-m}} = \frac{P}{W_m} \left(\frac{W_m}{W_{-m}} \right) \quad \text{(A2.20)}$$

we can now compute the employment in the rest of the economy:

$$N^*_{-m} = \frac{n-m}{n} \cdot \frac{1}{A} \left(\frac{P}{W_m} \cdot \frac{W_m}{W_{-m}} \right)^{1-\alpha} \frac{(\delta + i^K)^{1-\alpha} \alpha^{1-\alpha}}{(1-\alpha)^{1-\alpha}} \left(\frac{P_m}{P} \left(\frac{W_{-m}}{W_m} \right)^{\alpha} \right)^{-\eta} \frac{Y^D}{P}$$
(A2.21)

$$= \left(\frac{W_m}{W_{-m}} \right)^{1-\alpha+\alpha\eta} \left(\frac{n-m}{n} \left(\frac{W_{-m}}{W_m} \right)^{\alpha(1-\eta)} + \frac{m}{n} \right)^{\frac{1-\alpha+\eta\alpha}{\alpha(1-\eta)}}$$

$$\left(\frac{-\eta}{1-\eta} \right)^{\frac{1-\alpha}{\alpha}} \frac{1}{A^{\frac{1}{\alpha}}} \frac{(\delta + i^K)^{\frac{1-\alpha}{\alpha}}}{(1-\alpha)^{\frac{1-\alpha}{\alpha}}} \frac{n-m}{n} \frac{Y^D}{P}$$
(A2.22)

which can be rewritten as:

$$N^*_{-m} = \left(\frac{n-m}{n} \left(\frac{W_{-m}}{W_m} \right)^{\alpha(1-\eta)} + \frac{m}{n} \right)^{\frac{1-\alpha+\eta\alpha}{\alpha(1-\eta)}}$$

$$\cdot \left(\frac{-\eta}{1-\eta} \right)^{\frac{1-\alpha}{\alpha}} \frac{1}{A^{\frac{1}{\alpha}}} \frac{(\delta + i^K)^{\frac{1-\alpha}{\alpha}}}{(1-\alpha)^{\frac{1-\alpha}{\alpha}}} \frac{n-m}{n} \frac{Y^D}{P}$$
(A2.23)

Output in firms $1 \ldots m$ is given by:

$$y_m = \frac{m}{n} \left(\frac{P_m}{P} \right)^{-\eta} \frac{Y^D}{P}$$
(A2.24)

$$= \left(\frac{n-m}{n} \left(\frac{W_{-m}}{W_m} \right)^{\alpha(1-\eta)} + \frac{m}{n} \right)^{\frac{\eta}{1-\eta}} \frac{m}{n} \frac{Y^D}{P}$$
(A2.25)

Profits per unit of output in firms $1 \ldots m$ are given by:

$$\frac{\Pi_m}{y_m} = P_m - uc_m$$
(A2.26)

At the same time, we can use (A2.1) to get the share of profits from the sales price P_m:

$$P_m = \frac{-\eta}{1-\eta} uc_m \Leftrightarrow \frac{1-\eta}{-\eta} P_m = uc_m$$
(A2.27)

Real profits in firms 1 … m are given by multiplying profits per unit of output by output sold and dividing by the price level:

$$\frac{\Pi_m}{P} = \frac{\Pi_m}{Y_m} Y_m \frac{1}{P} \tag{A2.28}$$

$$= \frac{1-\eta}{-\eta}\left[\frac{n-m}{n}\left(\frac{W_{-m}}{W_m}\right)^{\alpha\,(1-\eta)} + \frac{m}{n}\right]^{-1} \frac{m}{n} \cdot \frac{Y^D}{P} \tag{A2.29}$$

$$= \frac{nW_m^{\alpha\,(1-\eta)}}{(n-m)W_{-m}^{\alpha\,(1-\eta)} + mW_m^{\alpha\,(1-\eta)}} \cdot \frac{1-\eta}{-\eta} \cdot \frac{m}{n} \cdot \frac{Y^D}{P} \tag{A2.30}$$

$$\tag{A2.31}$$

Differentiating real profits in this sector with regard to the wage paid in the firms concerned shows that profits are a negative function of W_m, just as one would have expected from a standard neo-classical model:

$$\frac{\partial \frac{\Pi_m}{P}}{\partial W_m} = \frac{(n-m)n\alpha\,(1-\eta)W_m^{\alpha\,(1-\eta)-1}W_{-m}^{\alpha\,(1-\eta)}}{[(n-m)W_m^{\alpha\eta}W_{-m}^{\alpha} + mW_{-m}^{\alpha\eta}]^2} \cdot \frac{1-\eta}{-\eta} \cdot \frac{m}{n} \cdot \frac{Y^D}{P} < 0 \tag{A2.32}$$

Aggregate demand

As real aggregate output in this chapter's model is determined by real aggregate demand, it is interesting to see whether real aggregate demand might change when wages in some firms are different from those in other firms. From (5.22) we know that equilibrium aggregate demand consists of three elements: a share c of the aggregate wage bill, a share δ of the real equilibrium capital stock and real autonomous consumption demand. As autonomous consumption demand is by definition independent from the model's other variables, we only have to check whether the equilibrium real capital stock or the real wage sum changes when a sector of the economy has a different wage than the rest.

Aggregate capital input in the firms 1 … m is given as

$$K_m^* = \frac{1}{A}\left(\frac{W_i}{P}\right)^{\alpha} \frac{(1-\alpha)^{\alpha}}{(\delta+i^K)^{\alpha}\alpha^{\alpha}}\left(\frac{P_i}{P}\right)^{-\eta} \frac{m}{n}\frac{Y^D}{P} \tag{A2.33}$$

Using (A2.14) and (A2.15) we get:

$$K_m^* = \left[\frac{n-m}{n}\left(\frac{W_{-m}}{W_m}\right)^{\alpha(1-\eta)} + \frac{m}{n}\right]^{-1} \frac{1-\eta}{-\eta}\frac{(1-\alpha)}{(\delta+i^K)}\frac{m}{n}\cdot\frac{Y^D}{P} \tag{A2.34}$$

And analogously for the rest of the economy:

$$K_{-m}^* = \left[\frac{n-m}{n} + \frac{m}{n}\left(\frac{W_m}{W_{-m}}\right)^{\alpha(1-\eta)}\right]^{-1} \frac{1-\eta}{-\eta}\frac{(1-\alpha)}{(\delta+i^K)}\frac{n-m}{n}\cdot\frac{Y^D}{P} \tag{A2.35}$$

The economy's aggregate capital stock is given by

$$K^* = K_m^* + K_{-m}^* \tag{A2.36}$$

$$K^* = \frac{1-\eta}{-\eta}\frac{(1-\alpha)}{(\delta+i^K)}\frac{Y^D}{P}\cdot\left[\frac{n-m}{n}\left(\frac{n-m}{n} + \frac{m}{n}\left(\frac{W_m}{W_{-m}}\right)^{(1-\eta)}\right)^{-1}\right.$$
$$\left. + \frac{m}{n}\left(\frac{n-m}{n}\left(\frac{W_{-m}}{W_m}\right)^{\alpha(1-\eta)} + \frac{m}{n}\right)^{-1}\right] \tag{A2.37}$$

$$= \frac{1-\eta}{-\eta}\frac{(1-\alpha)}{(\delta+i^K)}\frac{Y^D}{P}\cdot\left[\frac{n-m}{n}\left(\frac{(n-m)W_{-m}^{\alpha(1-\eta)}}{nW_m^{\alpha(1-\eta)}} + \frac{mW_m^{\alpha(1-\eta)}}{nW_m^{\alpha(1-\eta)}}\right)^{-1}\right.$$
$$\left. + \frac{m}{n}\left(\frac{(n-m)W_{-m}^{\alpha(1-\eta)}}{nW_m^{\alpha(1-\eta)}} + \frac{mW_m^{\alpha(1-\eta)}}{nW_m^{\alpha(1-\eta)}}\right)^{-1}\right] \tag{A2.38}$$

$$= \frac{1-\eta}{-\eta}\frac{(1-\alpha)}{(\delta+i^K)}\frac{Y^D}{P}\cdot\left[\frac{n-m}{n}\left(\frac{(n-m)W_{-m}^{\alpha(1-\eta)} + mW_m^{\alpha(1-\eta)}}{nW_{-m}^{\alpha(1-\eta)}}\right)^{-1}\right.$$
$$\left. + \frac{m}{n}\left(\frac{(n-m)W_{-m}^{\alpha(1-\eta)} + mW_m^{\alpha(1-\eta)}}{nW_m^{\alpha(1-\eta)}}\right)^{-1}\right] \tag{A2.39}$$

$$= \frac{1-\eta}{-\eta}\frac{(1-\alpha)}{(\delta+i^K)}\frac{Y^D}{P}$$
$$\cdot\left[\frac{(n-m)W_{-m}^{\alpha(1-\eta)}}{(n-m)W_{-m}^{\alpha(1-\eta)} + mW_m^{\alpha(1-\eta)}}\right.$$
$$\left. + \frac{mW_m^{\alpha(1-\eta)}}{(n-m)W_{-m}^{\alpha(1-\eta)} + mW_m^{\alpha(1-\eta)}}\right] \tag{A2.40}$$

$$= \frac{1-\eta}{-\eta}\frac{(1-\alpha)}{(\delta+i^K)}\frac{Y^D}{P} \tag{A2.41}$$

Thus, the aggregate capital stock employed in the economy is independent of both W_m and W_{-m} and exactly the same as in the monopoly union solution. Consequently, equilibrium investment is also the same as in the case with a uniform wage level.

Similarly, it can be shown that the real wage bill does not change when one union starts to lower its wages. For the sake of simplicity, we first define h as

$$h = \frac{n-m}{n}\left(\frac{W_{-m}}{W_m}\right)^{\alpha(1-\eta)} + \frac{m}{n} \qquad (A2.42)$$

The aggregate real wage bill is given as

$$\frac{\sum W}{P} = \frac{W_m N_m + W_{-m} N_m}{P} \qquad (A2.43)$$

$$= \frac{W_m \frac{m}{n} h^{\frac{1-\alpha+\alpha\eta}{\alpha(1-\eta)}} + W_{-m}\left(\frac{W_m}{W_{-m}}\right)^{1-\alpha+\eta\alpha} \frac{n-m}{n} h^{\frac{1-\alpha+\alpha\eta}{\alpha(1-\eta)}}}{\eta^{\frac{1}{\alpha(1-\eta)}} W_m}$$

$$\cdot \left(\frac{1-\eta}{-\eta}\right)\alpha \frac{Y^D}{P} \qquad (A2.44)$$

$$= \frac{W_m \frac{m}{n} + W_{-m}\left(\frac{W_m}{W_{-m}}\right)^{1-\alpha+\eta\alpha} \frac{n-m}{n} h}{h W_m} \cdot \left(\frac{1-\eta}{-\eta}\right)\alpha \frac{Y^D}{P} \qquad (A2.45)$$

$$= \frac{\frac{n=m}{n}\left(\frac{W_{-m}}{W_m}\right)^{\alpha(1-\eta)} + \frac{m}{n}}{h} \cdot \left(\frac{1-\eta}{-\eta}\right)\alpha \frac{Y^D}{P} \qquad (A2.46)$$

$$= \left(\frac{1-\eta}{-\eta}\right)\alpha \frac{Y^D}{P} \qquad (A2.47)$$

which is independent of both the wage in firms 1 … m and the wage in the rest of the economy. With the aggregate real wage bill being independent of the wages W_m and W_{-m}, real aggregate consumption is also independent of variations in the wages in the two wage bargaining areas. Thus, real aggregate demand does not change when one union starts to set a different wage level in its constituency. Since in this model aggregate output is determined by aggregate demand, aggregate output remains unchanged even when there are different wages in the economy.

The union's utility

A local extreme is at a point x_0 whenever the derivative of the function $f(x)$ changes its sign from positive to negative from the immediate left of the point x_0 to the immediate right (Chiang 1984, p. 235). As the union's utility derivative is positive to the left of $W_m = W_m^{\bar{N}}$, it needs to be negative to the immediate right of $W^{\bar{N}}$. Thus the condition for the existence of a high-employment/low-real wage local maximum in the union's utility function can be found as follows:

$$U_m^{union} = \gamma_{m1} \frac{W_m}{P}$$
$$-\gamma_{m2} \left| \frac{m}{n} \left(\frac{-\eta}{1-\eta} \right)^{\frac{1-\alpha}{\alpha}} \frac{(\delta+i^K)^{\frac{1-\alpha}{\alpha}}}{A^{\frac{1}{\alpha}}(1-\alpha)^{\frac{1-\alpha}{\alpha}}} \left(\frac{W_{-m}}{W_m} \right)^{1-\alpha+\eta\alpha} \frac{Y^D}{P} - \bar{N}_m \right|$$

$$(A2.48)$$

becomes for $W_m > W_m^{\bar{N}}$ (remember that the absolute term becomes 0 at $W_m^{\bar{N}}$, and the function has thus to be defined in the ranges $[0 \ldots W_m^{\bar{N}}]$ and $[W_m^{\bar{N}} \ldots \infty]$, respectively):

$$U_m^{union} = \gamma_{m1} \frac{W_m}{P}$$
$$+ \gamma_{m2} \frac{m}{n} \left(\frac{-\eta}{1-\eta} \right)^{\frac{1-\alpha}{\alpha}} \frac{(\delta+i^K)^{\frac{1-\alpha}{\alpha}}}{A^{\frac{1}{\alpha}}(1-\alpha)^{\frac{1-\alpha}{\alpha}}} \left(\frac{W_{-m}}{W_m} \right)^{1-\alpha+\eta\alpha} \frac{Y^D}{P}$$
$$- \gamma_{m2} \bar{N}_m$$

$$(A2.49)$$

Forming the first derivate yields as a condition for the existence of the maximum:

$$\frac{\partial U_m^{union}}{\partial W_m} =$$

$$\frac{\gamma_{m1}}{P} + \gamma_{m2} \left[(\alpha-1-\eta\alpha) W_m^{\alpha-\eta\alpha-2} W_{-m}^{1-\alpha+\eta\alpha} \frac{m}{n} N^* \right] < 0 \qquad (A2.50)$$

$$\Leftrightarrow \gamma_{m1} < \gamma_{m2} P \left[(1-\alpha+\eta\alpha) W_m^{\alpha-\eta\alpha-2} W_{-m}^{1-\alpha+\eta\alpha} \frac{m}{n} N^* \right] \qquad (A2.51)$$

$$\Leftrightarrow \gamma_{m1} < \gamma_{m2}(1-\alpha+\eta\alpha) \left(\frac{-\eta}{1-\eta} \right)^{\frac{1}{\alpha}}$$

$$\cdot \frac{(\delta+i^K)^{\frac{1-\alpha}{\alpha}}}{\alpha(1-\alpha)^{\frac{1-\alpha}{\alpha}}} \left(\frac{\frac{m}{n} N^*}{\bar{N}_j^{-2+\alpha-\eta\alpha}} \right)^{\frac{1}{1-\alpha+\eta\alpha}}$$

$$(A2.52)$$

Appendix 5.3 Disequilibrium Dynamics

Whenever the firms in the economy are faced with a change in aggregate demand, they are faced with a change in their *individual demand function*. In this model, it is assumed that they are able to vary their labour input at once, but that it takes some time to adjust the capital stock. Thus in the short run, given a change in Y^D (from the old level $\bar{Y}^D$), firms maximise their profit, varying their price P_i and labour employed N_i, given the equilibrium capital stock $\bar{K}_i = K_i^*$. From the production function

$$y_i = A N_i^\alpha \bar{K}_i^{1-\alpha}, 0 < \alpha < 1 \qquad (A3.1)$$

we get the labour employed as a function of output given the fixed capital stock:

$$N_i = \frac{y_i^{\frac{1}{\alpha}}}{A^{\frac{1}{\alpha}}(K_i^*)^{\frac{1-\alpha}{\alpha}}} \qquad (A3.2)$$

And thus the profit function:

$$\max_{P_i} \Pi_i = P_i y_i^D - W \frac{\left(y_i^D\right)^{\frac{1}{\alpha}}}{A^{\frac{1}{\alpha}}(K_i^*)^{\frac{1-\alpha}{\alpha}}} + P i^K K_i^* \qquad (A3.3)$$

$$= P_i \frac{1}{n}\left(\frac{P_i}{P}\right)^{-\eta} \frac{Y^D}{P} - \frac{W}{A^{\frac{1}{\alpha}}(K_i^*)^{\frac{1-\alpha}{\alpha}}}\left[\alpha_i \left(\frac{P_i}{P}\right)^{-\eta} \frac{Y^D}{P}\right]^{\frac{1}{\alpha}} + P i^K K_i^* \qquad (A3.4)$$

Differentiating yields:

$$\frac{\partial \Pi}{\partial P_i} = (1-\eta)\alpha_i P_i^{-\eta} P^\eta \frac{Y^D}{P} - \left(\frac{-\eta}{\alpha}\right) W P_i^{\left(\frac{-\eta-\alpha}{\alpha}\right)} P^{\frac{\eta}{\alpha}}\left(\frac{\alpha_i \frac{Y^D}{P}}{A(K_i^*)^{1-\alpha}}\right)^{\frac{1}{\alpha}} = 0 \qquad (A3.5)$$

$$\Leftrightarrow (1-\eta)P_i^{-\eta} P^\eta \frac{Y^D}{P} =$$

$$A^{-\frac{1}{\alpha}}\left(\frac{-\eta}{\alpha}\right) W P_i^{\left(\frac{-\eta-\alpha}{\alpha}\right)} P^{\frac{\eta}{\alpha}}\left(\frac{Y^D}{P}\right)^{\frac{1}{\alpha}}\left(\frac{-\eta(\delta+i^K)}{(1-\eta)(1-\alpha)}\right)^{\frac{1-\alpha}{\alpha}}\left(\frac{Y^D}{P}\right)^{\frac{\alpha-1}{\alpha}} \qquad (A3.6)$$

$$\Leftrightarrow P_i^{\left(\frac{-\eta+\eta+\alpha}{\alpha}\right)} =$$

$$W P^{\frac{\eta-\eta\alpha}{\alpha}}\left(\frac{Y^D}{P}\right)^{\frac{1-\alpha}{\alpha}} A^{-\frac{1}{\alpha}} \frac{1}{\alpha}\left(\frac{-\eta}{1-\eta}\right)^{\frac{1}{\alpha}}\left(\frac{\delta+i^K}{1-\alpha}\right)^{\frac{1-\alpha}{\alpha}}\left(\frac{Y^D}{P}\right)^{\frac{\alpha-1}{\alpha}} \qquad (A3.7)$$

Which gives us for the disequilibrium price level P^{Diseq} with $Y^D = P(y^D + \varepsilon)$ and $\bar{Y}^D = y^D$:

$$P^{Diseq} = P_i$$

$$= A^{-\frac{1}{\alpha}} \left(\frac{-\eta}{1-\eta} \right)^{\frac{1}{\alpha}} (\delta + i^K)^{\frac{1-\alpha}{\alpha}}$$

$$\cdot \frac{1}{\alpha(1-\alpha)^{\frac{1-\alpha}{\alpha}}} \left(\frac{y^D + \epsilon}{y^D} \right)^{\frac{1-\alpha}{\alpha}} W \qquad (A3.8)$$

$$= \left(\frac{y^D + \epsilon}{y^D} \right)^{\frac{1-\alpha}{\alpha}} P* \qquad (A3.9)$$

6
The Central Bank: Restrictions in a World of Endogenous Money

In the model presented in Chapter 5, it was shown that in a world without a real balance effect but in which the central bank sets the rate of interest, the price level is proportional to the nominal wage level. Output is determined not by the wage level, but by the central bank's interest rate. All the central bank has to do in this setting is to keep nominal wages from rising too sharply, either by signalling to strategically acting wage setters that it would punish excessive wage increases or by keeping unemployment high enough to lessen wage pressure.

However, this view of the world completely neglects the restrictions a central bank faces from financial markets. The model in Chapter 5 is a model of only part of the real sphere. This chapter will examine the financial sphere and show how it is connected with the real sphere. By modelling financial markets, it will show that the central bank might be restricted in its expansionary monetary policy by financial markets so that even with non-excessive wage contracts to begin with, the central bank might not be able to increase output and employment at will. Nevertheless, the central bank has a certain degree of freedom in setting the short-term interest rate.[1] This degree of freedom will be shown to depend on the openness of the economy in question.

The chapter will analyse in Section 6.1 how investment is initially financed in a world of endogenous money. It will then in Section 6.2 turn to the microeconomic portfolio allocation of a single wealth owner to show what happens to the money after it has been created. In Section 6.3, the individuals' considerations are translated into a macroeconomic portfolio model in which the limits to the central bank's discretionary interest rate setting are then examined. Appendices 1–4 consider further aspects of portfolio mathematics.

The argument is as follows: in a system of endogenous inside money, it is *money holdings* which macroeconomically finance the capital stock (in addition, of course, to direct real capital holdings). However, if the central bank cares about the sustainability of the monetary system, it can create only as much money as is desired by individuals to be held in their portfolios. Money has to compete in the portfolios with other possible investments, such as real capital or foreign currency. Changes in the monetary interest rate lead to changes in the prices of foreign assets (the exchange rate) and of real capital holdings. As long as this change in asset prices does not induce the individuals to reduce their real money holdings, the central bank can lower interest rates, thereby increasing the equilibrium capital stock and equilibrium output. Whether or not a central bank has this degree of freedom depends on the extent to which individuals perceive a depreciation or an increase in the price of real assets as a threat to their wealth position. The more domestically oriented an economy and its wealth owners, the less the exchange rate movement matters for perceived value stability of the domestic money.

Thus, in a departure from some Post-Keynesian works, this chapter concludes that a central bank might be constrained by financial markets to such an extent that full employment cannot be reached. In this chapter it is shown that, contrary to what some Post-Keynesians claim, it is the market logic and not always the maliciousness of central bankers which causes unemployment.[2]

6.1   Financing investment by money creation

The initial financing of the investment undertaken in Chapter 5 does not pose any problems in a world of endogenous money. While in a standard neo-classical model the entrepreneur would have to borrow capital which someone else had saved before (or which she herself had saved before), in a world of endogenous money, the saving to equilibrate macroeconomic savings and investments takes place after the investment has been conducted. The initial finance in order to pay for the investment good is provided by the banking system's money creation: the entrepreneur borrows from her bank, the bank in turn borrows from the central bank. The central bank creates the money demanded and hands it over to the commercial bank, which in turn loans it to the entrepreneur. The entrepreneur pays the investment with the newly borrowed (and created) money. As investment is increased, employment and aggregate income also increase. With higher aggregate incomes, aggregate savings also grow. In the model of Chapter 5 aggregate (net) savings always equal aggregate (net) investments. The investment here creates the income which finally provides for its financing.

Table 6.1 illustrates this process. A firm plans a real investment for which it has to buy labour worth €100. In step [1], the firm borrows €100 from its bank. The bank creates the deposit and has to refinance the loan. Note that as reserve requirements are to be fulfilled *ex post*, the loan comes before refinancing. Here, for simplicity, it is assumed that reserve requirements are 100 per cent. In step [2], the commercial bank refinances the loan at the central bank. The firm now takes its deposits and buys labour worth €100, thus creating a capital good worth €100. In this example, it is further assumed that the household saves all of its income. In the end, households have increased their wealth by €100 in bank deposits and the real capital stock of the economy has increased in value. Savings equal investments.

Table 6.1 Capital formation and money creation

Firms (F)			**Households (HH)**		
Assets		*Liabilities*	*Assets*		*Liabilities*
[1] Deposits D_F^{MFI}	+100	[1] Bank credits Cr_{MFI}^F	+100	[3] Deposits D_{HH}^{MFI}	+100	[3] House-hold wealth	+100
[3] Deposits D_F^{MFI}	−100				
[3] Capital good	+100				

Financial institutions (MFI)			**Central bank (CB)**		
Assets		*Liabilities*	*Assets*		*Liabilities*
[1] Credit Cr_{MFI}^F	+100	[1] Deposit from firm D_{MFI}^F	+100	[2] Credit Cr_{CB}^{MFI}	+100	[2] Deposit from *MFI* D_{MFI}^{CB}	+100
[2] Deposit at CB D_{MFI}^{CB}	+100	[2] Credit from CB Cr_{CB}^{MFI}	+100				
		[3] Deposit from firm D_F^{MFI}	−100				
		[3] Deposit from households D_{HH}^{MFI}	+100				

This is so far much in line which what many Post-Keynesians proclaim: if there were no pressure from wage costs, the central bank could, if it wished, impose full employment easily if it didn't have any additional goals as Wray (1990, pp. 184f) and Hewitson (1995, p. 298) note. The central bank would just have to push interest rates down enough so that aggregate demand was sufficient to guarantee full employment. This is in fact a view shared by the strain of Post-Keynesians dubbed 'horizontalists' such as Moore (1991).[3]

But this approach neglects an important fact. As Goodhart notes in his reply to Moore (1989), even money endogenously created in the credit process has to be *held* by the general public in equilibrium (emphasis as in the original text):

> I will accept always any money offered me in payment for some sale at an agreed price, so that any addition, e.g. caused by a bank loan, is always snapped up, but it does not mean that I will want to hold that amount of extra money in ultimate equilibrium. Demand for money, in the sense of the optimal amount that I would want to hold in *equilibrium* in a given context, is *not* the same thing as – or determined by – the credit-counterpart supply of money. The credit market is distinct and different from the money market ...
>
> I agree that at any moment the actual supply of money is determined, under present circumstances, primarily in the credit market – as the credit-counterparts approach indicates – and that it is willingly accepted. But I deny that this actual stock is necessarily also demanded in the equilibrium sense outlined above. (1989, p. 33, emphasis in the original)

At this point, the *portfolio theory* comes into play. As we know from models such as those described by Markowitz (1952, 1959) or Tobin (1958), rational investors diversify the risks related to their investments by allocating different shares of their wealth into different kinds of assets. Thus, they will hold a share of their wealth in money, depending on the rate of return on money (that is, the nominal interest rate on money less inflation), the rates of return on other assets, the volatility in the returns of each asset and the investors' expected need for liquid means of payment and their wealth.

This poses a limitation on the central bank's actions: monetary policy is able to set the short-term interest rate only in a range in which – while of course asset prices and yields on assets other than money are influenced – a new equilibrium is found. If the monetary authorities were to attempt to set the interest rates somewhere below that range, a downward cycle of depreciation and flight from the domestic currency would follow.

6.2   The microeconomics of endogenous money

To see how changes in the short-term interest rate affect the demand (and consequently the prices) of different assets, we will first take a look at the microeconomics of money and asset demand in a world of endogenous money, which we will then translate into an aggregate model of the asset markets in question.

'Money' in this chapter is defined as a very broad monetary aggregate, containing all liabilities of the financial sector fixed in nominal terms. The model thus does not distinguish between cash and demand deposits, but sees them as very close substitutes from the individual money-holder's point of view. This is not as strange a definition as it seems at first sight: in a system such as the monetary system of the euro-zone, in which the banks hold huge quantities of assets against which they can borrow actual cash from the central bank at any time, deposits in fact can be turned into actual currency, even at an aggregate level.[4] Moreover, from a macroeconomic perspective, it does not matter whether individuals hold actual currency or deposits. Table 6.2 shows what happens if the households decide not to hold deposits, but rather cash. The commercial bank's balance sheet shortens, while deposits in the central bank's and the households' balance sheets are substituted for cash. In the end, this shift from balances into cash in the households' portfolios does not change the real capital accumulation.[5]

What is important is that households decide to hold monetary assets at all. Only if households were willing to provide labour and take money (deposits or cash) into their portfolios in exchange, could capital good production take place. Money in a world of endogenous money is thus a complement to real capital holdings, not a substitute, as in Tobin's (1965) world.

Most of money from a very broad aggregate is primarily held for what Tobin (1998, p. 56) calls *investment motives*.[6] Of course, some part of monetary assets is not held for investment, but for transaction motives of both the household and the business sector (probably most of actual currency is). However, this part of monetary holdings covers a rather small portion of a broad money stock. Moreover, the transaction demand for money is probably less influenced by changes in the return of monetary assets or by changes in money's riskiness.

Table 6.2 Changing deposits into cash

Firms (F)		Households (HH)	
Assets	Liabilities	Assets	Liabilities
Capital good 100	Bank credits +100 Cr_{MFI}^F	Deposits +100 D_{HH}^{MFI} [4] Deposits −100 D_{MFI}^F [4] Cash +100	Household wealth +100

Financial institutions (MFI)		Central bank (CB)	
Assets	Liabilities	Assets	Liabilities
Credit 100 Cr_{MFI}^F	Deposit from households 100 D_{HH}^{MFI}	Credit 100 Cr_{CB}^{MFI}	Deposit from MFI 100 D_{MFI}^{CB}
Deposit 100 at CB D_{MFI}^{CB}	Credit from CB +100 Cr_{CB}^{MFI}		[4] Deposit −100 from MFI D_{MFI}^{CB}
[4] −100 Deposit at CB D_{MFI}^{CB}	[4] Deposit from households −100 D_{HH}^{MFI}		[4] Cash +100

As Tobin (1958) shows, in a world of risky assets and money, it is rational for risk-averse individuals to hold part of their wealth in the form of money in order to attain a combination of risk and return superior to what would be possible if they exclusively held only money or risky assets. This conclusion is not limited to a setting in which money is a completely safe asset. As early critics pointed out, return on money is uncertain as well: unexpected inflation might erode its value, unexpected deflation might even lead to strongly positive real returns. However, as is known from portfolio theory (Markowitz 1952, 1959), assets will be included in the portfolio when they help the individual reach a higher level of expected utility.

Following this definition, it is possible either to have positive or negative money holdings: when an individual's debts to the financial sector are larger than assets from the financial sector in the individual's portfolio, she has a negative monetary asset position. When an individual's monetary assets have a higher value than her monetary debts to the financial sector, her net money holdings are positive.

In a world of endogenous money, some individuals choose to invest more in real capital than their net wealth, financing their additional real capital investments by going into debt. At the same time, others decide to hold the money thereby created. Whether an individual goes short or long on money depends on her attitude towards risk.

Consequently, an approach with one single representative agent is not able to depict a world with endogenous money.[7] If all agents had the same net wealth and the same degree of risk aversion, either all agents would want to hold a negative net monetary position (thus having monetary debts larger than their monetary assets) or all agents would want to hold a positive net monetary position (having monetary assets larger than their monetary debts). With all money being inside money, neither of these two points would be possible. The only possible equilibrium in a world of endogenous money and identical representative agents would be one in which no one held any debt or any (net) monetary assets. However, this would not be a world of endogenous money, but a world without money.

I will thus illustrate the microeconomics of endogenous money using two kinds of individuals: entrepreneurs, who are sufficiently risk averse to decide to go into debt (and thus hold a negative share of their portfolio in monetary assets) and rentiers, who are risk averse and prefer to stick to safer assets, thus generally holding a positive part of their portfolios in monetary assets.

Figure 6.1[8] illustrates the idea in a standard μ–σ-diagram. μ (R) denotes the expected return of the portfolio, σ the risk measured as the standard deviation of returns on the portfolio. In a single-asset world in which investment only in real capital is possible, the only attainable risk return combination of an individual's portfolio is at point K. At this point, the individual holds all his wealth in real capital. Consequently, his expected return is the expected return on real capital holdings. The riskiness of his portfolio is that of real capital holdings.

If now money is added, which also carries some risk, but the return of which is not perfectly positively correlated with the return on real capital, all points on the line M–L are possible portfolios. Points to the left of K depict portfolios which include a positive share of money. At these points, the individual holds less than his total net wealth in capital. He also has a positive monetary asset position. Points to the right of K describe portfolios in which there is more real capital than the net wealth of the individual. This capital position is financed by the individual having gone into debt and thus having a negative monetary asset position.

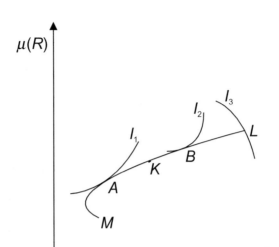

Figure 6.1 Possible portfolio positions in a world of endogenous money and investing all of the money borrowed in real capital

I_1–I_3 depict indifference curves for individuals with different attitudes towards risk. Both I_1 and I_2 belong – albeit to a different degree – to risk averse individuals. Since the individuals want to be compensated with additional expected return for any increased risk they incur, the indifference curves have a positive slope. I_3 belongs to a risk-loving individual. This individual would take on higher risks even if she were not compensated by higher returns. Instead, she would even take on greater risks if the expected return were lower. Consequently, her indifference curve in the μ–σ-space is negatively sloped.

Point M depicts the point in which the individual holds only money and no real capital at all. At the other end of the curve, point L depicts a point in which an individual has borrowed as much as the financial system is willing to loan him, having invested all the borrowed money in real capital.

Which point an individual chooses on the efficient frontier of possible portfolios depends on his attitude towards risk:[9] if the individual is rather risk averse, he might have an indifference curve I_1, bringing his portfolio to point A, thus giving him a positive net monetary position. If the individual is less risk averse, he might be so adventurous that he borrows some and invests more in real capital than his net worth, bringing him with an indifference curve I_2 to point B.[10] If an individual is risk-loving and thus has an indifference curve such as I_3, she will end up in the maximum risk position L, borrowing to the limit and investing all of the money borrowed in real capital.

Endogenous money thus allows less risk averse or even risk-seeking individuals to take on more risk, while it allows the risk averse a less risky portfolio. Or in Tobin's words (1998, p. 129):

> [F]inancial markets and the intermediary institutions ... in effect monetize capital. Loans permit the more adventurous members of society, those who are willing to assume risks, to invest in enterprise capital in excess of their net worth. The lenders, in return, acquire assets tailored to their more conservative tastes – less risky, more liquid, more reversible, more predictable.

But, the demand for monetary assets by those who are risk averse enough to hold monetary assets has to be the same as the (satisfied) demand for credit by those who are less risk averse. For a model with entrepreneurs and rentiers, this translates into

$$_Ex_M V_E = - {_R}x_M V_R \qquad (6.1)$$

with $_Ex_M$ and $_Rx_M$ denoting the portfolio shares entrepreneurs and rentiers want to hold in the form of monetary assets and V_E and V_R denoting entrepreneurs' and rentiers' respective net wealth.

If there were only two assets, real capital and money, and the stock of real capital were exogenously given (for example, by investment demand as in the model in Chapter 5), only one single interest rate would bring the two sides of (6.1) into equilibrium. However, in a world in which there are more than two assets, changes in the other assets' prices might also lead to an equilibrium.

The most obvious additional asset class for an open economy is foreign assets. In addition, it is the price for foreign assets, the *exchange rate*, which is probably the most important single asset price in an open economy. Formally, we can now deduce the portfolio shares an individual wishes to hold in any of the three assets money M, real capital K and foreign assets F by maximising a simple $\mu - \sigma$-rule in the form of

$$\max \mu - \beta\sigma^2 \qquad (6.2)$$

with μ as the portfolio's expected return and σ as the standard deviation of the portfolio's return. This maximisation is equivalent to maximising an expected utility function of any form as long as returns on the assets in question follow a normal distribution.[11]

For a portfolio of N assets of which each has the weight x_n in the portfolio and the expected return r_n and all portfolio shares add up to 1, expected return and variance are given by (remember that cov $[r_n, r_n]$ = var $[r_n]$):

$$\mu[r_{PF}] = \sum_{n=1}^{N} x_n \mu[r_n] \qquad (6.3)$$

$$\text{var } [r_{PF}] = \sum_{j=1}^{N} \sum_{n=1}^{N} x_j x_n \text{cov}[r_j, r_n] \qquad (6.4)$$

which gives us as a maximisation problem:

$$\max_{x_1 \dots x_n} \left(\sum_{n=1}^{N} x_n \mu[r_n] - \beta \sum_{j=1}^{N} \sum_{n=1}^{N} x_j x_n \text{cov}[r_j, r_n] \right) \qquad (6.5)$$

under the condition

$$\sum_{n=1}^{N} x_n = 1 \qquad (6.6)$$

Writing as a Lagrange-Function

$$L = \sum_{n=1}^{N} x_n \mu[r_n] - \beta \sum_{j=1}^{N} \sum_{n=1}^{N} x_j x_n \text{cov}[r_j, r_n] + \lambda \left(\sum_{n=1}^{N} x_n - 1 \right) \qquad (6.7)$$

and differentiating for all x_n yields N conditions in the form of:[12]

$$\frac{\partial L}{\partial x_n} = \mu[r_n] - 2\beta \sum_{k=1}^{N} x_k \text{cov}[r_n, r_k] + \lambda = 0 \qquad (6.8)$$

From these N conditions, we get by substituting for each $n, k \in 1 \dots N$, $n \neq k$:

$$\mu[r_n] - \mu[r_k] + 2\beta \sum_{j=1}^{N} [\text{cov}[r_k, r_j] - \text{cov}[r_n, r_j]] = 0 \qquad (6.9)$$

Taking $N - 1$ of these conditions plus the condition (6.6) gives us N equations with which we can solve the system for all portfolio shares

x_n. For the case of three assets, M, K and F, this gives us using Φ_{M1}, Φ_{M2}, Φ_{K1}, Φ_{K2}, Φ_{F1}, Φ_{F2} as representation for more complicated terms:[13]

$$x_M = \frac{\Phi_{M1} + 2\beta\Phi_{M2}}{2\beta\Phi_{den}} \qquad (6.10)$$

$$x_K = \frac{\Phi_{K1} + 2\beta\Phi_{K2}}{2\beta\Phi_{den}} \qquad (6.11)$$

$$x_F = \frac{\Phi_{F1} + 2\beta\Phi_{F2}}{2\beta\Phi_{den}} \qquad (6.12)$$

While the terms themselves are quite complicated to interpret, since the Φ_s do not have an obvious and simple meaning, we can obtain some conclusions as to how the portfolio shares depend on the returns of the single assets or their volatility. As we see by partially differentiating (6.10)–(6.12), the share of each asset the individual wishes to hold in his portfolio is a positive function of this asset's return and a negative function of the other assets' returns. Exemplarily differentiating the demand for monetary assets (6.10) with regard to each of the assets' returns yields:

$$\frac{\partial x_M}{\partial \mu[r_M]} = -\frac{\text{var}[r_K] + \text{var}[r_F] - 2\text{cov}[r_K, r_F]}{2\beta\Phi_{den}} \qquad (6.13)$$

$$\frac{\partial x_M}{\partial \mu[r_F]} = \frac{\text{var}[r_K] - \text{cov}[r_M, r_K] - \text{cov}[r_K, r_F] + \text{cov}[r_M, r_F]}{2\beta\Phi_{den}} \qquad (6.14)$$

$$\frac{\partial x_M}{\partial \mu[r_K]} = \frac{\text{var}[r_F] - \text{cov}[r_M, r_F] - \text{cov}[r_K, r_F] + \text{cov}[r_M, r_K]}{2\beta\Phi_{den}} \qquad (6.15)$$

Φ_{den} can be shown to be negative for independent or positively correlated asset returns[14] In this work, it will be therefore further assumed that Φ_{den} is negative.

As by definition,[15] $2\text{cov}[r_K, r_F] \leq \text{var}[r_F] + \text{var}[r_K]$, the share of money in the portfolio is an increasing function of the return on monetary assets (6.13). For the influence of the returns on capital and foreign assets on the portfolio's share of monetary assets, the interpretation is again more complicated. For relatively independent returns on the three asset classes, the share of money in the individuals' portfolios is clearly a decreasing function of the return on the other assets. When the returns on capital and foreign assets are strongly correlated, however, the share of money in the portfolio can actually even increase when one of the other returns increases.

As to the riskiness of any of the assets, we get for differentiating (6.10) with regard to var $[r_M]$:[16]

$$\frac{\partial x_M}{\partial \text{var}[r_M]} = \frac{-2\beta\,(2\text{cov}[r_K,r_F] - \text{var}[r_F] - \text{var}[r_K])(\Phi_{M1} + 2\beta\Phi_{M2})}{(2\beta\Phi_{den})^2} \qquad (6.16)$$

To interpret this term, we need to know more about the signs of $\Phi_M1 + 2\beta\Phi_M2$ and β. For both terms, entrepreneurs and rentiers differ. A relatively risk-averse rentier would have a high β_R, while a less risk-averse entrepreneur would have a low β_E. As we need a negative entrepreneur's demand for money $_E x_M$ in order to have an equilibrium in which money exists, this β_E must fulfil:

$$_E x_M < 0 \qquad (6.17)$$

$$\Leftrightarrow \frac{\Phi_{M1} + 2\beta_E\Phi_{M2}}{2\beta_E\Phi_{den}} \qquad (6.18)$$

$$\qquad (6.19)$$

This leads us for $\beta_E > 0$ and $\Phi_{M2} < 0$ to:[17]

$$\Phi_{M1} + 2\beta_E\Phi_{M2} > 0 \qquad (6.20)$$

$$\Leftrightarrow \beta_E < -\frac{\Phi_{M1}}{2\Phi_{M2}} \qquad (6.21)$$

Besides these somewhat risk-averse entrepreneurs, there might also be some real risk seekers who borrow up to their limit. Their (negative) demand for monetary assets is constrained only by the financial system's willingness to provide them with funds. As they find themselves in a corner solution no matter how high the return on monetary assets or how great their riskiness, their demand for credit (or negative money holdings) is not a function of assets' return or variance, but of the parameters of credit rationing.

Now we can interpret the reaction of the money demand to changes in the variance on the return on money (6.16). For rentiers money demand is positive. Consequently, $\Phi_{M1} + 2\beta_R\Phi_{M2}$ must be negative. Thus (6.13) is also negative for $\beta = \beta_R$: with an increasing riskiness of monetary assets, the rentiers' demand for money will fall.

For risk-averse entrepreneurs with $0 < \beta_E < -\dfrac{\Phi_{M1}}{2\Phi_{M:}}$, the story looks slightly different. Here, the second bracket in (6.16) is positive. Thus, the share of money they wish to hold in their portfolio increases with increasing variance of the return on monetary assets. The rationale behind this is simple: remember that the entrepreneurs' money demand is *negative* (they wish to borrow). An increase in their money demand thus means a decrease in their credit demand. With an increased variance of the return on monetary assets, having debts gets riskier. The entrepreneurs' nominal debt's real value is now more volatile. As entrepreneurs with a positive β_E are still risk averse, a reduction of their credit demand is a rational reaction.

Thus, both the demand for credit and the demand for money fall when the riskiness of monetary assets increases.

6.3   A macroecomic portfolio model of endogenous money

We could now use (6.10)–(6.11) for all three different classes of individuals (risk-averse and risk-seeking entrepreneurs, rentiers) to deduce a market equilibrium. However, this approach has two drawbacks. First, one would have to assume given proportions of these three kinds of individuals in the society as well as shares of nominal wealth owned by each of these groups. Second, the model would become very complicated.

Therefore, I will instead use a slightly modified Tobin (1982, pp. 183ff.) macroeconomic portfolio model. To Tobin's original contribution I will add endogenous money and an equilibrium capital stock as a function of the rate of return demanded by investors to invest in real capital. In order to interpret the effects of changes in the return of single assets or their riskiness, I will later return to the microeconomic foundation of Section 6.2. We thus get the following equations for the long-run equilibrium in the asset markets of real capital K, money M and foreign assets F with A^X being the aggregate (direct) demand function[18] for each asset, r^X the rate of return of each asset, V aggregate wealth, e the exchange rate, Cr credit demand and u a parameter denoting the individuals' propensity to hold money in their portfolios (depending on the perceived riskiness of monetary assets – see below):

$$A^K(r^K,r^M,r^F,u,V,...) + C_r(r^M,r^K,V,...) = K*(r^K) \qquad (6.22)$$

$$\frac{M}{P} \equiv A^M(r^K,r^M,r^F,u,V,...) = Cr(r^M,r^K,V,...) \qquad (6.23)$$

$$A^F(r^K,r^M,r^F,u,V,...) = \frac{e}{P}F \qquad (6.24)$$

Equation (6.22) describes the market for real capital. Real investment is financed either directly through households which hold shares of an enterprise (translating into direct demand for real capital A^K) or indirectly through entrepreneurs who borrow (translating into credit demand and credit supply Cr and indirectly into demand for real capital). As we have seen above, the demand for capital is a positive function of the return on real capital holdings and a negative function of returns on all other assets. In long-run equilibrium, the supply of real capital as a function of the interest demanded for real capital r^K needs to be equal the capital stock K^* firms want to hold at that given rate, as deduced in Chapter 5.

Equation (6.23) describes the money market (left-hand side) and the credit market (right-hand side). Money stock M here is defined as a very broad monetary aggregate, containing all liabilities of the financial sector fixed in nominal terms. Money is created only when entrepreneurs borrow from the financial sector. It is assumed that households do not borrow for consumption and that the government[19] does not borrow at all from the financial sector. As it can be assumed that interest rates charged by the banking sector for commercial loans depend positively on the interest rate in the money market r^M, and credit demand Cr can be expected to be negatively sloped in the interest rate on loans, credit demand is also a negative function of the money market interest rate. As we know from the entrepreneurs' demand for monetary assets (see Section 6.2), the credit demand (which in fact is only the negative demand of entrepreneurs for monetary assets) is also a positive function in the rate of return on real capital holdings and of aggregate net wealth.

Since the banking system (financial institutions and the central bank) accommodates any credit demanded at the exogenous central bank refinancing rate r^M by creating the monetary assets necessary, the money stock M is endogenous inside money.[20] At the same time, (6.23) guarantees that all money so created is also held by individuals. The left-hand side of (6.23) depicts the liability side of the monetary sector, while the right-hand side shows the sector's asset position. It is assumed that banks do not hold any equity.

Equation (6.24) shows the market for foreign assets. It is assumed that the stock of foreign assets F is fixed in the short run.[21] The rate of return on foreign assets r_F is exogenous.[22] In the long run current account surpluses or deficits would change the available amount of foreign assets. These considerations will be covered later in this chapter.

The equilibrium capital stock K^* is a function of the interest rate demanded by investors to invest in real capital r^K. In the context of

Chapter 5, this rate of return is equivalent to the interest rate which the single firm has to pay for obtaining funds to conduct real investment r^K. Thus, r^K and K^* are connected via (5.18). Each of these variables can be written as a function of only the other one and some additional parameters. Note that this demanded rate of return r^K is different from the *average* real rate of return R in (A1.28) on each unit of capital employed, as r^K is a marginal value, while R is an average value.

Adding (6.22), (6.23) and (6.24) leaves us with the economy's equilibrium net asset position (while the net asset position in the money/credit market is 0, since all money is inside money):

$$V = K^* + \frac{e}{P} F \tag{6.25}$$

The demand for any single asset type is an increasing function of this asset type's yield and a decreasing function of all other asset types' yields. In addition, the demand for money is an increasing function of the private agents' willingness to hold monetary assets in their portfolio u, while the demand for all other asset types is a decreasing function of u. This u can be interpreted as money's riskiness compared to the other assets' riskiness. u would thus be a decreasing function of var $[r_M]$ and an increasing function in var $[r_K]$ and var $[r_F]$. In addition, demand for all asset types increases with the economy's private wealth.

If we now consider the long-run equilibrium we see that both money holdings and real equity holdings finance the economy's capital stock:

$$A^K(r^K, r^M, r^F, u, V, ...) + A^M(r^K, r^M, r^F, u, V, ...) = K^* \tag{6.26}$$
$$A^F(r^K, r^M, r^F, u, V, ...) = \frac{e}{P} F \tag{6.27}$$

Or differently put, the larger the share of money in the individuals' portfolios, the larger the capital stock economic agents decide to hold directly and indirectly at a given exchange rate, and consequently the larger the capital stock available for productive purposes.[23] Tobin (1998, p. 129) uses a similar concept, calling capital which is held through monetary intermediation *monetised capital*. Appendix 4 to this chapter (p. 191) highlights parallels and differences between Tobin's concept and the concept used here.

In a world of endogenous money, a central bank that wants its economy to have a high long-term output (which in both a neoclassical world and the world as depicted in Chapter 5 comes with a large capital stock) should consequently aim at keeping the share of domestic monetary assets in the wealth owners' portfolios and thus also the individuals' preference for monetary assets u as high as possible.[24] It cannot increase output in any way it desires, but instead has to follow the logic of the asset markets and act as market participant (Riese 1995).

Investment, monetary policy and the capital stock: the long run

As long as one assumes both that the expected rate of return on all assets and their riskiness are independent of any changes in the exchange rate caused by a change in the central bank's interest rate,[25] and that a change in the exchange rate does not have any influence on domestic wage demands, the central bank is not confronted with any restrictions when choosing its interest rate. Totally differentiating and solving for de and dK^* yields with subscripts denoting partial derivatives:[26]

$$
\begin{aligned}
dK^* = \quad & \tfrac{1}{|H|}\tfrac{F}{P}\big[(A_M^V - Cr_V) \\
& \big((-A_{r^M}^K - Cr_{r^M})dr^M - A_{r^F}^K dr^F - A_u^K du - (A_V^K + Cr_V)\tfrac{e}{P}\,dF\big) \\
& \qquad\qquad -(A_V^K + Cr_V) \\
& \big((-A_{r^M}^M - Cr_{r^M})dr^M - A_{r^F}^M dr^F - A_u^M du - (A_V^M + Cr_V)\tfrac{e}{P}\,dF\big)\big]
\end{aligned}
\tag{6.28}
$$

$$
\begin{aligned}
de = \quad & \tfrac{1}{|H|}\big[(A_{r^K}^K r_K + A_V^K + Cr_V + Cr_{r^K}r_K^K - 1) \\
& \big((-A_{r^M}^M - Cr_{r^M})dr^M - A_{r^F}^M dr^F - A_u^M du - (A_V^M + Cr_V)\tfrac{e}{P}\,dF\big) \\
& \qquad\qquad -(A_{r^K}^M r_K + A_V^M + Cr_V + Cr_{r^K}r_K^K) \\
& \big((-A_{r^M}^K - Cr_{r^M})dr^M - A_{r^F}^K dr^F - A_u^K du - (A_V^K + Cr_V)\tfrac{e}{P}\,dF\big)\big]
\end{aligned}
\tag{6.29}
$$

with the main determinant H:

$$
|H| = \frac{F}{P}\left[\underset{+}{A_V^M}\left(\underset{+}{A_R^K r_K^K} + \underset{+}{Cr_{r^K}r_K^K} + \underset{-}{A_V^K + Cr_V - 1}\right)\right.
$$
$$
\left. - \underset{+}{A_V^K}\left(\underset{+}{A_R^M R_K} + A_V^M - Cr_V - \underset{+}{Cr_{r^K}r_K^K}\right)\right] < 0
\tag{6.30}
$$

For a constant riskiness of monetary assets, a constant stock of foreign assets and a constant return on foreign assets ($du = dF = dr^F = 0$)

we get as the effect of a central bank interest rate change on exchange rate and equilibrium capital stock:

$$\frac{dK^*}{dr^M} = \frac{1}{|H|} \underset{+}{\frac{F}{P}} \left[\underbrace{(A_V^M + Cr_V)}(\underbrace{-A_{r^M}^K + Cr_{r^M}}) - \underbrace{(A_V^K + Cr_V)}(\underbrace{-A_{r^M}^M + Cr_{r^M}}) \right] \qquad (6.31)$$

$$\frac{de}{dr^M} = \frac{1}{|H|} \left[\underbrace{(A_{r^K}^K r_K^K + A_V^K + Cr_V + Cr_{r^K} r_K^K - 1)}(\underbrace{Cr_{r^M} - A_{r^M}^M}) \right.$$

$$\left. + \underbrace{(A_{r^K}^M r_K^K + A_V^M + Cr_V + Cr_{r^K} r_K^K)}(\underbrace{A_{r^M}^K - Cr_{r^M}}) \right] \qquad (6.32)$$

As is shown in Appendix 2D, (6.31) and (6.32) are both negative. A cut in interest rates thus leads to a depreciation of the domestic currency just as can be expected in virtually any macroeconomic textbook model.

However, as (6.31) shows, a cut in interest rates also leads to a higher equilibrium capital stock of the economy and thus to a higher long-term output. The lower central bank interest rate leads to a fall in the demanded rate of return on real capital. This lower demanded rate of return leads to a higher desired capital stock by firms. Increased investment leads to higher employment and higher aggregate output, and thus also higher aggregate savings. The additional savings finance the capital stock and a higher capital stock equilibrium is attained.

By itself, the result that a lower interest rate comes with a higher capital stock is not surprising. In neo-classical textbook models, firms will demand a higher capital stock when interest rates are lower. However, usually the supply of capital is restricted by a saving function being foremost a *positive* function of the interest rate. In the model here, aggregate savings are a *negative* function of the interest rate. Higher interest rates lead to lower investment demand, lower aggregate output and consequently lower aggregate savings. Lower interest rates, on the other hand, cause the production that provides for their finance.[27]

These results can also be illustrated by a graphical representation of the portfolio model: figure 6.2 shows equilibria in each of the three asset markets. The *FF*-curve denotes all combinations of capital stock *K* and exchange rate *e* in which the market for foreign assets is in equilibrium; the *KK* and the *MM*-curves denote similar loci for the capital and the money market.[28]

Figure 6.3 shows what happens when the central bank lowers its interest rates. With lower interest rates on monetary assets, the entrepreneurs' demand for credit increases while the rentiers' demand for monetary assets decreases. The money market can obtain equilibrium again only at a higher capital stock or a higher exchange rate. Thus, the *MM*-curve shifts up. In the market for foreign assets, with a lower rate of return on domestic monetary assets, the demand for foreign assets increases, leading to an excess demand. Equilibrium here can be reached only at a higher exchange rate, thus shifting the *FF*-curve to the right. Finally, lower central bank interest rates lead to an increase in the real capital holdings demanded for portfolio purposes, by both lowering the return on monetary assets and by increasing the entrepreneurs' credit-financed demand for real capital. A new equilibrium here is found only with a higher capital stock, shifting the *KK*-curve up.

Obstacle I: import price hike

However, the assumption of independence of the return and risk of monetary assets from fluctuations in the exchange rate is implausible:

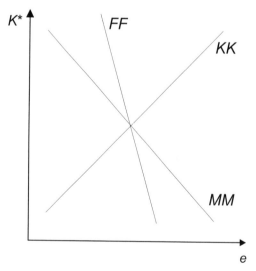

Figure 6.2   Asset markets in *K–e*-space

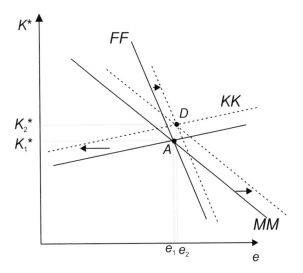

Figure 6.3   A cut in the central bank's interest rate

at least in an economy which is not completely closed (and why should there be any foreign assets in a completely closed economy?), the exchange rate influences exports, imports and their prices. Changes in these variables in turn can be expected to influence the return on monetary assets.

The consumption price level

As explained above, portfolio theory builds on an expected utility function. Expected utility depends on the utility in different future states of the world. In standard portfolio theory, utility is a function of wealth in these different states. However, from a microeconomic per-spective, it is not money (or wealth) itself that provides utility, but consumption or the option to consume (or the possibility to transfer this consumption or the option to consume to one's heirs). Consequently, the investor will measure the return on his portfolio (and on each single asset) by deflating the returns with his personal consumer price index (CPI.)

  The influence of a depreciation on the price level might thus be of particular relevance. There are two mechanisms by which a deprecia-tion influences consumer prices. First, imported goods which are directly consumed become more expensive. Second, as a depreciation affects net export demand, excess demand might push up prices. While the price push from increased export demand is a temporary phenomenon (as I will argue on p. 171), the shift in the exchange rate will alter the price level more permanently.[29]

By altering the price level for imported goods, changes in the exchange rate have a direct influence on the consumer price level. Extending the price level for a closed economy by an import sector, assuming that a share α_{Im} of consumed goods is imported, we get for the consumer price level P^{Cons}:

$$P^{Cons} = (1 - \alpha_{Im})P^{Dom} + \alpha_{Im}eP^{Foreign} \tag{6.33}$$

The consumer price level is the weighted average of domestically produced goods and imported goods which enter with their foreign price $P^{Foreign}$ converted into domestic currency. The domestic goods' price level P^{Dom} is a function of the nominal wage level, the interest rate, the degree of monopolisation in the economy and – in disequilibrium as described on p. 130 – excess demand (just as the price level in Chapter 5). The share of imported good prices α_{Im} in the consumer price level depends on the country's import share.[30]

A depreciation thus increases the equilibrium consumer price level, even if it does not change the price level for domestically produced goods. If unions now try to recoup their members' lost purchasing power through wage increases, the domestic price level will also rise, leading to an overall increase in prices.

But even if wages are kept stable, the depreciation also decreases a monetary asset's consumption value and thus the return of this asset by the same amount. As investors can be expected to be rational, they will expect such a depreciation when the central bank cuts interest rates. Thus, they will act as if the central bank had lowered interest rates not only by dr^M, but additionally by the depreciation-induced negative return.

If the initial depreciation has large enough an impact on the return of the monetary asset, it is possible that with a lower interest rate, no new equilibrium will be reached in the three asset markets. This would be the case in particular when the initial interest rate cut leads to a depreciation that decreases the monetary assets' return by more than the initial interest rate cut (as this would set in motion a downward spiral for the domestic currency – any additional devaluation would cause an expected fall in monetary assets' return in consumption terms, which would in turn lead to an even greater devaluation). Or in formal terms: if the depreciation alters only the consumption value of the return of monetary assets but not its riskiness, the central bank has the freedom to lower interest rates as long as:[31]

$$\left| \frac{\partial \mu[r_M]}{\partial e} \frac{de}{dr^M} \right| < \left| dr^M \right| \qquad (6.34)$$

Thus, with a price level like 6.33, we can deduce a condition for the central bank being able to cut interest rates to boost the capital stock. If the real rate of return on monetary assets r^M is in the eyes of investors the difference between the nominal rate on monetary assets i^M and the consumer price inflation π^{Cons}

$$r^M = i^M - \pi^{Cons} \qquad (6.35)$$

we get for $\dfrac{\partial \mu[r_M]}{\partial e}$

$$\frac{\partial \mu[r_M]}{\partial e} = \alpha_{Im} \frac{P^{Foreign}}{P^{Cons}} \qquad (6.36)$$

Looking now at (6.36) together with (6.32), we see what the central bank's degree of freedom depends upon. First and foremost, the smaller the share of imported goods in the investor's consumption basket, the more likely condition (6.34) is to hold, and thus the more likely the central bank is able to lower interest rates in order to increase the macroeconomic capital stock.

Second, as we see from (6.32) and (6.30), *portfolio composition* plays a key role in the central bank's abilities to use monetary policy to increase the capital stock: the larger the absolute value of the determinant H, the smaller is the depreciation following an interest rate cut, $\left| \dfrac{de}{dr^M} \right|$, thus the larger the central bank's degree of freedom. (6.30) shows us that the determinant's absolute value is greater the larger is the investor's marginal propensity to put any additional monetary unit of wealth into monetary assets or real capital. Since $A_V^M + A_V^K + A_V^F = 1$, a large share of monetary assets and real capital in the individuals' portfolios implies a low portfolio share of foreign assets. Thus, the smaller the portfolio share of foreign assets, the larger the central bank's degree of freedom.

So, both the financial openness (as measured by the individuals' share of wealth held in foreign assets) and the real openness (as measured by the share of imports in consumption) influence whether the central bank can use the interest rate to increase the capital stock: the more closed a country is financially and in real terms, the larger the central bank's degree of freedom.

Qualification: the riskiness of domestic assets

So far, it has been assumed only that the expected return on monetary assets changes when the domestic currency depreciates. The riskiness or the variance of the return on monetary assets has to be assumed to remain constant when the exchange rate changes. For an economy that is defined precisely by deterministic equations (as most macroeconomic models and also that presented in this book), this assumption would hold. Changes in the exchange rate cause an accurately foreseeable change in the price level, and there is no reason why the outcome should be any different from the expected outcome. $\frac{\partial var[r^M]}{\partial e}$ would be 0. Thus, investors in such a world should not perceive a depreciation and thus a change in the return of monetary assets as a change in the riskiness of monetary assets.

However, empirics show that in general higher rates of inflation also come with a higher variability of the rate of inflation.[32] While there are competing explanations for this fact, there is not yet a convincing and undisputed answer as to why this is the case. If investors perceived the devaluation and the subsequent hike in the consumer price level as an increase in the riskiness of domestic assets, they might demand a higher risk premium.

Moreover, if there is uncertainty about the unions' behaviour in the wake of a depreciation, it would be rational for investors to see monetary assets as riskier assets, with the domestic currency depreciating after a central bank interest rate cut. If the unions resort to aggressive wage bargaining in order to recoup real wage losses from the depreciation, the general price level will shift upwards. If this reaction cannot be ruled out, the *a priori* variance of monetary assets' return increases with a depreciation.

Taking this reasoning into account, the central bank can lower interest rates only if the effect on the individuals' portfolio choice from the additional riskiness *plus* the effect from a loss in return on monetary assets is not larger than the effect from the initial cut in interest rates. Again, since the pass-through from the exchange rate to consumption prices is larger the more open the economy is in terms of imports as a share of the consumption basket, and since unions will most likely measure their real wage development by deflating their nominal wages by the consumer price index, the more closed an economy, the smaller is the risk of igniting a wage–price spiral after a depreciation – thus the larger is the central bank's degree of freedom.

In addition, if the unions were to commit credibly not to try to regain real wage losses from depreciations following an expansionary monetary policy, the risk of a depreciation turning into a wage spiral would be reduced, and investors should thus perceive the central bank's interest cut as less risky.

Obstacle II: short-run dynamics

Besides the shift in the price of imported goods, an interest rate cut might have other effects on the domestic economy. First, as investment demand increases with lower interest rates, excess demand will lead temporarily to higher goods prices. At the same time, the price for real capital holdings will increase so that the current capital stock valued at current market prices equals the equilibrium capital stock. During this time, the marginal return on a unit of capital is larger than r^K, first because r^K is below the initial value of r^K, but also because excess demand leads to extra profits.[33] Only when investment increases the capital stock will the price for both real capital holdings fall again. With the increase of the capital stock, the general price level also falls as described on p. 130 (Collignon 2002a, Chapter 8).

The cut in interest not only influences aggregate demand via a lower interest rate. As we have seen, the cut also leads to a depreciation of the domestic currency. The higher exchange rate then will induce an effect on exports similar to that of the lower interest rate on investment demand. As long as demand for imports and exports is price-elastic, the volume of imports and exports is affected. This change in the trade balance will also affect aggregate demand. If we turn to Chapter 5's model and its aggregate demand, we could extend the model by adding net exports *ex* being a function of the exchange rate to the aggregate demand function:

$$Y^D = cNW + \xi P(K^* - K) + \delta PK + P(y_0^D + ex\,(e), \ldots) \tag{6.37}$$

With a fixed capital stock in the short run, a change in the net exports would change the price level in the short run just as would a shock on the autonomous demand or the increased investment demand described on p. 130. The consequence is that while increased demand would be satisfied, it would be satisfied only at a higher price. Only with capacities expanding in the medium run would this price hike from both investment as well as from increased export demand disappear again.

However, investors should anticipate this development. They therefore should not perceive this temporary price hike as a permanent fall in the rate of return on monetary assets. However, as the value of domestic monetary assets in consumption terms during a transition period will be below what it would have been without these temporary changes, they might perceive monetary assets as becoming more risky (as var $[r_M]$ has increased).

Just as in the case of the import price inflation, how unions react to the temporary price change is crucial. If they attempt to bargain aggressively to quickly regain the real purchasing power they have lost, a wage inflation might be induced which would then lead to a general inflation.

Here again, the extent to which one can expect a reaction to the depreciation depends on the magnitude of the temporary price change. The larger the reaction of aggregate demand to a change of the exchange rate, the more likely is a reaction by the unions. Besides the question of what kind of product a country is importing or exporting (as their demand's price elasticity in the world market is crucial), the effect on aggregate demand also depends on the degree of openness in trade. If a large part of the output is affected by the change in the exchange rate, one can also expect the reaction of aggregate demand to be stronger. And again just as in the case of the price hike for imported goods, the investors' perceptions of the riskiness of an interest rate cut for price stability depends upon their expectations of the unions' behaviour. If unions are committed to standing still and not pushing for wage increases to recoup lost real wages, investors should view the temporary price push from investment and export demand as less of a problem.

Obstacle III and qualification: accumulation of foreign assets

So far, we have assumed that the stock of foreign assets remains fixed. However, with exports and imports affected as described on p. 171, the stock of foreign assets will also change. In the short run, the depreciation leads to an improvement in the trade balance:[34] with a higher exchange rate e, foreign goods are more expensive in domestic terms while domestic goods are more competitive in the international market. If we assume a balanced current account (as the sum of trade balance plus interest payments, interest payments being positive since F is assumed to be positive) to begin with, a positive inflow of foreign assets will result.

From (6.28) we get that such an inflow does not change the equilibrium capital stock demanded for portfolio purposes by wealth owners since for dr^M, dr^F, $du = 0$ holds:

$$\frac{dK^*}{dF} = \frac{1}{|H|}\frac{eF}{P^2}\Big[(A_V^M - Cr_V)(-A_V^K - Cr_V$$
$$- (A_V^K + Cr_V)(-A_V^M + Cr_V)\Big] \qquad (6.38)$$
$$= \Big[-A_V^M A_V^K - A_V^M Cr_V + A_V^K Cr_V + Cr_V^2$$
$$+ A_V^M A_V^K - A_V^K Cr_V + A_V^M Cr_V + Cr_V^2\Big]$$
$$= 0 \qquad (6.39)$$

However, the exchange rate does not remain constant. From (6.29) we get:

$$\frac{de}{dF} = \frac{1}{|H|}\frac{eF}{P^2}\Big[(A_{r^K}^K r_K + A_V^K + Cr_V + Cr_{r^K} r_K^K - 1)(-A_V^M - Cr_V)$$
$$+ \Big[(A_{r^K}^M r_K + A_V^M + Cr_V + Cr_{r^K} r_K^K)(-A_V^K - Cr_V)\Big] \qquad (6.40)$$
$$= \frac{1}{|H|}\frac{eF}{P^2}\Big[\underbrace{A_V^M + Cr_V}_{+} - A_V^M A_{r^K}^K r_K^K - A_V^M r_K^K Cr_{r^K} + A_{r^K}^K r_K^K Cr_V$$
$$+ A_{r^K}^M r_K^K A_V^K - A_V^K C_{r^K} r_K^K + A_{r^K}^M r_K^K Cr_V\Big] \qquad (6.41)$$

With $A_V^M > Cr_V$, only $+ A_{r^K}^M r_K^K Cr_V$ of the terms in brackets is negative. All other terms are positive. Though without further assumptions about the magnitudes of the different partial derivatives, it is hard to prove analytically whether the term in brackets is positive, we can assume that the sum of positive terms will be larger in absolute terms than $+ A_{r^K}^M r_K^K Cr_V$. Moreover, this assumption can be shown to hold by using the graphical way of analysing the model. We can thus conclude that the whole bracket is positive. In consequence, $\frac{de}{dF}$ is negative, and an inflow of foreign assets leads to an appreciation.

Figure 6.4 shows a graphical representation of the inflow of foreign assets. In the capital market, the demand for real capital is increased as the total wealth increases. Only with a lower exchange rate or a higher capital stock can a new equilibrium be attained. Thus the KK-curve shifts up and to the left. In the money market, the increase of foreign assets also leads to an excess demand for monetary assets as a store of wealth. Here, an increase in the capital stock would only lower the return on capital, thus lowering the demand for credit and consequently increasing the excess demand. Hence, only a lower exchange rate or a lower capital stock can bring equilibrium to this market. The *MM*-curve shifts to the left and down. In the foreign exchange market, both demand and supply increase, though supply increases by a larger amount than demand. Here, a fall in the exchange rate would bring equilibrium. The *FF*-curve shifts to the left.

Consequently, the new equilibrium is one with an unchanged capital stock but an appreciated domestic currency. Thus, the inflow of foreign assets with an improved trade balance does not directly influence the economy's capital stock. However, there is a different caveat to this inflow of foreign assets: with an inflow of foreign assets and the appreciation this causes, net export demand will fall again. If we assume that in the long run current accounts are balanced, the amount of net exports in final long-run equilibrium will even be below that in the initial equilibrium: the current account consists of net

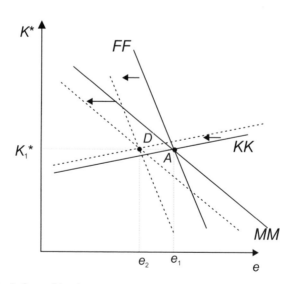

Figure 6.4   Inflow of foreign assets

interest payments and net exports given the nominal interest rate i^F on foreign assets:

$$CA = ei^F F + Pex(e) = 0 \qquad (6.42)$$

Thus, with a higher stock of foreign assets F, net exports need to be lower than in the initial situation to reach a balanced current account.

This fact limits the central bank's degree of freedom through two channels. First, if entrepreneurs anticipate the return to a balanced current account and normal export demand, they will not adjust their capital stock, but just deliver with the given capacities. Consequently, the temporary price hike from export demand following an initial depreciation will not disappear with increased capacities, but only when the current account again approaches its balanced state.

Second, in the long run, a central bank interest rate cut brings more employment only if the reaction of domestic demand (capital replacements $P\delta K^*$) to the cut in interest rates is greater than the reduction in net exports. Again, this depends upon the degree of openness of the economy: in a relatively closed economy, domestic investment plays a larger role relative to export demand, thus making it more likely that this condition is met.

However, it should be noted that the long-run reaction of the current account (with it returning to balance) for practical purposes probably plays the smallest role in the central bank's restrictions. Empirically, it has to be doubted that current accounts quickly return to equilibrium, especially for large industrialised countries. The USA has experienced a negative (and increasing) current account balance since the 1970s while Japan has run a huge surplus during that time. At least for a large number of the firms, it can be expected that they consequently do not calculate a quick return to a balanced current account and thus do adjust their capital stock.

It needs to be underlined that the conclusion of this section is valid only for countries which are not net debtors in foreign currency. If a country were a net debtor in a foreign currency,[35] the current account would worsen with a devaluation, as interest payments in domestic currency would increase. It would then be crucial that the reaction of the trade balance was greater than the reaction of interest payments in order to get back to a stable exchange rate. If the trade balance reacted less than the interest payments, the current account would worsen and a permanently increasing stock of foreign indebtedness would occur, leading to a permanent upward *trend* (as opposed to a one-time hike) in the exchange rate and thus to permanently imported inflation.

Degree of freedom

So, one can conclude that a central bank *has* a certain degree of freedom in choosing its interest rate on monetary assets r^M. However, this degree of freedom depends to a large degree on structural parameters of the economy. The more open an economy is both in trade and in the composition of its wealth owners' portfolios, the more limited is the central banks' degree of freedom. The more aggressively unions behave after an import price hike, the more limited is the monetary authority's scope of action.

Problems of small open economies

This analysis poses grave problems for small open economies. Being more open brings about two problems. First, as Schelkle (2001, pp. 185ff.) shows for reasonable assumptions, the share of foreign assets held by individuals is a positive function of the correlation between exchange rate movements and domestic prices.[36] The larger α_{lm}, the larger are both this correlation and thus the share of foreign assets held by domestic wealth owners, and thus the smaller the share of total wealth used to finance domestic capital stock. In addition, as we have seen above, a larger share of foreign assets in the portfolio also directly limits the scope for central bank actions.

Second, exchange rate movements become more important for the determination of the consumer price level. If α_{lm} is larger than 0.5, it is primarily the exchange rate and its fluctuations which determine the consumption purchasing power of the domestic currency. Moreover, the larger α_{lm}, the larger is the probability that unions will react with compensating nominal wage demands to a depreciation of the domestic currency, as a depreciation hits workers' purchasing power to a greater extent. Thus the larger α_{lm}, the less a central bank can practice *benign neglect* regarding its exchange rate.

For developing countries, this problem is further aggravated, since wealth owners in these regions often consider a different consumption price index as the measured CPI. Workers and small farmers in those countries usually do not save much and thus do not hold much wealth. At the same time, they consume primarily domestically produced goods such as food items. The affluent, on the other hand, often buy luxury goods which are usually imported.

In addition, they consider trips to the USA or Europe for medical treatment or they wish to send their children to college in the industrialised countries. All these consumption possibilities have to be paid for in foreign currency. Thus, the share α_{Im} of imported goods might in these countries understate the extent to which wealth owners consider a change in the exchange rate as a change in their purchasing power.

An additional problem arises for countries which already face a large degree of dollarisation: as Roy (2000) argues following Whalen (1966) and Tsiang (1969), individuals hold money in their portfolios for *precautionary motives*: they want to be prepared to meet sudden expenses or liabilities not anticipated in payment date or size. As long as there are liquidation costs for assets different from money and significant costs of illiquidity, economic agents will keep a certain share of their wealth in the asset generally accepted as means of payment. With debts and certain types of contracts denominated in a foreign currency, people will increasingly be reluctant to hold money for precautionary purposes. Again from a certain point of dollarisation onward, holding domestic currency instead of foreign currency brings about the risk of illiquidity, thus making foreign assets more attractive than domestic currency for precautionary motives – and making the wealth position in foreign currency the relevant point of reference for price stability.

Simply pegging the domestic currency to the currency in which imports are denominated does not help. As long as the domestic currency has a track record of higher inflation than the anchor currency, and it can be expected that the peg is regularly adjusted upwards (thus depreciating the domestic currency), such a move would only reduce the foreign assets' riskiness (as random fluctuations are eliminated). Consequently, wealth owners would replace the domestic currency in their portfolios with foreign assets at an earlier point than in a world of free float.[37]

Policy makers in a small open country are faced with a dilemma. Either they peg their currency to an anchor currency, taking the risk that it will be eliminated from the wealth owners' portfolios if they are not able to make it more stable than the anchor currency, and thus risking a decrease in the central bank's freedom to pursue a monetary policy which increases the domestic capital stock. Or they let their currency be in a managed float, possibly hindering trade and investment, but definitely forcing the central bank to use its interest rate in order to target the exchange rate.

Conclusions for the euro-zone

For the euro-zone, things are different. With regards to trade, the euro-zone is a relatively closed economy (imports from outside the currency-area account for roughly 10 per cent of GDP). And as French and Poterba (1991) and Tesar and Werner (1998) show, most industrialised countries, including the euro-area countries, show a strong home bias for equities.[38] Thus, the euro area can well be assumed to be relatively closed in portfolio terms as well. Consequently, the ECB has a certain degree of freedom on the financial market side.

However, the ECB still has to focus on keeping unit labour costs in check. It is thus confronted with two obstacles when conducting expansionary monetary policy. First, a cut in interest rates induces additional domestic demand. This will increase prices in the short run until an adjustment of the capital stock has taken place. Second, a depreciation will push up import prices. Unlike extra profits caused by the initial demand push after an interest rate cut,[39] which are only a disequilibrium phenomenon and will disappear after an adjustment period, the shift in the exchange rate might be at least a medium-term shift. Swings in the exchange rate might thus permanently alter the price level and induce unions to push for higher wage demands.

This possible wage pressure is potentially dangerous as it might help turn a one-time or temporary price hike into general inflation. As investors are aware of this danger, they might view any strategy of monetary expansion as an increase in the riskiness of monetary assets. These dangers could be alleviated by the trade unions' credible commitment not to push for wage increases in the wake of an interest rate cut. The scope for getting the unions into the boat for such an expansionary monetary policy strategy will be examined in depth in Chapter 7.

Appendix 6.1:   Microeconomic Portfolio Theory

Computing x_1 to x_n

For differentiating (6.7) with regard to x_n, we use a little trick introduced by Kruschwitz (1995, p. 193). For differentiating with regard to x_n only those terms of the middle term of (6.7) are of interest which contain x_n. Thus, the relevant terms for differentiating can be rewritten as:

$$x_n^2 \text{cov}[r_n, r_n] + 2 \sum_{\substack{j=1 \\ j \neq n}}^{N} x_n x_j \text{cov}[r_n, r_j] \tag{A1.1}$$

Differentiating (A1.1) with regard to x_n yields

$$2x_n\text{cov}[r_j,r_j] + 2\sum_{\substack{j=1 \\ j \neq n}}^{N} x_j\text{cov}[r_n,r_j] \qquad \text{(A1.2)}$$

$$= 2\sum_{j=1}^{N} x_j\text{cov}[r_n,r_j] \qquad \text{(A1.3)}$$

Thus we get from (6.7) to (6.8) or in detail for the case of three assets M, K, F:

$$\frac{\partial L}{\partial x_M} = \mu[r_M] - 2\beta\,(x_M\text{cov}[r_M,r_M] + x_K\text{cov}[r_M,r_K] + x_F\text{cov}[r_M,r_F]) + \lambda$$
$$= 0 \qquad \text{(A1.4)}$$

$$\frac{\partial L}{\partial x_K} = \mu[r_K] - 2\beta\,(x_M\text{cov}[r_K,r_M] + x_K\text{cov}[r_K,r_K] + x_F\text{cov}[r_K,r_F]) + \lambda$$
$$= 0 \qquad \text{(A1.5)}$$

$$\frac{\partial L}{\partial x_F} = \mu[r_F] - 2\beta\,(x_M\text{cov}[r_F,r_M] + x_K\text{cov}[r_F,r_K] + x_F\text{cov}[r_F,r_F]) + \lambda$$
$$= 0 \qquad \text{(A1.6)}$$

Substituting (A1.4) into (A1.6), (A1.4) into (A1.5) and (A1.5) into (A1.6) yields:

$$\mu[r_F] - \mu[r_M]$$
$$- 2\beta x_M(\text{cov}[r_F,r_M] - \text{cov}[r_M,r_M])$$
$$- 2\beta x_K(\text{cov}[r_F,r_K] - \text{cov}[r_M,r_K])$$
$$- 2\beta x_F(\text{cov}[r_F,r_F] - \text{cov}[r_M,r_F]) = 0 \qquad \text{(A1.7)}$$

$$\mu[r_K] - \mu[r_M]$$
$$- 2\beta x_M(\text{cov}[r_K,r_M] - \text{cov}[r_M,r_M])$$
$$- 2\beta x_K(\text{cov}[r_K,r_K] - \text{cov}[r_M,r_K])$$
$$- 2\beta x_F(\text{cov}[r_F,r_F] - \text{cov}[r_M,r_F]) = 0 \qquad \text{(A1.8)}$$

$$\mu[r_F] - \mu[r_K]$$
$$- 2\beta x_M(\text{cov}[r_F,r_K] - \text{cov}[r_M,r_K])$$
$$- 2\beta x_K(\text{cov}[r_F,r_K] - \text{cov}[r_K,r_K])$$
$$- 2\beta x_F(\text{cov}[r_F,r_F] - \text{cov}[r_K,r_F]) = 0 \qquad \text{(A1.9)}$$

Writing (A1.7)–(A1.9) as a matrix and using Cramer's rule yields (6.10)–(6.12):

$$x_M = \frac{\Phi_{M1} + 2\beta\Phi_{M2}}{2\beta\Phi_{den}}$$

$$x_K = \frac{\Phi_{K1} + 2\beta\Phi_{K2}}{2\beta\Phi_{den}}$$

$$x_F = \frac{\Phi_{F1} + 2\beta\Phi_{F2}}{2\beta\Phi_{den}}$$

with

$$\begin{aligned}
\Phi_{den} =\ & (\text{cov}[r_F,r_M] - \text{cov}[r_M,r_M]) \\
& (\text{cov}[r_K,r_K] - \text{cov}[r_M,r_K] - \text{cov}[r_K,r_F] + \text{cov}[r_M,r_F]) \\
& + \text{cov}[r_F,r_K] - \text{cov}[r_M,r_K]) \\
& (\text{cov}[r_K,r_F] - \text{cov}[r_M,r_F] - \text{cov}[r_K,r_M] + \text{cov}[r_M,r_M]) \\
& + \text{cov}[r_F,r_F] - \text{cov}[r_F,r_M]) \\
& (2\text{cov}[r_K,r_M] - \text{cov}[r_M,r_M] - \text{cov}[r_K,r_K])
\end{aligned} \tag{A1.10}$$

$$\begin{aligned}
\Phi_{M1} =\ & \mu[r_F](\text{cov}[r_K,r_K] - \text{cov}[r_M,r_K] - \text{cov}[r_K,r_F] + \text{cov}[r_M,r_F]) \\
& - \mu[r_M](\text{cov}[r_K,r_K] + \text{cov}[r_F,r_F] - 2\text{cov}[r_K,r_F]) \\
& + \mu[r_K](\text{cov}[r_F,r_F] - \text{cov}[r_M,r_F] - \text{cov}[r_F,r_K] + \text{cov}[r_M,r_K])
\end{aligned} \tag{A1.11}$$

$$\begin{aligned}
\Phi_{M2} =\ & (\text{cov}[r_F,r_K] - \text{cov}[r_M,r_K])(\text{cov}[r_K,r_F] - \text{cov}[r_M,r_F]) \\
& - (\text{cov}[r_F,r_F] - \text{cov}[r_M,r_F])(\text{cov}[r_K,r_K] - \text{cov}[r_M,r_K])
\end{aligned} \tag{A1.12}$$

$$\begin{aligned}
\Phi_{K1} =\ & \mu[r_F](\text{cov}[r_K,r_F] - \text{cov}[r_M,r_F] - \text{cov}[r_K,r_M] + \text{cov}[r_M,r_M]) \\
& - \mu[r_M](\text{cov}[r_K,r_F] - \text{cov}[r_K,r_M] - \text{cov}[r_F,r_F] + \text{cov}[r_M,r_F]) \\
& + \mu[r_K](2\text{cov}[r_F,r_M] - \text{cov}[r_M,r_M] - \text{cov}[r_F,r_F])
\end{aligned} \tag{A1.13}$$

$$\begin{aligned}
\Phi_{K2} =\ & (\text{cov}[r_F,r_F] - \text{cov}[r_M,r_F])(\text{cov}[r_K,r_M] - \text{cov}[r_M,r_M]) \\
& - (\text{cov}[r_F,r_M] - \text{cov}[r_M,r_M])(\text{cov}[r_K,r_F] - \text{cov}[r_M,r_F])
\end{aligned} \tag{A1.14}$$

$$\begin{aligned}
\Phi_{F1} =\ & \mu[r_F](\text{cov}[r_K,r_M] - \text{cov}[r_M,r_M] - \text{cov}[r_K,r_K]) \\
& - \mu[r_M](\text{cov}[r_F,r_K] - \text{cov}[r_K,r_M] - \text{cov}[r_F,r_M] + \text{cov}[r_K,r_K]) \\
& + \mu[r_K](\text{cov}[r_F,r_K] - \text{cov}[r_M,r_K] - \text{cov}[r_F,r_M] + \text{cov}[r_M,r_M])
\end{aligned} \tag{A1.15}$$

$$\begin{aligned}
\Phi_{F2} =\ & (\text{cov}[r_F,r_M] - \text{cov}[r_M,r_M])(\text{cov}[r_K,r_K] - \text{cov}[r_M,r_K]) \\
& - (\text{cov}[r_F,r_K] - \text{cov}[r_M,r_K])(\text{cov}[r_K,r_M] - \text{cov}[r_M,r_M])
\end{aligned} \tag{A1.16}$$

Sign of Φ_{den}

We can show that Φ_{den} is negative. We use the definition of the correlation coefficient ρxy:

$$\rho_{XY} = \frac{\text{cov}[X,Y]}{\sqrt{\text{var}[X]\text{var}[Y]}} \tag{A1.17}$$

We also know that $-1 \le \rho xy \le 1$. From this definition, we can write any cov $[r_i, r_j]$ with $i, j = M, F, K$ as a product of a correlation coefficient and a square root of the product of two variances:

$$\text{cov}[r_i, r_j] = \rho_{ij}\sqrt{\text{var}[r_i]\text{var}[r_j]} \tag{A1.18}$$

Substituting (A1.18) for all covariances in (A1.11), multiplying and regrouping thus yields:

$$\begin{aligned}
\Phi_{den} = {} & (2\rho_{MF} - 2\rho_{MK}\rho_{KF})\sqrt{\text{var}[r_K]^2\text{var}[r_M]\text{var}[r_F]} \\
& + (2\rho_{KF} - 2\rho_{MF}\rho_{MK})\sqrt{\text{var}[r_M]^2\text{var}[r_K]\text{var}[r_F]} \\
& + (2\rho_{KM} - 2\rho_{MF}\rho_{KF})\sqrt{\text{var}[r_F]^2\text{var}[r_K]\text{var}[r_M]} \\
& + (\rho_{MF}^2 - 1)\sqrt{\text{var}[r_M]^2\text{var}[r_F]^2} \\
& + (\rho_{KM}^2 - 1)\sqrt{\text{var}[r_M]^2\text{var}[r_K]^2} \\
& + (\rho_{KF}^2 - 1)\sqrt{\text{var}[r_K]^2\text{var}[r_F]^2}
\end{aligned} \tag{A1.19}$$

Again using the definition of the correlation coefficient, this can be rewritten as:

$$\begin{aligned}
\Phi_{den} = {} & 2\rho_{MF}\sqrt{\text{var}[r_K]^2\text{var}[r_M]\text{var}[r_F]} - 2\text{cov}[r_M, r_K]\text{cov}[r_K, r_F] \\
& + 2\rho_{KF}\sqrt{\text{var}[r_M]^2\text{var}[r_K]\text{var}[r_F]} - 2\text{cov}[r_M, r_F]\text{cov}[r_K, r_M] \\
& + 2\rho_{KM}\sqrt{\text{var}[r_F]^2\text{var}[r_K]\text{var}[r_M]} - 2\text{cov}[r_M, r_F]\text{cov}[r_K, r_F] \\
& + (\rho_{MF}^2 - 1)\text{var}[r_M]\text{var}[r_F] \\
& + (\rho_{KM}^2 - 1)\text{var}[r_M]\text{var}[r_K] \\
& + (\varphi_{KF}^2 - 1)\text{var}[r_K]\text{var}[r_F]
\end{aligned} \tag{A1.20}$$

Regrouping yields:

$$\begin{aligned}
\Phi_{den} = &-2\text{cov}[r_M,r_K]\text{cov}[r_K,r_F] \\
&-2\text{cov}[r_M,r_F]\text{cov}[r_K,r_M] \\
&-2\text{cov}[r_M,r_F]\text{cov}[r_K,r_F] \\
&(\rho_{MF}^2-1)\text{var}[r_M]\text{var}[r_F]+2\rho_{MF}\text{var}[r_K]\sqrt{\text{var}[r_M]\text{var}[r_F]} \\
&(\rho_{KM}^2-1)\text{var}[r_M]\text{var}[r_K]+2\rho_{KM}\text{var}[r_F]\sqrt{\text{var}[r_K]\text{var}[r_M]} \\
&(\rho_{KF}^2-1)\text{var}[r_K]\text{var}[r_F]+2\rho_{KF}\text{var}[r_M]\sqrt{\text{var}[r_K]\text{var}[r_F]}
\end{aligned} \quad (A1.21)$$

This term can be shown to be negative for $\rho_{MF}, \rho_{KF}, \rho_{KF} \geq 0$ as follows: the first three lines of this expression are all negative as long as asset returns are not negatively correlated (all covariances are by definition positive when correlation is positive). For the other lines, the terms can be positive or negative, depending on the correlation coefficients. However, it is obvious that the terms are all negative for $\rho_{MF} = \rho_{KF} = \rho_{KF} = 0$ as all positive terms then disappear:

$$\Phi_{den} = -\text{var}\,[r_M]\,\text{var}\,[r_F] - \text{var}\,[r_M]\,\text{var}\,[r_K] - \text{var}\,[r_K]\,\text{var}\,[r_F] < 0 \quad (A1.22)$$

Moreover, we can easily see that the partial derivatives of Φ_{den} with regard to $\rho_{MF}, \rho_{KF}, \rho_{KF}$ are all positive. Finally, we see that for the case of perfect correlation of the returns on all three assets $\rho_{MF} = \rho_{KF} = \rho_{KF} = 1$, (A1.19) becomes:

$$\Phi_{den} = 0 \quad (A1.23)$$

Φ_{den} is thus a positively sloped, from some negative value to 0 monotonously growing function over the range $\rho = 0 \ldots 1$. Thus, as long as returns are positively correlated, Φ_{den} is negative. In addition, there is a wide range of negative ρs over which the term Φ_{den} remains negative: As can be seen in (A1.19), lines 4–6 definitely remain negative even for negative ρs. Lines 1–3 get positive only when some of the ρs get strongly negative, while others remain positive or only slightly negative. Only if the returns on some of the three assets are *strongly* negatively correlated, can thus Φ_{den} be positive.

Appendix 6.2:   Aggregate Portfolio Mathematics

Equations (6.22)–(6.25) are given. It is useful to remember that with increasing u, wealth is shifted from real capital and foreign asset holdings into monetary asset holdings, thus:

$$-A_u^M = A_u^F + A_u^K \tag{A2.1}$$

An increase in wealth has to be held in any of the three asset types:

$$-A_V^M + A_V^F + A_V^K = 1 \tag{A2.2}$$

Since we only have two endogenous variables, the exchange rate e and the capital stock K^* (r_K^k being only a function of K^* and vice versa), we need only two of the asset market conditions, as Walras' law states that when $n - 1$ markets are in equilibrium, the nth is also in equilibrium.[40] Totally differentiating (6.22) and (6.23) gives us (subscripts denoting partitial derivatives):

$$(A_{r^K}^K r_K^K + A_V^K + Cr_V + Cr_{r^K} r_K^K - 1)dK^* + (A_{r^M}^K + Cr_{r^M})dr^M$$
$$+ A_{r^F}^K dr^F + A_u^K du + (A_V^K + Cr_V)\frac{F}{P}de + (A_V^K + Cr_V)\frac{e}{P}dF = 0 \tag{A2.3}$$

$$(A_{r^K}^M r_K^K + A_V^K + Cr_V + Cr_{r^K} r_K^K - 1)dK + (A_{r^M}^M + Cr_{r^M})dr^M$$
$$+ A_{r^F}^M dr^F + A_u^M du + (A_V^M + Cr_V)\frac{F}{P}de + (A_V^M + Cr_V)\frac{e}{P}dF = 0 \tag{A2.4}$$

Or written as a matrix:

$$\begin{pmatrix} (A_{r^K}^K r_K^K + A_V^K + Cr_V + Cr_{r^K} r_K^K - 1) & (A_V^K + Cr_V)\frac{F}{P} \\ (A_{r^K}^M r_K^K + A_V^M + Cr_V + Cr_{r^K} r_K^K) & (A_V^M + Cr_V)\frac{F}{P} \end{pmatrix} \begin{pmatrix} dK^* \\ de \end{pmatrix} =$$
$$\begin{pmatrix} (-A_{r^M}^K - Cr_{r^M})dr^M - A_{r^F}^K dr^F - A_u^K du - (A_V^K + Cr_V)\frac{e}{P}dF \\ (-A_{r^M}^M - Cr_{r^M})dr^M - A_{r^F}^M dr^F - A_u^M du - (A_V^M + Cr_V)\frac{e}{P}dF \end{pmatrix} \tag{A2.5}$$

To use Cramer's rule, we first need to get the determinant of the matrix (6.30):

$$|H| = \frac{F}{P}\left[A_V^M \underbrace{\left(\underbrace{A_R^K r_K^K}_{+} + \underbrace{Cr_{r^K}\, r_K^K}_{+} + \underbrace{A_V^K + Cr_V - 1}_{-} \right)}_{-} \right.$$

$$\left. - A_V^K \underbrace{\left(\underbrace{A_R^M R_K + A_V^M - Cr_V - Cr_{r^K}\, r_K^K}_{+} \right)}_{+} \right] < 0$$

When assuming $A_V^M \geq Cr_V$,[41] it can be shown that H is negative. For dK and de we get (6.28) and (6.29):

$$dK^* = \frac{1}{|H|}\frac{F}{P}\Big[A_V^M - Cr_V$$
$$\big((-A_{r^M}^K - Cr_{r^M})dr^M - A_{r^F}^K dr^F - A_u^K du - (A_V^K + Cr_V)\tfrac{e}{P}\, dF \big)$$
$$-(A_V^K + Cr_V)$$
$$\big((-A_{r^M}^M - Cr_{r^M})dr^M - A_{r^F}^M dr^F - A_u^M du - (A_V^K + Cr_V)\tfrac{e}{P}\, dF \big)\Big]$$

$$de = \frac{1}{|H|}\Big[(A_{r^K}^K r_K + A_V^K + Cr_V + Cr_{r^K} r_K^K - 1)$$
$$\big((-A_{r^M}^M - Cr_{r^M})dr^M - A_{r^F}^M dr^F - A_u^M du - (A_V^K + Cr_V)\tfrac{e}{P}\, dF \big)$$
$$-\big([(A_{r^K}^M r_K + A_V^M + Cr_V + Cr_{r^K} r_K^K)$$
$$(-A_{r^M}^K - Cr_{r^M})dr^M - A_{r^F}^K dr^F - A_u^K du - (A_V^K + Cr_V)\tfrac{e}{P}\, dF \Big]$$

(6.28) can be simplified for dr^F, $du = 0$, $dF = 0$ to:

$$\frac{dK^*}{dr^M} = \frac{1}{|H|}\frac{F}{P}\underbrace{\left[\underbrace{A_V^M - Cr_V}_{} \underbrace{(-A_{r^M}^K - Cr_{r^M})}_{+} \underbrace{A_V^K - Cr_V}_{+} \underbrace{(-A_{r^M}^M + Cr_{r^M})}_{-} \right]}_{+} < 0$$

(A2.6)

For dr^M, $dr^F = 0$, $dF = 0$, we get:

$$\frac{dK^*}{du} = \frac{1}{|H|}\frac{F}{P}\underbrace{\left[\underbrace{-(A_V^M - Cr_V)A_u^K}_{+} \underbrace{(A_V^K + Cr_V)A_u^M}_{+} \right]}_{+} < 0$$

(A2.7)

184

(6.29) can be simplified for dr^F, $du = 0$ to:

$$\frac{de}{dr^M} = \frac{1}{|H|}\left[\underbrace{\underbrace{(A_{r^K}^K r_K^K) + A_V^K + Cr_V + Cr_{r^K} r_K^K - 1)}_{-}\underbrace{(Cr_{r^M} - A_{r^M}^M)}_{-}}_{+} \right.$$

$$\left. + \underbrace{\underbrace{(A_{r^K}^M r_K^K) + A_V^M + Cr_V + Cr_{r^K} r_K^K)}_{-}\underbrace{(A_{r^M}^K + Cr_{r^M})}_{-}}_{+} \right] \qquad (A2.8)$$

The term in brackets can be rewritten as

$$(A_{r^K} r_K^K + Cr_V + Cr_{r^K} r_K^K - A_V^M - A_V^F)(Cr_{r^M} - A_{r^M}^M)$$
$$- (Cr_V + Cr_{r^K} r_K^K - A_R^M R_K - A_V^M)(Cr_{r^M} - A_{r^M}^K) \qquad (A2.9)$$

As $|A_R^K| > |A_R^M|$ (the demand for real capital reacts more strongly than the demand for monetary assets to a change in the return of real capital) and A_V^M, $A_V^F > 0$, $|A_{r^K} r_K^K - A_V^F + Cr_V + Cr_{r^K} r_K^K - A_V^M| > |-A_{r^K}^M r_K^K - A_V^M + Cr_V + Cr_{r^K} r_K^K|$. From $|A_{r^M}^M| > |A_{r^M}^K|$ we get $|Cr_{r^M} - A_{r^M}^M| > |Cr_{r^M} + A_{r^M}^K|$. Thus the first term in (A2.9) is larger than the second term. In consequence, the numerator in (6.32) is positive, $\frac{de}{dr^M} < 0$.

For dr^M, dr^F, $dF = 0$, we get:

$$\frac{de}{du} = \frac{1}{|H|}\left[\underbrace{-A_u^M(A_{r^K}^K r_K^K + A_V^K + Cr_V + Cr_{r^K} r_K^K - 1)}_{+} \right.$$

$$\left. + A_u^K\underbrace{\underbrace{(A_{r^K}^M r_K^K + A_V^M - Cr_V - Cr_{r^K} r_K^K)}_{+}}_{-} \right] \qquad (A2.10)$$

The term in brackets can be rewritten as

$$-A_u^M(A_{r^K}^K r_K^K - A_V^M - A_V^F + Cr_V + Cr_{r^K} r_K^K) + A_u^K(A_R^M - A_V^M + Cr_V + Cr_{r^K} r_K^K) \qquad (A2.11)$$

As $|A_u^M| > |A_u^K|$ and $|A_{r^K}^K r_K^K - A_V^M - A_V^F + Cr_V + Cr_{r^K} r_K^K| > |A_{r^K}^M + A_V^M - Cr_V - Cr_{r^K} r_K^K|$, the term in brackets is positive, thus $\frac{de}{du} < 0$.

Appendix 6.3:   Graphical Representation

Each of (6.22), (6.23) and (6.24) represents possible equilibria in the particular asset market. Each possible equilibrium in any of these markets can be depicted as a combination of an equilibrium capital stock K^* and a corresponding exchange rate. Each of the equations can thus be represented by a graph in the capital stock exchange rate space. With the implicit function theorem, we can easily get the slopes of each of the three curves:

$$A^K(r^K, r^M, r^F, u, K^* + \frac{e}{P}F, \ldots) + Cr(r^M, r^K, K^* + \frac{e}{P}F, \ldots)$$
$$-K^*(r^K) = 0$$
$$\equiv \Gamma \qquad \text{(A3.1)}$$

$$A^M(r^K, r^M, r^F, u, K^* + \frac{e}{P}F, \ldots) + Cr(r^M, r^K, K^* + \frac{e}{P}F, \ldots) = 0$$
$$\equiv \Omega \qquad \text{(A3.2)}$$

$$A^K(r^K, r^M, r^F, u, K^* + \frac{e}{P}F, \ldots) - \frac{e}{P}F = 0$$
$$\equiv \Psi \qquad \text{(A3.3)}$$

Applying the theorem yields for the slope of the capital market equilibrium (*KK*)-curve:[42]

$$\frac{dK^*}{de} = \frac{-\Gamma_e}{\Gamma_K} = \frac{F}{P}\left(\frac{\overset{+}{A_V^K} + \overset{\shortmid}{Cr_V}}{\underbrace{A_{r^K}^K r_K^K}_{-} + \underbrace{A_V^K + Cr_V - 1}_{-} + \underbrace{Cr_{r^K} r_K^K}_{-}} \right) > 0 \qquad \text{(A3.4)}$$

And for equilibrium in the money market (*MM*-curve):

$$\frac{dK^*}{de} = \frac{-\Omega_e}{\Omega_K} = \frac{F}{P}\left(\frac{\overset{+}{A_V^M - Cr_V}}{\underbrace{A_{r^K}^M r_K^K}_{-} - \underbrace{Cr_{r^K} r_K^K}_{-} + \underbrace{A_V^M - Cr_V}_{-}} \right) < 0 \qquad \text{(A3.5)}$$

As for the *MM*-curve, the slope for the *FF*-curve (equilibrium in the foreign asset market) is also negative:

$$\frac{dK^{\star}}{de} = \frac{-\Psi_e}{\Psi_K} = \frac{F}{P}\left(-\frac{\overbrace{A_V^F + 1}^{+}}{\underbrace{A_{r^K}^F r_K^K + A_V^F}_{+}}\right) < 0 \qquad \text{(A3.6)}$$

As $A_V^F + 1$ is significantly larger than A_V^M, the *FF*-curve can be expected to be steeper than the *MM*-curve. With these pieces of information, we can draw the simultaneous equilibrium in all three asset markets (see Figure 6.2).

Regarding the equilibrium equations (6A3.1)–(6A3.3), we can now deduce in which way each curve will shift when the exogenous parameters F, r^M, r^F or u change: an increase in F increases the demand for real capital. With constant K, this market only finds equilibrium with a lower exchange rate e. Thus, the *KK*-curve (Figure 6A3.1) shifts left with a higher F. Just the opposite, an increase in r^M, r^F or u decreases the demand for real capital, which can be equilibrated only with an increased exchange rate, thus shifting the *KK*-curve to the right.

In the money market (Figure 6A3.2), an increase in either r^M, F or u increases the demand for money (an increase in r^M also decreases the demand for credit, thus amplifying the net effect). This increase in the demand for monetary assets can be offset only if nominal wealth falls, which can be brought about by a falling exchange rate. Thus the *MM*-curve shifts left. On the other hand, an increase in the return on foreign assets r^F leads to a falling demand for monetary assets, which in turn makes an increase in the exchange rate necessary, thus leading to a shift of the *MM*-curve to the right.

In the foreign exchange market, things get a little more complicated, as the nominal stock of foreign assets $\frac{e}{P}F$ is not only an argument for the demand for foreign assets, but also represents the supply of foreign assets. An increase in r^M or u here leads to a decrease in the demand for foreign assets. However, a rise in the exchange rate that rebalances the demand for foreign assets to its old level would lead to a disequilibrium in the foreign asset market: it would also increase the supply, thus widening the gap between supply and demand. An equilibrium can be brought about only by a fall of the foreign exchange rate, and a corresponding appreciation

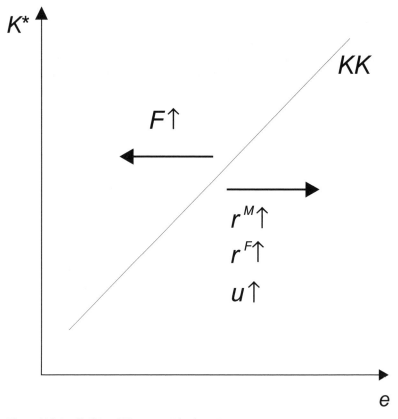

Figure 6A3.1   Shifting *KK*-curve with changing parameters

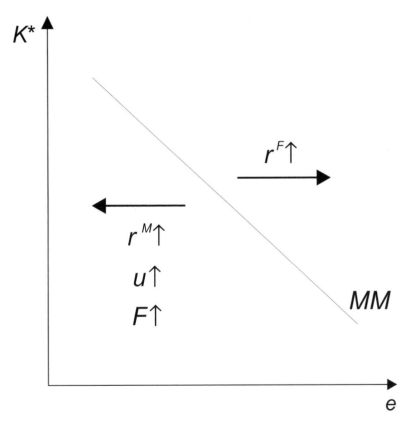

Figure 6A3.2 Shifting *MM*-curve with changing parameters

of the domestic currency. Consequently, the *FF*-curve shifts left. The same is true for an increase in the stock of foreign assets *F*. Once again an excess supply of foreign assets is the consequence, which can be cured only by a depreciation of the domestic currency and a resulting shift of the *FF*-curve to the left. On the other hand, a rising return on foreign assets r^F leads to an increased demand for foreign assets, which can be offset only by an increase in the nominal stock of foreign assets, and thus a shift of the *FF*-curve to the right (Figure 6A3.3).

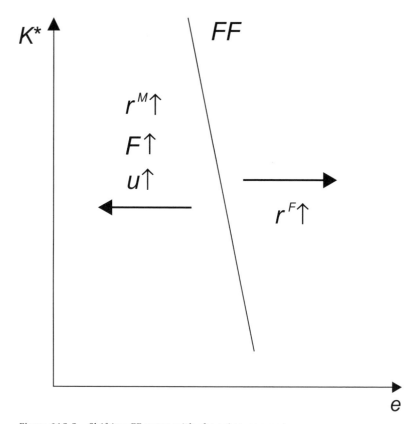

Figure 6A3.3   Shifting *FF*-curve with changing parameters

Appendix 6.4: Inside Money, Tobin's Monetised Capital, and Public Debt

The fact that the stock of inside money finances real capital accumulation is also embodied in Tobin's (1998, p. 129ff) concept of *monetised capital*:

> [F]inancial markets and the intermediary institutions that play important roles in those markets in effect monetize capital. Loans permit the more adventurous members of society, those who are willing to assume risks, to invest in enterprise capital in excess of their net worth. The lenders, in return, acquire assets tailored to their more conservative tastes – less risky, more liquid, more reversible, more predictable.

However, given the institutional setup of the US monetary system, in which the central bank issues currency only in exchange for government bonds, currency proper does not finance private productive capital:

> Many of the assets [inside money, author] are, for them [lenders], close if not perfect substitutes for government issued currency. These inside loans, debt of some private agent to other private agents, do double duty. They finance borrowers' holdings of capital, and they substitute, albeit imperfectly, for lenders' holding of currency. The greater the extent of this 'monetization' of capital, the greater is the aggregate demand for capital and the smaller is the aggregate demand for currency proper.

In the euro-area, in which money is created against private liabilities, and holdings of currency proper thus also finance real productive enterprises, a shift from currency proper to other monetary assets does not increase the demand for real capital. Here, it is foremost a shift out of foreign assets and into domestic monetary assets which increases the demand for capital.

However, Tobin's considerations about currency proper as part of the government debt should lead to some thoughts about the government debt's role in the monetisation of capital. Government debt is a monetary asset for the private sector, as it is denominated in nominal terms. One can thus expect that government bonds are close substitutes for prime rate corporate bonds and that short-term treasury bills are close substitutes for time deposits. Alternatively, one could imagine the financial system financing government debt and creating corresponding deposits. In this case, both asset and liability side of the financial system grow. The private agents have to be willing to hold the additional money stock created by the expansion of the financial system's balance sheet. In short, on the asset side of the financial sector, government debt B is a substitute for private real capital financing:

$$A^K(\underset{+}{r^K}, \underset{-}{r^M}, \underset{-}{r^F}, \underset{-}{u}, \underset{+}{V}, ...) + Cr(\underset{-}{r^M}, \underset{+}{R}, ...) = K \qquad (A4.1)$$

$$A^M(\underset{+}{r^K}, \underset{-}{r^M}, \underset{-}{r^F}, \underset{-}{u}, \underset{+}{V}, ...) = Cr(\underset{-}{r^M}, \underset{+}{R}, ...) + B \equiv \frac{M}{P} \qquad (A4.2)$$

$$A^F(\underset{+}{r^K}, \underset{-}{r^M}, \underset{-}{r^F}, \underset{-}{u}, \underset{+}{V}, ...) = \frac{e}{P} F \qquad (A4.3)$$

Aggregating (A4.2) with (A4.1) shows that in long-run equilibrium, the aggregate amount of capital demanded for productive purposes decreases with higher government debt, at least if government debt is not counted as net wealth for the private sector:

$$A^K(\underset{+}{r^K}, \underset{-}{r^M}, \underset{-}{r^F}, \underset{-}{u}, \underset{+}{V}, ...) + A^M(\underset{-}{r^K}, \underset{+}{r^M}, \underset{-}{r^F}, \underset{-}{u}, \underset{+}{V}, ...) - B = K \qquad (A4.4)$$

There is thus a crowding out from government debt. With government debt not being a net asset for the economy, total net wealth would remain unchanged. Individuals would thus not be willing to hold the additional deposits if the rate of return on monetary assets increased, thereby leading to a lower demand for credits and a higher demanded return on real capital holdings and thus a smaller equilibrium capital stock. Alternatively, the additional deposits could be expected to be held by the general public if the exchange rate depreciated. However, if the central bank were to defend the domestic currency's exchange rate, a higher government debt would inevitably come with a higher interest rate and a lower capital stock.

Ceteris paribus, a higher stock of outstanding government debt thus means that less of the money stock can be used to finance private real capital expenditure. This does not mean, however, that deficit spending has only negative consequences: as long as unions do not push for higher wages and thus trigger a central bank response, deficit spending increases output and employment, thus also increasing aggregate saving, consequently financing part of the initial deficit itself.

Moreover, by stabilising price and profit volatility, fiscal policy might be able to decrease risk premia on real investment, thus boosting private investment and the holding of real capital. To this end, especially the use of automatic stabilisers seems to be suitable. In the context of this chapter's portfolio model it is important, however, that government debt will be reduced again in times of strong private demand.

7
The Optimal Policy Mix and Logic of a Social Pact

From the reasoning of the preceding chapters, one can deduce how an optimal policy mix would look with regard to monetary policy and wage increases. From Chapter 5, we know that in a world of endogenous inside money, nominal wage developments are central for the path of the equilibrium price level. Wage moderation by itself cannot change output or employment. For output to increase, aggregate demand has to be increased, which can be done by cutting interest rates.[1] As wage bargainers thus cannot by themselves increase employment, while the central bank cannot by itself ensure price stability, some kind of cooperation is desirable if the target of both high employment and low and stable inflation is to be achieved.

The whole setting is further complicated by the fact that the central bank is constrained by financial markets, as has been argued in Chapter 6. With any change in the central bank interest rate, other asset prices such as the exchange rate or the price for real capital holdings also change. These price changes may influence the return and riskiness of monetary assets in the eyes of investors. A strong depreciation may especially be regarded as a threat to the domestic currency's function as a store of value, inducing investors to shift out of domestic monetary assets. Since endogenous inside money macroeconomically finances the economy's capital stock, a central bank wanting to increase equilibrium output and employment cannot neglect the financial market's reactions to its interest rate decisions. It might be forced by financial markets to choose a higher interest rate than it would otherwise prefer.

An optimum policy mix would thus have two elements. First, wages should grow at a rate which would ensure that unit labour costs grow at the central bank's target rate of inflation. At the same time, the central bank should act as expansionary as possible given the necessity to maintain price stability,[2] which stems from asset market considerations, as explained in Chapter 6.

This chapter will examine the reasons why an optimal cooperative policy mix might not be achieved. It will do so by again underlining in Section 7.1 what role each of the policy actors would have to play in an optimal policy mix. It will in Section 7.2 use game-theoretic approaches to look for reasons why such a Pareto-optimum might not be reached. In a final step (Section 7.3), it will examine whether the EU macroeconomic dialogue, as initiated by the Cologne process, might help to overcome obstacles on the path to the optimum policy mix.

To keep the exposition manageable, I will restrict it to the question of coordination between wage setters and the central bank. Fiscal policy will be assumed to remain unchanged, as has been done throughout this book. I will also abstract from the highly interesting questions of coordination between wage setters in different sectors or the coordination between different levels of wage setting. Instead, following Soskice and Hancké (2002), I will assume that wage setting in the euro-zone takes place as an implicitly coordinated process in which wage setters in other countries set their wages relative to certain core countries following the German wage standard.[3] However, the conclusions from this chapter do not rely on this assumption. If it should turn out that wage setting in the euro-zone is not coordinated along the lines described by Soskice and Hancké (2002), the basic problems of communication between wage setters and the central bank would remain the same. The central bank would then have to communicate to a group of wage setters which are large enough that they together significantly influence the overall EMU wage level. In addition, problems concerning both the coordination of wage setters across sectors and across countries and the processing of central bank signals among wage setters would arise. However, because for the time being we can only speculate about forms of coordination other than that argued by Soskice and Hancké (2002), I will stick to their hypothesis.[4]

7.1 The optimal policy mix in EMU

For EMU, the above considerations about an optimum policy mix would translate into wage increases in line with macroeconomic trend productivity gains plus about 1 percentage point: the target range of inflation for the euro-zone was defined until 2003 as 'a year-on-year increase in the Harmonised Index of Consumer Prices (HICP) for the euro area of below

2%' (ECB 1998b). However, the ECB has repeatedly underlined that it would consider an actual fall in prices as a violation of this target as well (ECB 2001, p. 39). In 2003, this target was clarified towards 'below, but close to 2% over the medium term' (ECB 2004).[5] The inflation target range of the ECB can thus be considered as being around 1.5–2.0 per cent.

As has been shown in Chapter 5, an expansionary monetary policy would bring about transitional price hikes via extra profits (or, in Collignon 2002a, terms q-values above $\bar{q}$): when interest rates are lowered, demand at first exceeds supply. This leads to price increases which are only competed away after firms have adjusted their productive capacities to the new level of aggregate demand. So that the headline inflation does not rises above 2 per cent after a cut in interest rates, trend growth of unit labour costs should stay safely below the upper limit of the central bank's inflation target range.

On the other hand, with extra profits (q-values) disappearing again and prices being competed down again as capacities increase, prices will return to the equilibrium price level. If the equilibrium price level remained constant with unit labour cost changes being zero, this would actually lead to *falling* prices in the later adjustment process. In order not to encounter deflationary problems in this phase, constant unit labour costs do not seem to be an optimal solution either. Therefore it seems sensible to aim for the middle of the ECB's target band with a 1 per cent increase in unit labour costs.

How does this conclusion differ from policy mix conclusions drawn from a SICCD model? A policy mix exactly like the one presented in this chapter is seemingly at work when the central banker is 'non-accommodating' or 'conservative': as he then does not react to a change in nominal wages with a change in nominal money supply, real money supply and aggregate demand become a negative function of nominal wages. Wage restraint thus automatically leads to higher output when the central bank follows its policy rule.

However, even if there are some parallels between the conclusions of Chapter 5 and SICCD models, the approach presented in this book differs in two important aspects. First, in the world depicted here, a wage restraint which leads to falling prices is not favourable. Second, in a world without real balance effects, for a central bank to act as expansionary requires more than just following a simple money supply rule.

Constructive and destructive wage restraint

From an output and employment perspective, nominal wages cannot be too low in the SICCD approach as long as unemployment exists.

Without any limit, the lower the nominal wages, the higher aggregate demand and hence output. Thus a fall in nominal wages is beneficial until full employment is reached. In this book, the story is different. As we know from the model of monopolistic competition in Chapter 5, in a world without real balances, nominal wages influence prices but not aggregate output. A fall in nominal wages (or if we assume rising productivity, a fall in unit labour costs) does not do any good. At best, when such a fall is fully anticipated by both wealth owners making their portfolio decisions and firms fixing their prices, such a fall is neutral to output and employment. Then, as a result of the mark-up pricing derived in Chapter 5, lower wages would lead only to lower prices, leaving real variables unchanged.

If, however, such a fall in wages is not anticipated or prices are sticky, wage restraint can have undesired consequences. If demand and output react faster than prices, the mechanism would be as follows: falling wages lead to a fall in aggregate demand, thus depressing output (5.21). Only with prices adjusting to the new equilibrium would real aggregate demand and employment recover to their original values. During the transition period, employment and output would even be lower than in the original situation, and after the transition they would be exactly the same as before the wage cut. Alternatively, one could imagine a transition path in which employment does not suffer even with sticky prices: if consumption demand is as sticky as prices (and thus workers hang on to their consumption patterns for a while even after their incomes have changed, which means they consume a higher share of their wage income during a transition period), this could bolster output and prevent a fall in output and employment during the transition period. However, such behaviour is not very plausible, as it would imply workers consuming their savings during the transition period without recovering them later, which in turn would imply either some nominal illusion or some non-rational saving behaviour.

Of course, one could argue that even with consumption demand reacting faster than prices to wage cuts, profits would increase during a transition period, which might induce additional investment. However, this argument has two caveats. First, it is not entirely clear whether aggregate real profits truly increase with wage restraint. While there is surely an effect of increased profits per unit of real output sold, output also falls. Without further assumptions about the elasticity of substitution η of the single good in the individuals' utility function and the consumption share, we cannot determine whether the price or the quantity effect dominates. Second, even if aggregate profits were to increase during the transition period, this would most likely not translate into additional investment: this increase in aggregate profits comes about with a *falling* capacity utilisation. Moreover, firms can anticipate that profits will return to normal levels as soon as prices have adjusted. Additional investment would therefore just not be rational.

A wage cut would lead only to higher aggregate output if profits increased during the transition period *and* individuals receiving profit incomes had a higher propensity to consume than individuals living off wage incomes. Such a scenario conflicts with the empirical observation that households which receive profit incomes are usually those with a lower propensity to consume and a higher savings rate. At first sight, this statement seems to be refuted by the US experience of the 1990s when the savings rate for the wealthiest households turned negative while it increased in households with the lowest incomes and savings. But as Maki and Palumbo (2001) show, this change of the familiar consumption pattern can almost entirely be explained by large unexpected capital gains for the wealthiest Americans during that time.

The argument against wage cuts or excessive wage restraint becomes even stronger when one introduces financial intermediation into the model: as in the baseline model, a cut in wages (or even wage increases below the trend productivity growth) would lead to a falling price level and thus falling sales prices for the firms' products. If now firms and banks have nominally fixed liabilities, this would worsen their balance sheet position. This in turn would cause banks to ration credit supply, thus hindering further investment by the firms and consequently dampening aggregate demand. Additional downward pressure on prices and aggregate profits would consequently develop. In the end, such a policy might even lead to a downward spiral of prices and thus a full-fledged deflation.

Thus, contrary to the SICCD conclusions, a fall in wages and prices does not have any beneficial effects in a world of endogenous money. This conclusion is a direct consequence of the fact that money is endogenous and not net wealth to the private sector. Without the nominal money stock as some nominal fixed wealth of the private sector, falling prices simply fail to increase aggregate demand.

Instead, a cut in wages might even depress output and employment further during a transition period, depending on the speed of adjustment of prices, demand and output. The only role wage restraint plays here is that of stabilising the price level and keeping one-time price hikes from feeding into a general wage inflation. Such a wage restraint will be called *stability-oriented wage restraint* in the rest of this chapter. While the SICCD approach places the responsibility for unemployment in a setup with a conservative or non-accommodating central bank into the unions' hands (since they can restrain wages enough to achieve full employment), the approach presented in this book makes the unions responsible for keeping trend inflation low.

Active and passive central bank, or: what is a conservative central bank?

The second stark difference is in the central bank's reaction to wage restraint. While in the SICCD approach the monetary authorities simply have to follow a simple money supply rule to be expansionary, in the approach presented here the central bank has to turn actively to an expansionary monetary policy stance to increase output and employment. In the SICCD setting, the money supply rules are, respectively:

$$M = P^\alpha \tag{7.1}$$
$$m = \nu_0 + \nu_1 w \tag{7.2}$$

with $0 \leq \alpha \leq 1$ and ν being positive for 'liberal' central banks and being non-positive for sufficiently conservative central banks.[6] Prices are set by monopolistically competitive firms and are a positive function of wages and aggregate demand, the latter of which is a function of real balances. With lower wages, prices are thus lower and the real balances higher, thus output and employment higher. What is interesting about the money supply rules (7.1) and (7.2) is the way they change when a central bank becomes more 'non-accommodating' or more 'conservative': for wages above the level normally compatible with price stability (or some price target of the monetary authorities), the larger the degree of non-accommodation (or the smaller α) or conservativeness, the more restrictive the monetary policy. This is well in line with what one would expect from a conservative monetary policy. If wages are below what would be compatible with price stability, however, things get blurry. Rogoff (1985) originally dubbed a central banker 'conservative' when he puts a larger weight on low inflation than on higher output. Of course, a conservative central banker who has an interest in price stability (that is, he detests both inflation and deflation) would have to react expansionary when wages are below what is necessary to keep prices from falling. Coricelli,

Cukierman and Dalmazzo's (2000) definition of an 'ultra-conservative' central banker who actually decreases the nominal money supply when wages are rising and increases the nominal money supply when wages are falling, also fits this pattern. Even though it might contradict common sense that an ultra-conservative central banker is the one among the central bankers to act as the most expansionary when wages are falling, there is at least no problem deducing this reaction from a central banker's utility function.

This kind of definition becomes problematic only when a 'liberal' or 'populist' central banker is introduced. By definition, things are clear: the liberal central banker would like to keep output stable and thus accommodates any price change that occurs. In the SICCD approach, however, this liberal central banker would react to a fall in wages and prices by *decreasing* the money supply, thus aggravating deflation. It is hard to imagine how this policy could be 'popular'. Moreover, while there might well be real-world central bankers who accommodate wage increases by a lax monetary policy to increase the money stock because they are afraid of inflicting the real costs of disinflationary policy on the economy, there is simply no plausible motive for a central banker to decrease the money supply when prices and wages are falling. For with falling wages and prices, expansion would come as a 'free lunch'.

In the setting proposed in this book, a central bank's possible reactions are more rational over the whole range of possible wage developments: in order to be expansionary, the central bank has to react with bold interest rate cuts to the unions' stability oriented wage restraint. This expansionary monetary policy comes with some risks: the central bank cannot be entirely sure how financial markets will react to the move. A standard reaction to expect would be a depreciation of the domestic currency. This depreciation would lead to an increase in import prices, which could potentially feed back into new wage demands. Even if the unions exercise stability oriented wage restraint once, the central bank does not know how they will react to a price hike. On the other hand, if the central bank remains passive in face of a constructive wage restraint, it does not lose much: prices will remain stable, but there will be no expansion in output. Thus, for a central bank which does not care at all about output developments, it is completely rational not to be expansionary.

This conclusion is unrelated to the question of whether a central bank will react in an accommodating or a non-accommodating manner to inflationary wage increases. Even a central bank which cares about output can be non-accommodating in this case. As we have seen in Chapter 6, long-term output is a function of domestic monetary assets held in the individuals' portfolios. High and volatile rates of inflation induce wealth owners to hold less of their wealth in domestic monetary assets. Inflation thus has harmful long-term effects on output, and a central bank which cares about output must take these into account. Inflation thus has no positive effects. The only reason why a central bank would refrain from fighting wage increases in the very beginning could be that such a disinflationary policy would place short-term burdens on real activity. When a central bank was subject to the influence of politicians who might have a short horizon (e.g. with elections coming up), accommodation might be rational from the central bankers' perspective.

To take both the degree of accommodation and the degree of expansionary monetary policy in the face of stable unit labour costs into account, a two-dimensional index for the central bank's monetary policy stance seems sensible: the first indicator of 'non-accommodation' would measure how sharply a central bank reacts to wage increases which endanger price stability, the second indicator of 'boldness' would measure how strongly the central bank reacts in an expansionary matter when there are no risks for its inflation target from the wage side. Thus a central bank is considered 'non-accommodating' when it reacts in a contracting manner when unit labour cost developments are inflationary. It is 'accommodating' when it does not react by contracting monetary policy to inflationary unit labour cost increases. It is called 'bold' when it is courageous enough to run an expansionary policy when faced with stable and low unit labour cost developments. And it is called 'not bold' when it timidly sticks to a non-expansionary monetary policy stance even when unit labour cost developments are low enough not to cause any inflationary dangers. From a policy mix perspective, a central bank with a high degree of both boldness and non-accommodativeness would be desirable, as it would deter inflationary wage demands and at the same time be as expansionary as possible.

To compute such indices for different countries, unit labour cost increases are plotted against the average output gaps in the two years following the change in labour costs.[7] The degree of non-accommodation is now computed by counting the number of instances in which excessive wage increases (as defined as unit labour cost increases above the central banks' target rate of inflation) are followed by negative output gaps in the following years. The degree of boldness, on the other hand, is defined as the share of positive output gaps following wage increases below the target rate of inflation. Figure 7.1 illustrates this approach. In quadrant I, when unit labour costs growing faster than compatible with the central banks' target rate of inflation are not followed by a negative output gap, monetary policy is accommodating. On the other hand, when a contraction occurs as a reaction, monetary policy is non-accommodating (quadrant II). When, despite wage restraint, the output gap is negative in the years following the unit labour cost change, monetary policy has been too timid (quadrant III). A bold monetary policy (quadrant IV) would have lowered interest rates enough so that the output gap was positive.

If we now compute the degrees of monetary policy non-accommodation and boldness for the US (Figure 7.2), Germany (Figure 2.14, p. 41) and the EU-11 (Figure 2.18, p. 45) from 1980 to 1998,[8] we find that the US Fed was both more non-accommodating than the Bundesbank and bolder in acting in an expansionary matter when inflationary risks from unit labour cost increases were absent. When compared to the effects of the Bundesbank's monetary policy on the rest of Europe (as it influenced monetary policy in all EMS countries), it is found that monetary policy for EU-11 was more non-accommodating and less bold than US policy (Figure 7.3, Table 7.1). This startling result as to the 'accommodativeness' of the Bundesbank's policy can be explained by the aftermath of German reunification, which brought about high positive outputs gaps

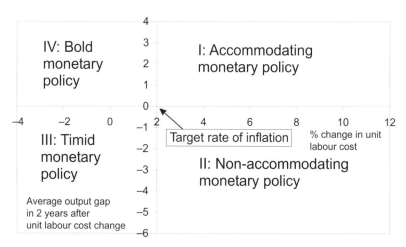

Figure 7.1   Accommodating, non-accommodating, bold and timid monetary policy

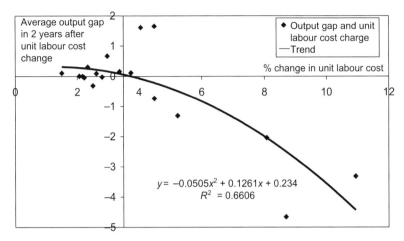

Figure 7.2 Unit labour cost changes and output gaps in the following two years, USA, 1980–98

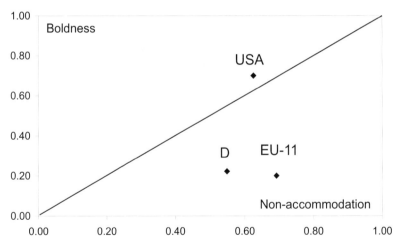

Figure 7.3 Degree of non-accommodation and boldness for US, German and European monetary policy, 1980–98

caused by demand factors not influenced by monetary policy while unit labour costs grew strongly. The four 'accommodating' points stem from the years 1990–3. If one excluded this episode, the Bundesbank would be perfectly non-accommodating. It is not surprising that the resulting policy was non-accommodating and not at all expansionary for the rest

Table 7.1   Degree of non-accommodation and boldness for US, German and
European monetary policy, 1980–98

Country	Degree of non-accommodation	Degree of boldness
USA	5/8 = 0.63	7/10 = 0.70
Germany	5/9 = 0.56	2/9 = 0.22
EU-11	9/13 = 0.69	1/5 = 0.2

of Europe. Unit labour cost increases above the German level were punished not only by losses in export markets, but also by market-induced increases in the risk premia of the country concerned, causing interest rates to rise and domestic demand to contract. Wage restraint in the other EU-11 countries was at the same time not honoured by the Bundesbank, as it was its task to make monetary policy for Germany, not for the EU-11.

What remains startling is the low degree of boldness in the Bundesbank's policy reaction, which might be a hint that Solow (2000b, p. 9) was correct when he noted:

> To be more blunt, I mean to suggest that American fiscal and monetary policy has been more successful than Europe has been in supporting aggregate demand, and above all more aggressive in taking advantage of opportunities to expand whenever inflationary pressure has been weak.

Anecdotal evidence hints that the ECB's policy reaction is not much bolder to date than was the Bundesbank's in the 1980s and 1990s. Though the ECB did indeed switch to an expansionary stance at the beginning of EMU, it tightened monetary policy quickly in the wake of oil price increases in late 2000 – early 2001, without really taking into account that unit labour cost pressure was very moderate.[9]

7.2   EMU: coordination failure or cooperation failure?

A lack of boldness in the central bank's monetary policy has consequences far beyond the forgone expansion. It might just change the policy mix between wage increases and monetary policy structurally for the worse. If unions learn that the central bank will not react to their stability-oriented wage restraint with an expansionary monetary policy, they may push for higher wage increases. The wage round of 2002 is an example of this logic. In late 2001 – early 2002, though the economy was evidently in a downturn, unions began to bring forward excessive wage demands. In Germany, union rhetoric again focused on 'redistribution' and making up for wage restraint exercised earlier after having signed a moderate, long-running wage contract two years earlier, since in their eyes wage restraint had not brought the improvement in unemployment which had been hoped for.

At first sight, getting into this kind of 'policy mix trap' cannot be desirable for any of the policy actors: the central bank's task of maintaining price stability becomes harder. At the same time, the possibility of higher growth and lower unemployment is forgone. Thus, in principle, a policy mix containing stable unit labour costs[10] and an expansionary monetary policy should be preferred. None of the interest groups and institutions responsible for monetary policy or wage contracts, so it seems, would lose out. Unions would profit from a higher degree of employment while their real wage position would not deteriorate.[11] Employers could even increase their (absolute) real profits since profits are a function of aggregate demand.

The question is thus: why is the seemingly optimal outcome not reached? To answer this, we will use game-theoretic considerations. Following Silvestre (1993) and Horn (2001), who elaborate on coordination and cooperation of macroeconomic actors, three possible explanations can be proposed:[12]

1. *Coordination failure:* Due to incomplete information or a failure to react to this information, an inefficient outcome arises.
2. *Cooperation failure:* Due to the rules of the game and the participants' incentives, an inefficient outcome arises.
3. The seemingly optimal outcome is *not optimal* for at least one of the institutions/groups involved.

Possible problems with coordination in EMU

In order to see whether a coordination or a cooperation failure lies at the heart of a sub-optimal policy mix in EMU, and how this problem can be tackled, we first need to ask what exactly the difference is between the two problems.

Basic considerations of non-cooperation

We talk of *coordination failure* in situations in which an outcome which is not a Pareto-optimum is reached due to uncertainty or lack of information (Horn 2001, p. 30). The best-known example of a coordination failure is a slight variation of the standard game 'battle of the sexes': Chris and Pat work at different workplaces and want to spend the evening together. Chris would rather go to the opera than to the prize fight, while Pat prefers to watch the fight. Both would prefer to spend the evening together rather than alone. Their payoffs are shown in Table 7.2. Due to a problem in Pat's company's phone system, they are not able to communicate about where to go but must travel there directly. Game theory does not answer where each of them should go in order to effectively maximise utility.

The point about the battle of the sexes is that without further information, which of the four outcomes will be reached is not predictable. If both Pat and Chris were flipping coins in order to determine where to go, in 50 per cent of the cases they would both reach a payoff of 0. This uncoordinated situation with 0-payoff outcomes is clearly not Pareto-optimal, since in both (Fight; Fight) and (Opera; Opera) outcomes Pat *and* Chris are better off. Only with additional information or the possibility to communicate can the (0,0)-payoffs effectively be avoided.

However, the example of the battle of the sexes cannot be transferred one-to-one to the analysis of interaction between monetary policy and wage bargaining. For the possible coordination problems here, Silvestre's (1993) example (see Table 7.3) might be a better illustration. Player 1 has the choice between Left and Right while player 2 can choose between Up and Down. Clearly the combination Top-Left is Pareto-superior to Bottom-Right. However, both outcomes are possible Nash equilibria. When player 1 thinks player 2 will choose Bottom, she is better off choosing Right. When player 2 is convinced that player 1 will choose Right, Bottom would be the best choice. Once in this inefficient equilibrium, there is no way to reach the efficient equilibrium without coordination. Neither player 1 nor player 2 has an incentive to opt for Top or Bottom if she is not sure that the other player will do so as well.

Table 7.2 Payoffs in the classic game 'battle of the sexes'

	Pat: Opera	Pat: Fight
Chris: Opera	(2,1)	(0,0)
Chris: Fight	(0,0)	(1,2)

Table 7.3   Payoffs in a coordination problem

	Left	Right
Top	(4,4)	(0,0)
Bottom	(0,0)	(1,1)

Source: adapted from Silvestre (1993).

While, of course, payoffs for unions and the central bank might be more complex than in the example presented here, it can be used as a simple parable. For unions, the possible alternatives Left and Right could represent long-term wage contracts with moderate wage demands (as described above) on the one hand (*stability-oriented wage restraint*),[13] and short-term wage contracts with wage demands strongly reacting to losses in purchasing power on the other – due to import price increases or transitory changes in q as well as to perceived opportunities to improve distribution (*aggressive wage bargaining*).[14] For the central bank, the alternatives would be an expansionary monetary policy or a restrictive monetary policy.

Assuming that the central bank has an interest in growth and high employment as well as low inflation, one could argue that both unions and the central bank prefer the combination of stability-oriented wage restraint with an expansionary monetary policy to all other outcomes. At the same time, one could argue that the situation of aggressive wage bargaining with a restrictive monetary policy is preferred to the other two options: in a situation of an expansive monetary policy combined with aggressive wage bargaining, inflation would surge and the central bank would have to restrict monetary policy again. The ensuing policy of disinflation would lead to at least temporarily higher unemployment.

With inflation averse unions, this situation would not have incurred any benefits for either unions or for the central bank. Wage restraint combined with a restrictive monetary policy, on the other hand, would force the union leaders to explain to their constituencies why they restrained their wage demands in the first place and would put pressure on the central bank for having choked off growth.[15] In this model, one would argue that in EMU, the situation of a restrictive monetary policy with wage bargaining somehow has been reached and now the central bank has no incentive to move to the expansionary situation, nor do the unions have one to move to the state of stability-oriented wage restraint.

But how plausible is this explanation? In order to answer this question, it is useful first to change the static design of the game as presented above into a dynamic two-stage setup:

1. *Wage bargainers decide on their nominal wages.* They can choose between stability-oriented wage restraint and aggressive bargaining.
2. *The central bank observes the wage increases and decides on its monetary policy.* It has two options: to run a restrictive or an expansive monetary policy.

The reason for the dynamic setup of the game is an empirical one: while wage contracts are usually agreed upon for some longer period (occasionally even several years), central banks can set and reset interest rates whenever they want to. The ECB council, for example, meets every two weeks[16] to decide whether their key interest rates are still appropriate.[17]

With the payoffs as explained above, given complete information,[18] backward induction shows that unions will choose the stability-oriented wage restraint option since they know the central bank will react with an expansionary monetary policy. This path is shown in the tree representation of this game (Figure 7.4). Coordination problems here could arise only if wage bargainers did not know the central bank's payoffs. If unions expected the central bank not to react with an expansionary monetary policy to their wage restraint, it would be rational for them to bargain aggressively.

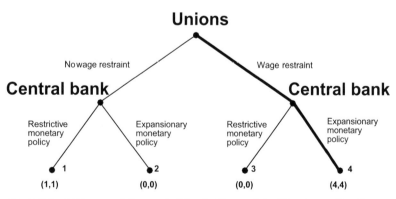

Figure 7.4 Unions and the central bank: the world without coordination or cooperation problems

Model uncertainty

Of course, such expectations on the unions' side violate the following standard assumptions and definitions of rational expectations:[19]

1. The individuals' expectation is equal to the mathematical expectation based on the information available.
2. The individuals know the underlying macroeconomic model.
3. All individuals have the same information set.

These assumptions are standard to many modern macroeconomic models. Nevertheless, in reality they are seldom fulfilled. It is not only quite possible but even very likely that unions use a different underlying model for explaining the macroeconomy than does the central bank: even in the academic community there is no consensus among the different strands of macroeconomics as to how the economy works.[20] Also in politics, different individuals, parties, and even governments of different countries disagree about the consequences of economic policies (Eichengreen and Ghironi 1996). These different views of the working of the economy are not simply an academic argument. As Hanappi (1995, p. 95) observes, players in macroeconomic simulation games behave differently depending on their ideological background, a fact which cannot be observed in microeconomic simulation games.

The possibility of a misunderstanding between the ECB and wage bargainers is further increased as the ECB itself does not clearly explain what it is looking at when deciding on its key interest rate. While the ECB claims it relies for its monetary policy on a strategy of 'two pillars' (ECB 2001, pp. 46ff.) with one pillar being a 'reference value' of growth of the monetary aggregate M3 and one being an analysis of 'developments in overall output, demand and labour market conditions, in a broad range of price and cost indicators, and in fiscal policy, as well as in the balance of payments' (ECB 2001, p. 51), it is not clear what it focuses on in practice. Von Hagen and Brückner (2001, p. 10) make the criticism that:

> No framework was specified how these variables would be used to assess price developments, nor their relative weights in such assessments. The Second Pillar thus adds an opaque part to the ECB's strategy.

Moreover, they conclude from central bankers' statements during the first years of EMU that in fact the second pillar has changed since its introduction.

This impression can also be drawn from the ECB's statements after the review of its monetary policy strategy in early 2003: while during the first years of the ECB, the pillar focusing on monetary aggregates was dubbed the 'first pillar' and the pillar focusing on other indicators was called the 'second pillar' (ECB 2001, pp. 55ff.), the bank changed its wording in ECB (2004): the assessment of current economic development is now called the 'first perspective', that of monetary aggregates the 'second perspective'.

Even Issing *et al.* (2001) at least partially admit that the ECB's two-pillar strategy might be difficult to comprehend. Even worse, the ECB states that the two-pillar-strategy reflects the uncertainties about the 'imperfect understanding of, the economy in general – and the transmission mechanism of monetary policy in particular' (ECB 2001, p. 54). It continues:

> Therefore, any single model – while potentially offering a useful perspective on economic developments – is necessarily incomplete. In such circumstances, it would be unwise to rely exclusively on a single approach or a single indicator in order to take monetary policy decisions.

Uncertainty about which model the central bank is using is not necessarily a feature only of the euro-zone. In the USA it is also not always easy to predict what course monetary policy is taking. However, if one takes market expectations as a measure of how well the public understands what the central bank is doing, it becomes obvious that the ECB is still slightly less predictable than the US Fed. Even the US Fed is much less than perfectly predictable, as it from time to time surprises markets with its interest rate moves.

Figure 7.5 illustrates this point, demonstrating the ECB's monetary policy steps and the spread of one-month-money in the money market over the ECB's target interest rate.[21] Prior to a change in interest rates, one could expect the spread in the money market to reach the magnitude of the expected interest rate change. As we see in Figure 7.5, markets had wrong expectations about the ECB's moves during much of the period from the beginning of 2000 until the end of 2001. This is not only true for the time after September 11, 2001, which might understandably have led to increased uncertainty and unpredictability, but also for the interest rate steps in 2000 and early 2001. While the interest rate increases in February 2000 and June 2000 were correctly anticipated, markets expected stronger hikes in March and April 2000.

They also expected a stronger hike in September 2001 and an additional increase in late November. When the economy weakened in 2001, they expected rate cuts in late March 2001 and early April 2001, but were convinced that the central bank would not act when the cut finally came in May 2001.

The picture for the US Fed[22] (Figure 7.6) looks slightly better: not were only the cuts after September 11, 2001 better anticipated, most other policy moves were expected, though the cuts in January 2001 and March 2001 were misjudged in size. Moreover, there have not been extended periods (as with the ECB in 2001) during which markets expected monetary policy moves without anything happening.[23]

With even market prices which should – according to standard economic theory – include all relevant information not being able to predict the central banks' monetary policy moves, it is plausible to conclude that unions also do not know what exactly the central bankers are looking at and what influence the choice between aggressive wage bargaining and wage restraint has had on the monetary authority's actions.

Moreover, the market prediction of imminent interest rate moves might even overstate the extent of public understanding of the central bank's actions. The US Fed is known for leaking imminent interest rate

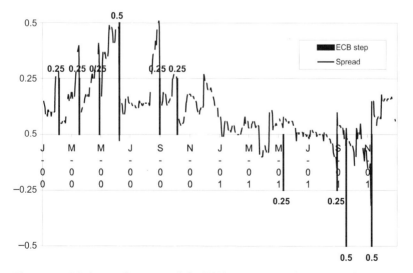

Figure 7.5 Market predictions and the ECB's monetary policy moves, 2000–1

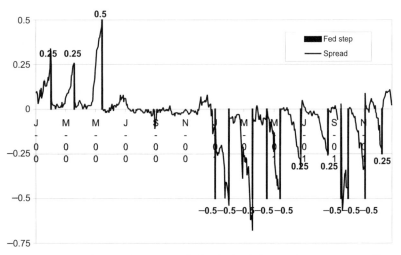

Figure 7.6 Market predictions and the Federal Reserve's monetary policy moves, 2000–1

moves to financial markets via central bankers' speeches or newspaper interviews. Thus the (correct) market expectations about interest rate changes might even stem from correctly reading short-term signals from the central bank rather than from understanding the central bank's view on the economy.

Signal uncertainty

In principle, this problem of model uncertainty could be overcome simply by playing the game repeatedly. Even if the central bank did not reveal that it closely monitored unit labour cost developments, some economists might tell the unions that the central bank did so. As a permanent shift to outcome 4 would increase the unions' payoffs for all future rounds, unions might decide that exercising wage restraint was worth a try even if they were not sure of the central bank's reaction.[24] Following their wage restraint, they would then observe the central bank's reaction and draw their conclusion about the bank's payoffs. With the central bank reacting to a wage restraint with expansionary policy moves, unions would quickly get to know the monetary authority's true payoffs.

In practice, however, things are more complicated. As the central bank is not only reacting to unions' wage demands but also has to take into account how autonomous demand components (investment, budget deficits) are developing, as well as how the exchange rate and asset prices are reacting, it is seldom clear whether an interest rate decision is a reaction to the unions' behaviour or to other factors. Of course, central bankers would argue that they explicitly state their reasoning not only at the press conference after an interest rate decision, but also in their monthly bulletin. However, central bank publications are not necessarily clear to those who have to read and comprehend them from the outside, especially when readers and writers come from different ideological (unions on the one hand and the financial community on the other) or cultural backgrounds.[25] Thus, there remains room for signal uncertainty.

Moreover, if the unions have a different model for the mechanisms behind the economy, they might well interpret a monetary policy decision as a restrictive monetary policy stance, while the central bank would consider it an expansionary path. There might thus not only be model uncertainty, but also signal uncertainty.

But even if unions were eventually to learn what the central bank is targeting, this could take a long time. It took roughly two decades from 1974, when the Bundesbank announced that it would be following a monetary target, until an academic article showed that the bank's behaviour could be better described using a Taylor rule (Bernanke and Mihov 1997). During this time, a failure to coordinate would lead to significant output and welfare losses.

Fragmentation of wage bargaining

A further reason why unions could fail to act as would be rational in Figure 7.4 has been pointed out by Hall and Franzese (1998): only if wage bargainers are in principle able to react to the central bank's signals, can a coordination be successful? Small unions bargaining only for a small share of the workers, in particular, might not have the expertise to recognise the macroeconomic consequences of their behaviour, or might by themselves in fact not even have a notable impact on the macroeconomy. Moreover, coordination might be hindered by collective action problems. For a single union working in a sector which produces a good with a low elasticity of substitution, it might well be sensible to go for higher nominal wages while the effects of their behaviour are externalised. In addition, as we have seen in Chapter 5, for a small union it might be optimal to try to reach a high-real wage/low-employment point. If all unions were small and their actions uncoordinated and they had such a utility function, coordination would fail.

As wage bargaining in the euro-zone is highly heterogeneous and traditions and structures differ from country to country, one could argue that in such an environment unions are simply not able to react to the central bank's signals in a coordinated way. However, as it has been argued in Chapter 2, the centre of the euro-area comprising Germany, France, Austria and Belgium works – even if not formally but *de facto* – as a coordinated wage area, with the German unions still setting the pace. Those German unions were well able to coordinate their wage setting behaviour in interaction with the Bundesbank (Hall and Franzese 1998, pp. 512ff.). Thus, in principle they should still be able to coordinate their wage setting with the ECB. Therefore it is more likely that a coordination failure here results more from model or signal uncertainty than from a structural inability to react to the central bank's signals.

The problem of non-cooperation

But a lack of coordination does not necessarily explain the whole story of a sub-optimal policy mix between wage increases and monetary policy in EMU. A possibility is that unions' and the central bank's payoffs are of such a form that simple coordination does not lead to a Pareto-efficient outcome.

Basic considerations of non-cooperation

The basic game which shows the problem of non-cooperation is the prisoner's dilemma. Table 7.4 shows the payoffs of this game in a bi-matrix. Both players have the choice between confessing and not confessing. If both confess, they each go to prison for six years. If only one of them confesses, the player confessing walks free while the other has to spend nine years in jail. If both decide not to confess, each will be put in prison for one year. Without cooperation, the dominant strategy for both players is to confess since confessing yields superior payoffs no matter whether the other player confesses or not. Consequently, the Nash equilibrium is an inefficient outcome in which both players go to jail for six years.

Table 7.4   Payoffs in the classic game 'prisoner's dilemma'

	Player 1: Confess	Player 1: Not Confess
Player 2: Confess	(6,–6)	(–9,0)
Player 2: Not Confess	(0,–9)	(–1,–1)

In contrast to the situation of cooperation failure, it is not sufficient that the players communicate clearly. Even if both players agreed on not confessing, they would still have an incentive to confess. Thus, in order to remove the inefficiency (and to keep both players from confessing), it is necessary to alter either the mode of behaviour or the rules of the game.

Cooperation failure in EMU

It is easy to plausibly change the payoffs in the game between unions and the central bank (p. 208) in such a way that a non-cooperative Nash equilibrium similar to the prisoners' dilemma emerges: Table 7.5 shows the union's payoffs, Table 7.6 the central bank's payoffs in such a situation.[26] In this world, stability-oriented wage restraint comes with a cost for the unions: even when real wages eventually adjust in such a way that a nominal wage restraint does not lead to a real wage loss, there are political costs connected with wage restraint. Union leaders have to explain to their members why they have exercised wage constraint. Moreover, during the transition to a new equilibrium, real wages *are* lower than they would have been had nominal wages grown at a faster pace. However, the union is still strongly interested in an increase in employment. As a high level of unemployment makes the threat of finding oneself unemployed even more gruesome, one can assume that employment enters the individual union member's utility function along with the real wage and should thus also enter into the union leader's utility function.

For the central bank, stability-oriented wage restraint is to be preferred to aggressive wage bargaining: it makes the task of keeping inflation under control much easier. At the same time, central bankers who are 'conservative' in Rogoff's (1985) sense,[27] might not like expansionary monetary policy even in times of stability-oriented wage restraint: as such a policy comes with a certain risk from the exchange rate and asset

Table 7.5 Unions' payoff

Event	Payoff
Wage restraint	−1
No wage restraint	0
Expansionary monetary policy	5
Restrictive monetary policy	0

Table 7.6 Conservative central banker's payoff

Event	Payoff
Wage restraint	5
No wage restraint	0
Expansionary monetary policy	−1
Restrictive monetary policy	0

price side (and requires monitoring those developments more closely), they might have a slightly negative payoff from such a policy.

Backward induction helps us to solve the situation from Figure 7.4 with the new payoffs. Figure 7.7 shows what happens in a world of complete information in which the unions know the conservative central banker's payoff function. As the unions anticipate that the central banker will not react to stability-oriented wage restraint with an expansionary monetary policy, they are reluctant to exercise wage restraint. In reaction, the central banker would not loosen its restrictive course and the sub-optimal outcome 1 would be reached.

Strategies to escape the prisoner's dilemma

As in the static prisoner's dilemma, the non-cooperative behaviour can – at least partially – be corrected when the game is played repeatedly for an indefinite number of periods.[28] If both players know the payoffs from Table 7.4, the players might begin to cooperate. As they know that cooperation will cease if one of the players stops cooperating, they will continue with their cooperation as long as their discounted future return from cooperation is larger than the gain from non-cooperation.

However, in this chain of cooperation, each player will form a strategy for reacting to non-cooperation by the other player. If they were simply cooperating no matter what the other player was doing, the other player would have an incentive not to cooperate, as he would thereby maximise his payoff. One strategy which is found to lead to a subgame-perfect Nash equilibrium is the *trigger strategy* (Gibbons 1992) or *grim strategy* (Rasmusen 1994): the player would cooperate until the other player behaved in a non-cooperative way. From this moment onwards, the player would switch to a non-cooperative behaviour as well and remain non-cooperative thereafter (Gibbons 1992, pp. 95ff.). With the trigger strategy, one problem arises: non-cooperative behaviour for all future games is the harshest punishment one player can inflict on the other. It also inflicts heavy costs on the punisher himself.

If there is the possibility of a misunderstanding, the costs of this misunderstanding are extremely high.

A similar argument applies for the *tit-for-tat strategy*, which is often considered an ideal solution for the repeated prisoner's dilemma (Myerson 1991, pp. 324ff.), and which Heise (1999) even proposes as the preferable solution for the prisoner's dilemma between central bank and wage bargainers: the strategy consists simply in copying the other player's behaviour in the preceding round. If the other player did not cooperate in the preceding round, one is not to cooperate in the current round. According to its proponents, this strategy has several advantages:

- It is simple
- It never initiates non-cooperation
- It retaliates instantly against non-cooperative behaviour
- It forgives a non-cooperative player who goes on to cooperate after a deviation from cooperation, the welfare costs of punishment are thus limited.

This argument neglects an important fact: if there is the possibility of misunderstanding, tit-for-tat will lead to substantial welfare losses (Dixit and Nalebuff 1997, pp. 106f.). Suppose at least one player cannot perfectly determine whether the other player has cooperated in the preceding round or not. In this case, there will be situations in which player 1 believes player 2 has not cooperated, though in fact player 2 did cooperate. Player 1 would then begin to retaliate. As player

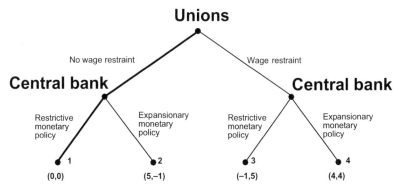

Figure 7.7 Unions and the central bank: the non-cooperative subgame-perfect Nash equilibrium

2 has not done any wrong, he would interpret the retaliation as a simple failure to cooperate by player 1 and retaliate in the next round. This phase of mutual retaliation would go on until one of the players again made a mistake in judging the other player's action and wrongly believed that the other player did cooperate. As Dixit and Nalebuff (1997) note, it is not even important how likely it really is that a player has made such a mistake. If the probability of making a mistake is very low, the average time lapse before a retaliation period starts may be longer, but on average, retaliation will last for a greater number of rounds, and the probability that a new mistake is necessary to end mutual retaliation will have decreased as well. With an infinite number of games played, regardless of the probability of mistake, half of the periods will be retaliation periods with welfare forgone.[29]

This argument is especially important for the game between unions and central bankers. As the central bank not only has to react to wage developments, but also – to a certain extent – to keep an eye on asset markets, as described in Chapter 6, the unions cannot be sure whether the central bank has reacted to their wage behaviour or to some outside pressure. Particularly when both sides are using different models of the macroeconomy, it is easily possible that the unions mistake a policy stance considered by the central bank to be expansionary as a restrictive response, and thus a failure to cooperate. If they now ended the phase of stability-oriented wage restraint by signing only short-term wage contracts and aggressively trying to compensate any real wage losses due to changes in the exchange rate or q, the central bank would have to react with a restrictive monetary policy, and the economy would again find itself with outcome 1 in Figure 7.7. Some new mistake in judging the central bank's action would now be necessary to begin a new phase of cooperation.[30] Until this happens, the economy has to live with sub-optimal output and employment.

Being stuck with an overly conservative central banker

Another possibility for explaining why the seemingly optimal outcome of stability-oriented wage restraint and an expansionary monetary policy is not reached is that the players' payoffs simply do not allow for cooperation or coordination. Such a situation would occur if there were an overly conservative central banker. One could imagine a monetary authority who does not care at all for employment and output and who believes that no matter what wage increase unions demand and wage bargainers agree upon, with the stroke of a pen it will be able to increase interest rates enough to keep inflation down. Of course, the

central bank may have to inflict severe losses on the economy's companies, as he has to push q down violently when wage increases are too
high. But as changing interest rates is not hard for the head of a central
bank, one could imagine such behaviour. Fortunately, the real world
does not know many central bankers who do not care at all about
output and employment. Moreover, there might be an automatic
mechanism for preventing such central bankers from being in power
for too long: a central bank that acts in the way described would probably risk losing its independence. But as academic literature often
seems to imply that a central banker cannot be too conservative, such
a setting might well be worth a little thought.

In such a world, the central banker's payoff in an uncooperative situation with a restrictive monetary policy and without stability-oriented
wage restraint would be the same as in the situation of wage restraint
and restrictive monetary policy. In such a case, unions would anticipate that the central banker would follow a restrictive policy stance;
and no matter what the unions did, they would at least try not to bear
the political cost of wage restraint and would go for aggressive wage
bargaining. Moreover, in this setting, there is no way to get unions and
the central bank to cooperate since the central banker cannot improve
his situation by cooperating. If society as a whole has any interest in
output and employment (as one can usually assume), this outcome is
highly sub-optimal.

To get into this kind of trap does not even require a central banker
who cares nothing about output and employment. It is sufficient to
have a policy maker running the central bank who puts sufficient
weight on price stability and is highly risk averse: as has been argued
above, an expansionary monetary policy might bring about the depreciation of the domestic currency and consequently the risk of a wage –
price spiral. The depreciation would hurt workers' real wage position,
and they in turn might try to regain lost real wages through increased
nominal wage demands. As the equilibrium price level is a function of
nominal wages, this would lead to inflation. If the central banker considers this risk as sufficiently high, he might not want to get involved
in an expansionary policy.

Thus in a world without real balance effects and with strategically
acting unions, it is not ideal to appoint an extremely conservative
central banker as (Rogoff 1985) proposes. At the same time, of course,
it is not optimal to appoint someone who cares more about short-run
output and employment than about price stability. In such a setting,
the central bank will choose an expansionary policy no matter what

the unions do. As soon as they know the populist central banker's payoff function they will no longer engage in wage restraint but will instead shift to aggressive bargaining. The result will be a higher rate of inflation. This cumulative process could lead to a decline in the preference for monetary assets, thus reducing the equilibrium capital stock and leading to a lower output in the long run. The ideal candidate for the post of the central banker should therefore dislike inflation but still care enough about employment and output that he is willing to boldly use expansionary monetary policy as long as the risk for a wage-price spiral is kept under control. His monetary policy would ideally show a degree of both non-accommodativeness and boldness close to one.

7.3   A social pact as a possible remedy

Coordination failure, cooperation failure and an overly conservative banker – the explanations are plausible to a varying degree. The assumption that unions and the central bank have a rather symmetrical interest, as would be the case in Silvestre's (1993) example of coordination failure, is a rather stark one. On the other hand, we do not know whether the central bank does in fact have a utility function that weights output lightly enough to run into the prisoner's dilemma described on p. 214. Taylor rules which take into account the current output gap can be shown to give a good approximation of the ECB's monetary policy during the first years of its existence.[31] This suggests that European monetary policy at the moment is not run by central bankers who do not care at all for output and employment. Yet, without knowing the actual actors' utility functions we can say very little of the true reasons for the unfavourable macroeconomic environment in EMU. However, we can still look at a possible remedy – namely the attempt to create a 'cooperative macroeconomic policy mix' agreed upon by the European Council at the Cologne summit in 1999.

By starting a macroeconomic dialogue, the Union has tried to add a 'third pillar'[32] to its employment strategy (European Council 1999). This macroeconomic dialogue is divided into two levels: technical and a political. On the technical level, economic developments are monitored and analysed by a working party 'set up in the framework of the Economic Policy Committee in collaboration with the Employment and Labour Market Committee, with the participation of representatives of both committees (including the European Central Bank), of the Commission and of the Macroeconomic Group of the Social Dialogue' (European Council 1999). This working group meets bi-annually.

On the political level, a confidence-building and confidential exchange of ideas between decision makers is supposed to be initiated. 'To this end, meetings will take place twice a year in the framework of the ECOFIN Council in collaboration with the Labour and Social Affairs Council, with the participation of representatives of both formations of the Council, of the Commission, of the European Central Bank and of the social partners' (European Council 1999). To keep the group efficient, each participating institution is to appoint only two members. The country which holds the presidency of the European Council is also to preside over the political level of the macroeconomic dialogue (Köhler 2001).

With regard to goals, the macroeconomic dialogue is supposed to make it possible for the major economic actors responsible for fiscal policy, monetary policy and wage increases to 'exchange ideas on how they think a policy mix can be achieved which promotes growth and employment while safeguarding price stability', 'while maintaining their respective responsibilities and preserving their independence' (European Council 1999). These respective responsibilities are further defined as:

- *Fiscal policy* is required to respect the objectives of the Stability and Growth Pact (SGP), which implies bringing budgets securely close to balance or to a surplus over the medium term. Beyond that, public budgets should also be restructured towards higher investment and with a view to meeting forthcoming challenges such as an ageing population. At the same time, it must not lose sight of macroeconomic developments.
- *Wages* must keep to a sustainable path, with wage developments that are consistent with price stability and job creation.
- The primary objective of *monetary policy* is to maintain price stability. For this, it is crucial that monetary policy be underpinned by fiscal policies and wage developments of the type described above. Without prejudice to the objective of price stability, monetary policy will support the general economic policies in the Community with a view to contributing to sustainable and non-inflationary growth and a high level of employment.

While these responsibilities show at least some kind of deviation from the neo-classical assignment of policy goals to different actors, the standard conclusion remains intact: job creation is foremost the task of social partners who decide on wage developments. Price stability, on the other hand, is to be achieved by monetary policy. This is in contrast to this book's conclusions: in the models presented in the preceding chapters, wage policy is central to price stability. At the same time, wage restraint by itself cannot create employment. Wage restraint is thus a necessary, but not a sufficient, condition for more employment and higher growth, but only to the extent that wage developments do not become deflationary. The assignment of policy goals presented in this work is thus completely different from that in the founding documents of the macroeconomic dialogue. The question is thus: if we accept the mechanics of macroeconomics described in this work, is it possible to improve the macroeconomic environment by the macroeconomic policy dialogue as initiated in 1999?

Improving coordination

Basically, getting rid of coordination problems, as described on p. 205, is fairly simple: coordination failure is a problem of insufficient information. If each player knew what the others were doing, coordination failure would not occur. A social pact could create an institutional frame in which the macroeconomic actors have the possibility to communicate what they will do both clearly and confidentially. Since improving coordination works in the interest of all participants, there will be no danger that any of the players will send the wrong signals in order to deceive the other macroeconomic actors. Coordination problems could therefore be easily solved by implementing a social pact.[33]

However, in practice we must ask whether the actors themselves are capable of using and distributing the information gathered and exchanged in the macroeconomic dialogue. For the ECB as a relatively centralised institution, this should not be a problem with two senior officials taking part in the meeting. The case is slightly different for the unions. Though many of them are organised in the European Trade Union Confederation (ETUC), their formal ties are much weaker than those of monetary authorities. However, as Hancké (2002) notes, informal information exchange in industrial sectors such as metals and textiles has been strengthened by the *Doorn* process between Dutch, German, Belgian and Luxembourg confederations. Consequently, at least for the large unions, one can expect the flow of information to work reasonably well.

If it is true that the German wage setters still set the pace for wage contracts in the core of the euro-zone (via implicit coordination between wage setters across the euro-zone as described above), it would be important only for German unions to receive the ECB's signals. As the German unions, and especially the tradable sector union *IG Metall*, which most of the time sets the pilot contract, are well organised and integrated into ETUC, they can be expected to get information from the macroeconomic dialogue. The existing macroeconomic dialogue should thus be expected to deal with problems of coordination failure within EMU.

Improving cooperation

In principle, the problems of cooperation failure could at least be alleviated by a *social pact*. First, the macroeconomic dialogue could help the players to learn what strategy the other player is using in the repeated prisoners' dilemma (p. 216). If, for example, one of the players uses the *grim* strategy, it might be helpful for the other player to know this so he does not have to test which strategy is being employed: remember that testing under this strategy implies a permanent non-cooperation for the future. Second, even when the players are using gentler strategies, the dialogue process could help. With both players playing tit-for-tat, for example, a better communication could help to limit mutually harmful punishing periods: an institution through which policy actors can talk about current economic developments and can communicate about their strategies for dealing with each other might lower the probability of wrongly accusing the other party of deviating from cooperation. But as we have seen above, just lowering the probability of a misunderstanding does not solve the problem. In addition, it would be necessary to create a mechanism that helps to end a retaliation phase of non-cooperation without having to wait for a new misunderstanding. Here again, simple communication and the mutual change of strategies away from simple tit-for-tat could help to bring the actors back to a cooperative stance. If it were thus possible to lower the probability of an initial misunderstanding and limit the lengths of retaliation periods,[34] much would be won.

However, one of the actors could try to use the macroeconomic dialogue to convince the other party that he had not deviated from cooperation in a situation in which he in fact had broken the (informal) agreement to cooperate.[35] At this point, simple communication would lose much of its value, as the actors could not be sure whether the information they were getting in the dialogue was 'true' pieces of information or just sand in their eyes in order to cover up a non-cooperation by the other side. The basic problem of potential misunderstandings remains.

In order to effectively get around this problem, one needs a way to determine whether a player has actually defected. To this end, it would be useful to have an impartial monitoring institution or referee as Heise (2002) proposes. As punishment in the form of non-cooperation is harmful not only to the actors, but also to the economy as a whole, such retaliatory episodes should be avoided as far as possible. One possibility could be to reprimand publicly the defecting actor as a milder form of punishment before moving to a (limited) phase of mutual non-cooperation.

Unfortunately, such a setup or even the development toward such a setup is not imaginable within the Cologne process as it has been organised to date. A cooperation agreement would have to admit that it is not the central bank alone which is responsible for price stability and not the social partners' wage increases alone which determine the number of unemployed. Agreeing on those conclusions, however, would force the actors to break with the assignment given to them by the European Council. Unions and employers would be made responsible for price stability and could be reprimanded by the referee for wage increases that endanger low rates of inflation. At the same time, the central bank would have a joint responsibility for output and growth and could be called to account for being too tight given actual wage developments. With the assignment of policy goals to the respective actors as described above, there would simply be no need for a monitoring institution. If you want to judge the central bank's performance in the neo-classical world, you just have to measure the rate of inflation. If you want to judge whether wage demands are appropriate, the public just has to take a look at the (cyclically adjusted) rate of unemployment.[36] Clearly, a social pact with a referee and a changed and shared distribution of responsibility is not what the European Council intended (European Council 1999) or what current EU governments would push for.

Opposition would most likely also come from the ECB, which does not seem to have any interest in coordination or cooperation between macroeconomic policy actors which goes further than simple information exchange, as ECB chief economist Otmar Issing (2002, p. 313) emphasises:

> The central message I wish to convey here, however, is that there are no convincing arguments in favour of attempts to co-ordinate macroeconomic policies ex ante in order to achieve an overall policy mix favourable to growth and employment. On the contrary, attempts that extend beyond the informal exchange of views and information give rise to the risk of confusing the specific roles, mandates and responsibilities of the policies in question.

Moreover, as von Hagen and Mundschenk (2001) note, so far, the wage bargainers in the social dialogue themselves cannot enforce the agreements made. The EU federations of trade unions and employers do not have the authority to represent a common view of their partners in all of the countries and cannot ensure the enforcement of any agreement on guidelines for wage policies.

Thus, although a social pact could in principle be able to lessen the negative impact of a natural tendency towards cooperation failure, the current setup of the macroeconomic dialogue in Europe will not be able to do so.

Dealing with an overly conservative central banker

As long as the central banker is not so conservative that he does not care at all about output and employment, but is only overly risk averse, a social pact might provide a remedy: first, long-term wage contracts agreed upon within the framework of the macroeconomic dialogue decrease the risk that one-time depreciation and import price hikes will turn into a wage–price spiral, thus altering probabilities and consequently expected payoffs for different monetary policy stances. With lower risks, the central banker's expected costs of an expansionary monetary policy decrease while the benefits remain constant. Such a shift in expected payoffs can be expected to change the central bank's policy. The social pact would become a macroeconomic safety net for engaging in expansionary monetary policy.

Unfortunately, for very high degrees of risk aversion or completely conservative central bankers, even reducing the risk to price stability will not be sufficient. Simply providing a framework for communication like the macroeconomic dialogue will not change this banker's actions as he does not have anything to gain from a cooperation. His utility function simply has the wrong shape.

However, if one really takes the social pact and especially the idea of an impartial referee able to reprimand the policy actors further, there might even be a solution to the problem of the overly conservative central banker. If the macroeconomic dialogue were to be followed closely by the media, academics and the public, the dialogue might even change the participants' preferences. At the end of the day, even central bankers are human beings who like to earn respect and praise from their peers. If the macroeconomic dialogue is able to shift the awareness of academics, the general public and the financial community towards the role of the central bank in achieving lower rates of unemployment, this could alter the monetary authority's payoffs. This does not necessarily mean a shift in the central banker's utility function. One could argue that the central banker's utility depends, among other things, on the amount of favourable feedback he receives from media, academics and the financial community. If the perception in these groups changes about what a central bank can and should do, the central banker's payoff will also change – without a change in the utility function itself.

As the overly conservative central banker himself would not enter into any social pact or any cooperative framework, the social pact would have to be equipped with a mandate to foster cooperation no matter whether the actors prefer cooperation or not. It would have to be able to monitor which actor does not behave cooperatively and would need the power to at least publicly reprimand the defector. Forming such a setup would of course be very delicate since the impression might arise that the central bank's independence is infringed upon. Given the high symbolic and legal weight of the ECB's independence, it is very improbable that the real-world macroeconomic dialogue in EMU will ever progress in this direction.

With the current setup of the macroeconomic dialogue, not much will be achieved in the face of an overly conservative central banker. Not only is the dialogue a long way from assigning joint responsibility for price stability and employment to the macroeconomic actors, but it also does not provide for reporting to the public. In contrast to the provisions regarding the Luxembourg and the Cardiff processes, there are not even any requirements for giving a regular report on progress or the working of the dialogue (Heise 2002). In addition, the Cologne process does not seem to be taken very seriously by politicians currently in power.[37] With such a weak public standing, the macroeconomic dialogue will hardly be able to change the public's or the financial community's view on the work and tasks of the central banker and thereby influence his behaviour. Fortunately, there are few signs that the ECB's central bankers are of such an overly conservative type as described in this section. Moreover, this type of central banker is probably more of an academic invention than a real-world problem.

In conclusion, a social pact could in principle be able to get rid of the coordination failure between monetary policy makers and social partners, could to a large extent alleviate the cooperation failure resulting from a prisoner's dilemma between unions and central bank and might even have a chance to limit the negative consequences of an overly conservative central banker on the economy. Unfortunately, the European macroeconomic dialogue is not fit to reach those aims. As it relies on the standard assignment of macroeconomic policy goals to single actors as known from the standard neo-classical model, it will not be able to motivate the actors to a cooperative behaviour in a world without the real balance effect as depicted in this work. The only thing it might achieve is to get rid of possible coordination failures by distributing information more effectively.

8
Conclusions and Outlook

This book started with a question: how do wage bargainers and monetary policy jointly influence output, employment and inflation? While older standard models concluded that it was wage bargainers who set real wages, which determine output and employment, while the central bank just set the growth rate of money supply, thus determining the rate of inflation, recent literature, as represented by the SICCD models has come to a different conclusion: the setup of a monetary policy rule can change the wage setters' behaviour. If, for example, it is clear that the central bank will set a given nominal money supply no matter what the wage setters are doing, unions can increase the real money supply (Soskice–Iversen 2000) by lowering their wage demands and thus pushing down prices. The increased real money supply would then lead to higher output and employment. If wage setters are a large enough force to be acting strategically, and if they care enough about unemployment, they can be expected to make use of this possibility. A monetary policy rule can thus have non-neutral effects in the long run.

The empirical cases studied in Chapter 2 cast some doubt on this conclusion. Although it seems that wage setters in some of the EMU countries were able to increase aggregate demand by exercising wage restraint, this result was mostly observed in smaller and more open EMU countries. Germany, as the largest EMU economy, on the other hand, did not seem to have benefited much from wage restraint, although it seems to have followed a similar strategy as well.

This book has argued that the reason for the proclaimed effect's failure to show up in large EMU countries is the absence of a real balance effect. This theoretic construction, which lies at the heart of the SICCD models, claims that with falling prices real money balances increase and thus investment and/or consumption demand is pushed up. As was shown in Chapter 3, this mechanism cannot be at work in a world of endogenous inside money. Since money is created as a consequence of real investment or consumption decisions, the nominal money stock cannot be assumed to remain constant when prices change. Moreover, since money is created as a consequence of loans granted by the banking sector, it is not net wealth for the private sector. Changes in the price level might therefore have consequences for the distribution between debtors and creditors. However, they do not make the private sector richer or poorer and should thus not increase real consumption demand. Chapter 3 also argued that the euro-zone – as any modern monetary economy – is a system of endogenous inside money, so the real balance effect will not be at work.

That small EMU countries such as the Netherlands or Ireland were nevertheless able to benefit from wage restraint stems from the fact that they were able to improve their competitive position relative to the rest of EMU and thereby increase export demand. However, for a large, relatively closed economy such as EMU as a whole, wage restraint cannot be expected to lead to positive output or employment effects by itself, as could have been expected if the SICCD models were correct.

In Chapters 4 and 5, this book went on to model an economy in which real balances do not cause real economic variables to change. With regard to firms which are monopolistically competing with each other, it has been shown that prices are set as a mark-up over labour costs. The exact magnitude of this mark-up depends positively on the interest rate and the monopoly power. Thus, the less monopolised the product markets, the lower the mark-up; the lower the interest rate, the lower also the mark-up. Output has been shown to be a function of interest rates. Since monopolistically competitive firms maximise their profits given the demand function they face, higher demand also leads to higher output. As lower interest rates lead to higher investment demand, a lower interest rate thus leads to higher output.

Consequently, it is the development of nominal wages which determines the path of equilibrium prices and thus inflation. At the same time, it is monetary policy which determines output and employment through the interest rate. With wage setters able to influence price stability and the central bank able to influence growth, the variables to be more directly controlled by each of the two policy actors are exactly opposite from what they are assumed to be in standard models where wages determine output and employment, while monetary policy determines the price level.

However, as was explored in detail in Chapter 6, the central bank is not free to choose any interest rate it wishes. Instead, it is constrained by financial markets. Since in a world of inside money the capital stock of the economy is financed in part by investors' money holdings, to achieve high output and employment it is crucial that individuals keep a high share of monetary assets in their portfolios. The central bank has thus to convince private agents to hold monetary assets. As wealth owners might see a depreciation as a possible threat to the stability of monetary assets' purchasing power, and such a depreciation can be expected to come with a cut in interest rates, the central bank's degree of freedom is limited.

Whether a depreciation turns into permanent inflation depends in part on how wage setters react to transitory price hikes. A depreciation will always increase import prices; only if wage setters do not react to these price spikes with increased nominal wage demands, can low and stable rates of inflation be guaranteed following a depreciation.

As was argued in Chapter 7, for an optimum policy mix, wage setters will keep their nominal wage growth low so that the equilibrium price level does not change faster than what the central bank's inflation target allows for, even when a depreciation or demand spikes temporarily push up prices. The central bank, in turn, will lower interest rates as far as the financial markets' restrictions allow. An optimum outcome with high output and employment can be reached only by a (implicit or explicit) cooperation between the central bank, trade unions and employers.

The problem is that each actor incurs costs from his perspective when he follows a strategy as described above without knowing for sure whether the other actor will cooperate. The unions are faced with the risk that their wage restraint will not be answered with an expansionary monetary policy. The central bank, on the other hand, cannot be sure whether unions will react with strong *ex post* compensation demands when an expansionary monetary policy leads to depreciation and hence a hike in import prices. Such compensation demands will push up nominal wages and will thus lead to an increase in domestic inflation.

These possible costs do not *a priori* have to keep actors from cooperating. In a situation in which both sides can win from a cooperative outcome, an implicit agreement might be reached when both actors try different strategies, as was explained in Chapter 7. However, without a formal mechanism of coordination, the risk will remain that due to misunderstandings, misperceptions or outright attempts by one side to cheat the other, prolonged episodes of non-cooperation will occur. Such episodes will inevitably incur heavy costs in the form of increased unemployment and forgone output in the euro-zone economies.

This book has thus given a possible explanation for how the macroeconomic setup of the euro-zone might make it hard to achieve a permanently high-employment/low-inflation solution. Contrary to what conventional wisdom claims, it is not microeconomic labour market rigidities which lead to this outcome, but simply the economic mechanisms of an economy in which real money balances cannot act in a way to balance aggregate supply and demand. Contrary to what some Post-Keynesians claim, it is not the central bank's malevolence that keeps unemployment high. Instead, it is the failure of monetary policy and wage bargainers to act jointly in a way that increases unemployment at low and stable rates of inflation.

As has been discussed in Chapter 7, there might be a possibility to improve the cooperation between policy actors by strengthening the macroeconomic policy dialogue. In the logic of the book, a certain caution against reforming the macroeconomic dialogue is justified: as the central bank has to take into account the financial markets' reaction to its monetary policy actions, any reform that will actually keep it from observing these restrictions and thus hurt the long-term outlook for low and stable inflation will be counterproductive. Attempts to push the interest rate and thus employment beyond the point at which a depreciation becomes destabilising only hurt long- and medium-run growth prospects, as the capital stock formation will be impaired. However, if a reform were to be carried out in a careful manner, it could help to alleviate the problems of insufficient cooperation and coordination, not only lowering unemployment in Europe, but also making the central bank's task easier. Unfortunately, the current political discussion does not seem likely to push for any reform of this economic policy instrument.

Appendices: Monetary and Wage Policy in Standard Models

In this Appendix, I will briefly review the way monetary policy and money are modelled in standard textbook models. This has two aims. First, it is supposed to remind readers how the real balance effect is working. This reasoning is not only important for understanding my critique of the SICCD approach, as presented in Chapter 3, but is also important for understanding why the central bank cannot easily set the rate of inflation, as implied in models building on Barro and Gordon (1983) in absence of a real balance effect. Second, this Appendix is supposed to show the central role that the real balance effect plays in the most widely used textbook models.

I will concentrate on the Aggregate Supply/Aggregate Demand (AS-AD) Model (e.g. McCallum 1989, Chapter 5 or Romer 1996, Chapter 5) and the New Classical Model (based on Lucas 1972, 1973). I have chosen these models since they are not only the baseline models in most economic textbooks, but also the foundation of much of the research in monetary macroeconomics of the last few years.

Even in models which have structures different from the AS-AD or the New Classical approach, the basic transmission mechanisms of monetary policy often remain the same.[1] For example, those Real-Business-Cycle (RBC) models which try to incorporate monetary shocks into their analysis rely on the Keynes effect or the Pigou effect to explain how monetary policy influences real values in the wake of special constraints.[2] Moreover, to the present day the Pigou effect remains at the heart of monetarist argumentation as presented in Meltzer (1999) or Nelson (2000).

Appendix A.1: The Transmission of Monetary Policy

Monetary policy is usually modelled as an exogenous change in the stock of money M^s. There are two ways in which such a change affects the real economy: the Keynes and the Pigou effect, which both increase aggregate demand. In short, the Keynes effect focuses on the individuals' choices of allocating their savings between bonds and cash holdings. An increase in the money stock here leads to lower interest rates and consequently higher investment. The Pigou effect focuses on the effects of an increased money supply on consumption: since an increased money stock increases the individuals' net wealth, it also increases consumption demand. As Keynesian economists focus on the direct effects of monetary policy on investment rather than consumption,[3] the standard IS-LM model relies heavily on the Keynes effect and neglects the Pigou effect altogether.[4] Thus, I will use the AS-AD model which is derived from Hicks's (1937) IS-LM model for explaining the Keynes effect.

I will then turn to the Lucas (1972) model to explain the Pigou effect. This special case of a New Classical model only incorporates the Pigou effect, so the effect can be nicely demonstrated. However, neglecting the Keynes effect is not a constituent feature of New Classical models. Instead, in a monetarist tradition,[5] most New Classical models such as Sargent and Wallace (1975) incorporate effects of money stock changes both on (nominal) consumption and (nominal) investment demand.[6] As I will later need not only the narrow mechanics of the Keynes and the Pigou effects, but also considerably more of the economic reasoning behind both the AS-AD and the New Classical models to explain the role of wage policy in the standard textbook models (see Section A.3), I will also outline the basic properties of both models in the next two sub sections.

The Keynes effect in the AS-AD model

In the AS-AD model, an increase in money supply M^S leads to increased investment and thus to increased aggregate demand Y^D. The mechanism is the same as in the IS-LM model since the AS-AD model's demand equations are taken from IS-LM.

The IS-LM model consists of two equations. The LM curve presents the combinations of output Y and nominal interest rate i that lead to equilibrium in the money market for a given price level. The opportunity costs for holding money instead of lending it out equals the nominal interest rate. Thus, the demand for real money balances L is decreasing in the nominal interest rate. Since the volume of transactions is greater when output is higher, the demand for real balances is an increasing function of output Y:

$$\frac{M^s}{P} = L(i, Y), \quad \frac{\partial L}{\partial i} < 0, \quad \frac{\partial L}{\partial Y} > 0 \qquad (A.1)$$

The IS curve presents equilibrium values of output and interest rate in which planned and actual expenditures are the same. Expenditure consists of private consumption C, investment I and state consumption G. Private consumption is increasing in Y and investment is decreasing in i:

$$Y = C(Y) + I(i) + G, \quad \frac{\partial C}{\partial Y} > 0, \quad \frac{\partial I}{\partial i} < 0 \qquad (A.2)$$

Monetary policy now increases the money supply M^S. This is accomplished by a process which is characterised by Friedman's helicopter parable:[7] overnight the individual's money balances are increased. Suddenly, economic agents find themselves with real money holdings which are higher than what they would prefer. The individuals try to lend out their excess money holdings. They buy bonds. The bonds' price increases. This is equivalent to a fall in the interest rate i. With falling interest rates, investment I increases. With increased investment, aggregate demand and output also increase. This in turn leads to a higher demand for transaction services, which then leads via (A.1) to a higher demand for money balances. In the new equilibrium, I, Y, and M^S have increased, while i has fallen. The process by which an increased money supply lowers interest rates and thus leads to a higher investment demand is called the *Keynes effect* or *liquidity effect* (Duwendag *et al.* 1999, p. 147).

This story changes slightly when we add the AS curve. Aggregate supply is then determined not by aggregate demand, as in the original underemployment IS-LM model, but by a macroeconomic production function. Since the stock of capital is assumed to be fixed in the short run, real output y^s becomes a function of employment N:

$$y^s = f(N), \quad \frac{\partial f}{\partial N} > 0, \quad \frac{\partial f}{\partial^2 N} < 0 \tag{A.3}$$

Firms choose employment so that the marginal product of labour equals the real wage:

$$\frac{\partial f}{\partial N} = \frac{W}{P} \tag{A.4}$$

Thus, labour demand becomes a decreasing function of the real wage:

$$N^D = N^D\left(\frac{W}{P}\right), \quad \frac{\partial N^D}{\partial \frac{W}{P}} < 0 \tag{A.5}$$

At the same time, workers offer labour until their marginal disutility from working equals the real wage paid. Thus labour supply is increasing in the real wage.

$$N^S = N^S\left(\frac{W}{P}\right), \quad \frac{\partial N^S}{\partial \frac{W}{P}} > 0 \tag{A.6}$$

If wages are free to adjust and there is no money illusion among workers, labour demand and labour supply equalises at an equilibrium real wage rate. All unemployment in equilibrium is voluntary:

$$N = N^S\left(\frac{W^*}{P^*}\right) = N^D\left(\frac{W^*}{P^*}\right) \tag{A.7}$$

Finally, aggregate supply and aggregate demand have to be equal in equilibrium:

$$Py^s = C(Y) + I(i) + G \tag{A.8}$$

If the stock of money is now increased, individuals again find themselves with excessive money balances. Interest rates fall and investment demand, and consequently aggregate demand, rise. However, since aggregate supply is fixed by (A.3) and (A.4), only the price level P can adjust. With rising prices, nominal wages rise proportionally, since equilibrium real wages are given by (A.7) and wages are free to adjust. Rising prices diminish real money balances (and thus real money supply) and increase nominal output Y. In new equilibrium only the price level has changed; real values have not been affected.

However, if either the assumption of flexible nominal wages or the assumption of absence of any monetary illusion is relaxed, monetary policy does have real effects via the Keynes effect.

Special case I: fixed nominal wages

When nominal wages are fixed at $\overline{W}$, employment and output are determined by firms' profit-maximising choices:

$$N = N^D\left(\frac{\overline{W}}{P}\right) \tag{A.9}$$

Thus, with a given nominal wage, employment N and output Y become a positive function of the price level P. Rising prices lead to a lower real wage, which lowers the marginal product of labour required by the firms. In this case, monetary policy can be effective in the AS-AD model. An increased money supply (and thus increased real balances) leads to a fall in interest rates and to higher investment and aggregate demand. As the increased aggregate demand leads to higher prices, real wages fall. This increases employment and aggregate supply. In the end, employment, real output and the price level will have increased, real wages and the interest rate have fallen.

Special case II: the money illusion

Monetary policy is also effective in the AS-AD framework in the case of the money illusion. Here, workers underestimate price increases; they thus believe their real wages to be higher than they actually are.

Under these assumptions, the monetary transmission mechanism works as follows: an increase in the money supply leads to a falling interest rate and increased investment and aggregate demand. The excess demand pushes up the price level. As workers do not fully take into account this increase in prices, they do not push for higher nominal wages. With the firms paying marginally higher nominal wages (but lower real wages than in the beginning), more workers offer their labour, which is employed as the required marginal product of labour has fallen in line with (new and lower) real wages. Higher employment then leads to higher output.

Thus, in the case of the money illusion, an increase in the money stock increases real output, employment and the price level. Real wages and interest rates fall while nominal wages increase slightly.

The Pigou effect in New Classical models

In Lucas (1972), monetary policy is modelled slightly differently from the AS-AD model. Lucas' model knows young and old individuals. The young generation works and produces output. This output is either consumed by the young or sold to the old against money which the old have earned during their youth.

The money supply is increased only via a direct government transfer of newly printed money to the old (Lucas 1972, p. 105). Since the old do not save but only consume (it is not possible to inherit in Lucas' model), this transfer leads to an increased consumption demand. This mechanism works much like the mechanism Pigou (1943, p. 349) describes for the classical model:[8] Pigou assumes that the individuals (there are no different generations in Pigou's argument) have the goal of holding a given real amount of money. If the individuals find themselves with larger real balances than desired, they will stop saving and will consume more. However, Pigou does not assume the increases in real balances to stem from newly printed money but from a fall in the price level. The basic rationale of both effects is that an increase in real balances (either by an increase in nominal balances through newly printed money or by a fall in the overall price level) leads to higher wealth and consequently to higher consumption demand.

In order to show how a monetary shock affects the economy in the New Classical model, I will now turn to Lucas' (1973) simplification of his original model. Aggregate demand is given as a function of some 'exogenous shift variable' x (changes which are later interpreted as changes in the nominal money supply) and the price level P in period t. In log notation, we get:[9]

$$y_t = x_t - P_t \qquad \text{(A.10)}$$

Aggregate supply in Lucas' world is determined by the supply decisions of individual agents in a large number of different markets. Demand for goods in each period is distributed unevenly over markets, leading to relative as well as aggregate price movements. The individual supplier knows only the history of money and demand shocks (the distribution of which is assumed to be normal) and the price level observed in her own market. Any systematic changes in the money supply are rationally expected by the individuals. Given these pieces of information, the suppliers estimate the overall price level. With this overall price level, they can now estimate the real value of the money they are paid for their products. Given their preferences they will then supply as much output (and thus as much labour) so that their marginal disutility from working equals their marginal utility from the estimated real value of one unit of output.

Thus, aggregate supply becomes a function of the estimation error that the individuals make because they are not perfectly informed. Given y_n as the 'normal' trend output, ν as the persistence of cyclical fluctuations, γ as the influence of relative price changes on supply, the variance in the overall price level σ^2 around its mean $\overline{P}_t$ and the variance in the deviation of a partial market's price level from the overall price level ρ^2, we get:

$$y_t = y_{n,t} + \frac{\tau^2}{(\sigma^2 + \tau^2)} \gamma(P_t - \overline{P}_t) + \nu(y_{t-1} - y_{n,t-1}) \qquad \text{(A.11)}$$

If we interpret this equation, we see that the slope of the aggregate supply curve depends on the fraction of total variance in a single market which is due to relative price variation. If τ^2 is relatively small, so that price changes in individual markets almost certainly reflect general price changes, the supply curve is nealy vertical. Or, put differently: In an environment in which the overall price level is relatively stable, nominal shocks have a larger influence on real output.

As long as there are no unexpected shocks and the individual agents estimate the price level correctly, all individuals are in their optimum. Unemployment in this model is always voluntary,[10] fluctuations in real output and employment reflect unexpected nominal shocks.

Appendix A.2: The Money Stock as an Automatic Stabiliser

Both the Keynes and the Pigou effect not only explain how monetary policy transmits to the real economy. The existence of each of these effects is also a sufficient condition for a monetary economy with flexible wages and prices to attain equilibrium.

The money stock thus keeps aggregate demand from ever falling short of aggregate supply: if it was assumed that there was a shift in consumer preference expressed in a fall in the marginal propensity to consume,[11] aggregate demand would be lower than initial aggregate supply. Owing to the excess supply in the goods market, the price level would fall. As a falling price level would lead to increased real balances, the Keynes effect would lead to higher investment demand and the Pigou effect to higher consumption demand until aggregate demand again equalled aggregate supply.

A positive demand shock would have exactly the opposite consequences: prices would rise, real balances fall and the Keynes and Pigou effects would lower investment and consumption until aggregate demand and aggregate supply were again in line. Positive or negative supply shocks would have the same consequences as negative or positive demand shocks and would be balanced just the same. Thus, in an economy like that described by the AS-AD model, without fixed wage contracts, or by basic New Classical models, there is no need or reason for active monetary policy in order to stabilise the economy.

Simply for the sake of completeness, it should be noted that a case for active fiscal stabilisation policy can be made in models which incorporate only the Keynes and not the Pigou effect, such as the basic AS-AD model described on p. 233. The two instances in which the money stock fails to balance aggregate supply and aggregate demand are usually denoted the *liquidity trap* and the *investment trap*. The liquidity trap is a case in which the nominal interest is so low that the opportunity costs of holding cash become negligible (Keynes 1936, p. 207). The individuals do not buy bonds but hold all additional real balances as cash. In this case, a falling price level does not lower interest rates and consequently does not influence investment, but increases only the individuals' real balances. The investment trap describes a situation in which confidence in future returns on investment is so low that even a falling interest rate does not induce the firms to invest more. In this case, a falling price level and increased real balances lead to falling interest rates but do not affect investment or aggregate demand. Since in the two cases described supply falls short of demand and prices consequently begin to fall, an increase in government consumption in order to stabilise the deflationary process makes sense.

Appendix A.3: The Role of Wage Policy

As stated above, in both the AS-AD model and the New Classical model, aggregate demand and aggregate supply balance easily when prices and wages are flexible.[12] Demand and supply of labour are balanced by changes in the real wage, which is determined in the labour market. In equilibrium, all observed unemployment is voluntary.

Long-term wage contracts

Long-term wage contracts, collective bargaining or minimum wages consequently enter in the model only as disturbing frictions. The famous Fischer (1977) formulation, which builds on a New Classical framework, is a good example: here-overlapping wage contracts which run for two periods while unforeseen supply and demand shocks appear every single period are the reason that real wages might be higher than labour market equilibrium would require. Unemployment consequently emerges in the wake of a negative shock. Long-term wage contracts in this model are directly responsible for unemployment.

For the AS-AD model, the case of fixed wages shows the same logic. As real wages are somehow too high (e.g. due to a long-running wage contract agreed upon before the emergence of some negative supply shocks), unemployment exists. If there were no long-term contracts, wages could adjust freely to the new equilibrium and unemployment would vanish.

Collective bargaining

Similarly, no economic case can be made for collective bargaining in the textbook approaches presented in this chapter. Real wages are determined on the labour market, and all collective wage contracts are only frictions which keep the economy from attaining equilibrium. As Burda and Wyplosz (1997, p. 150) put it:

> Collectively, through their unions, workers feel that they have more strength and accordingly aim at better outcomes. In particular, for a given amount of labour supplied, they ask for higher real wages: the union-driven collective labour supply curve lies above the individual labour supply curves ... Individuals would be willing to provide employment at a wage below the current wage. They cannot however, because the wage ... is set through negotiations between the firms and the trade union, and individuals cannot simply underbid their employed colleagues. Unemployment is involuntary for affected individuals.

It is thus assumed that unions deliberately accept unemployment in order to attain higher real wages for their members.[13] However, as unions represent individual workers, they cannot completely ignore unemployment. Since rising aggregate unemployment increases the employed workers' risk of being laid off, the union has to take into account these negative consequences.[14] A typical union can thus be thought of as having a utility function which is positively sloped in the real wage and negatively sloped in unemployment (Burda and Wyplosz 1997, pp. 147f).

The weights that unions attach to their members' real wage increases and to aggregate unemployment depend on the economy's wage bargaining structure. In the literature on wage bargaining structures and macroeconomic outcomes, it is often argued that a large union which covers most of the economy with some centralised wage bargaining will give more weight to unemployment. On the other hand, small and fragmented unions only representing a small group of workers put more weight on real wage increases than on aggregate unemployment. Thus, while a completely decentralized wage bargaining between individual workers and companies would be the best solution, a very centralized bargaining process with a high degree of union coverage could also provide reasonable results.

Minimum wages or welfare

Equally, no economic case for minimum wages or welfare can be made in the standard approach.[15] If minimum wages are legally set below the marginal productivity of the workers concerned (that is, if we assume heterogeneous labour, the least qualified workers), it does not have any effect at all. If, on the other hand, minimum wages are set above the workers' marginal productivity, real wages are above what would be necessary to attain equilibrium in the labour market, thus causing unemployment. The imposition of a minimum wage may in this model not only affect those at the bottom of the wage distribution to whom it directly applies, but also those further up the scale as higher-paid workers attempt to restore wage differentials (Bean 1994, p. 595). Consequently, minimum wages either have no effect or cause involuntary unemployment.

In contrast to minimum wages, welfare or unemployment benefits do not cause involuntary, but voluntary unemployment. As individuals are provided with an income for which they do not have to work, their reservation wage increases. If welfare or unemployment benefits are sufficiently high to push the reservation wage above equilibrium wage, some unemployed will decide to stay out of work instead of accepting a low-paid job (Barro and Grilli 1994, p. 266). Unemployment thus occurs.

Notes and References

1 Introduction: The Unsolved Unemployment–Inflation Puzzle

1. The standard reference is Samuelson and Solow (1960).
2. Throughout this book, *macroeconomic policy* means monetary policy as well as the fiscal policy stance, such as the share of government expenditure and taxes of GDP or deficit/surplus position of the government budget. Questions of inefficiencies due to details of a particular tax implemented are not considered to be macroeconomic policy questions.
3. For an in-depth criticism and discussion of the NAIRU concept, see Galbraith (1997), Staiger, Stock and Watson (1997) and the other contributions in the Winter 1997 issue of the *Journal of Economic Perspectives*.
4. Though not all agree on the way to achieve them. While Modigliani (1997) and Collignon (2002a) are in favour of lower central bank interest rates, Betz (2001b) argues that interest rates are solely a market result and thus cannot be directly influenced by the central bank, but only by improving the quality of the domestic currency by ensuring price stability.

2 Bargaining Structures and the Central Bank: Literature and Empirics

1. 'Corporatism' was gauged by an index in which different measures of institutional labour market and government features such as centralisation of union movements, shop floor autonomy, the involvement of work councils, etc. were added up, while the misery index is simply the sum of unemployment and inflation.
2. Schmidt (1996) even cites an example in which an alphabetical ordering has been wrongly taken as a rank order.
3. For references, see Calmfors (1993).
4. See, for example, Blanchard and Wolfers (2000).
5. Of course, in a world of perfect rationality, this argument would be invalid. However, as will be discussed in greater depth in Chapter 7, it is not necessarily useful to assume rational expectations when analysing the interaction of a central bank and wage bargainers.
6. See Figure 2.1. As Franzese (2001) does not focus on the underlying structure of the model, his survey is classified differently.
7. Iversen (1998a, 1999b) provide a similar model.
8. Skott (1997) derives a similar result using a Barro–Gordon setup and unions which only care for real wages and inflation, albeit not employment.
9. Note that in this setting the central bank does not care about EMU unemployment, but about unemployment in each EMU country.

240

10. More precisely, in the Soskice–Iversen (2000) setting, it is the unions who directly set the prices for the goods produced with their labour, while Coricelli, Cukierman and Dalmazzo (2000) use profit-maximising firms as intermediaries.
11. In Soskice–Iversen's (2000) terms.
12. In Coricelli, Cukierman and Dalmazzo's (2000) terms.
13. Following Cukierman and Lippi (1999), as well as the general tendency in central bank literature, 'conservativeness' is here equated with central bank independence.
14. Of course, it cannot be expected that a stylised model can explain all the developments observed in the real world. Economic models always work under the *ceteris paribus* condition. However, if a model systematically fails to capture one aspect of reality or works well for one group of countries but not for another, it is reasonable to research the reasons for these differences in performance.
15. For an in-depth criticism of the Barro–Gordon approach, see Spahn (1999).
16. For a recent survey on the deflation debate, see Svensson (2003).
17. For discussion, see Calmfors (2001, p. 334) or Franzese (2001, pp. 469f).
18. Of course, for the case of public pensions this is true only in countries where pensions are not indexed to the price or wage level.
19. Of course, one could add a simple quantity equation to explain how the central bank sets the rate of inflation by simply setting the money supply and thus influencing aggregate demand in a way that the desired price level is reached. When relying on this mechanism, however, the model works via the real balance effect for monetary policy transmission, an approach which I will call into question in Chapter 3.
20. Or, in Coricelli, Cukierman and Dalmazzo's (2000) terms a shift to a conservative central banker.
21. For the Netherlands, the hard phase of EMS began with the devaluation in 1979, after which the guilder followed the German mark's realignments. For the rest of EMS, the hard phase began in 1987.
22. In fact, as Iversen (1999a, p. 59) points out, the hard currency index might even exaggerate shifts in monetary policy, as Dornbusch (1976) had shown that in a monetarist model with rigid goods markets the exchange rate overshoots when monetary policy changes.
23. Austria had also pegged its currency to the German mark and followed the Bundesbank's monetary policy very closely. However, it was not part of EU or EMS at that time.
24. On 24 September 1979, the German mark appreciated 2 per cent *vis-à-vis* the other currencies. The guilder did not follow this revaluation.
25. For an overview of realignments in the EMS, see Collignon (1994, p. 252).
26. *'Unvermeidlicher' Preisanstieg.*
27. In fact, until shortly before the beginning of EMU, most other EMS countries had higher real interest rates than Germany.
28. The Irish punt was depreciated in 1986, but not realigned in 1987. The Irish punt was again depreciated by 10 per cent in 1993. However, this last realignment was not due to inflation having run out of bounds in Ireland, but rather to the sharp depreciation of the British pound which had dropped out of the EMS in 1992 and had eroded Irish competitiveness on its main export market.

29. The output gap is defined as the difference between potential and actual GDP as a percentage of potential GDP. Negative output gaps stand for actual output below potential GDP while positive output gaps show actual GDP in excess of potential GDP.
    For Figures 2.7, 2.8, 2.11 and 2.14, European Commission (1998) has been used instead of European Commission (2002) in order to permit Chapter 7's comparison with the USA, for which only European Commission (1998) provides data.
30. Admittedly, Ireland and the Netherlands have pushed down their relative unit labour costs far more than the other countries reviewed in this chapter. However, this does not change the basic notion that the other countries should at least have experienced *some* positive results from their falling unit labour costs. Instead, it seems that their unemployment problem even worsened with falling unit labour costs.
31. Of course, it is the unions and the employers who agree on wages.
32. The fall of unit labour costs in ECU as shown in Figure 2.9 in 1981 and 1982 is largely a result of two devaluations of the French franc within the EMS, by 3.0 and 5.75 per cent, respectively.
33. The lira was forced out of the EMS by speculative attacks on 17 september 1992.
34. In Figure 2.17, growth accounting is used. For details see the Appendix to this chapter.

3   The Real Balance Effect: Shortcomings

1. The term seems to have been coined by Patinkin (1948, p. 556). For the distinction between the Pigou and Keynes effect, see also Tobin (1980, pp. 5ff).
2. It should be noted that Keynesian models generally know some *investment trap*, when the mood among businesses is so bad that even falling interest rates cannot increase investment any longer. For details see the Appendix.
3. Of course, one could object that the microeconomic working of the effect is different in the interaction models than in the standard textbook models, as real money holdings enter directly into the utility function instead of changing only the budget constraint. However, as the macroeconomic chain of causation from falling prices to higher real money holdings and higher consumption demand remains the same, I think it is justified to treat it as equivalent to the standard Pigou effect. Moreover, all scepticism voiced in this chapter about the real balance effect applies equally to the effect in the interaction models.
4. This is the case in an extended AS-AD model in which consumption is a function of net wealth as well as in a New Classical model.
5. In this subsection, I completely abstract from credit money, which I will cover in the next section.
6. That is, fulfilling the standard functions of money: measure of value, medium of exchange and means of payment.
7. The foreign currency used differs from country to country, but is usually an internationally acknowledged reserve currency. Argentina, for example, has been using the US dollar, while Estonia and Bosnia are using the euro.

8. M3 in the ECB's definition consists of currency, deposits with agreed maturity up to two years, deposits redeemable at notice up to three months, money market shares, repurchase agreements, money market papers and debt securities up to two years. For the ECB's definition of monetary aggregates, see ECB (2000b, p. 23).

9. Of course, the financial sector has to provide adequate reserves and adequate capital in order to expand its balance sheet. While adequate capital is seldom a problem in sound and developed economies, the reserve requirements could pose a problem. I will discuss all problems related to the banks' reserve positions on p. 68.

10. The ECB regularly publishes such a consolidated balance sheet for the financial sector of the euro-zone in its *Monthly Bulletin.*

11. For the simplicity of the argument, I do not distinguish between maturities of deposits at this point. I will come to the differences in M2 and M3 later.

12. For the counterparts of monetary aggregates, see also ECB (1999a).

13. For a closed economy without gold, only the government's nominal debt is left as wealth being open to the Pigou effect (Tobin 1993, p. 59).

14. Interventions in the foreign exchange market or the sale of gold do not change the private sector's net wealth as only assets are swapped.

15. In fact, the ECB hardly buys any security on a definite base.

16. For the ECB's instruments see ECB (1998a) and Duwendag, *et al.* (1999, pp. 346ff).

17. See, for example, Bernanke (2002) or the elaboration on that topic in Svensson (2003).

18. Table 3.7 builds on the original state of the economy shown in Table 3.1.

19. However, as Tobin (1998, p. 266) notes, monetarist Ricardians assume precisely that an increase in government debt is neutral while an increase in the money stock at least has an influence on prices. (That is, a 'bond rain' is neutral while a 'money rain' affects economic variables.) While one can find this conclusion in a vast range of monetarist literature, I have not been able to find any piece of work in which a rationale is given for this assumption.

20. Of course, the government does have to pay interest to the central bank, but that interest is returned to the government at the end of a fiscal year as the central bank's profits go into the government's budget.

21. At first sight, one could blame me for having overlooked that the individual could invest her money in some real capital, earning its marginal product. However, this is not true. Only if the individual is to *hold* the additional money stock is it compatible with price stability. Currency held, however, does not yield any interest.

22. Of course, there would be additional effects of monetary policy. In order to increase the money stock, the stock of government bonds in the hands of the public would have to decrease. For individuals to be in their optimum, the interest rate would have to fall. However, as a fall of interest rates makes debtors richer while taking away the same amount of wealth from creditors, this does not have a net wealth effect and is not considered in this section.

23. Currency in circulation and deposits at the ECB.

24. For simplicity, it is assumed that the government finances consumption and not investment. If it financed investment, the government's assets

would also change. If it bought real assets from the private sector, net private wealth would not change even in a non-Ricardian world.

25. The so-called 'quantitative easing' which the Bank of Japan announced in early 2001 could be seen as one of the rare exceptions to this rule. But even in this case, the Bank of Japan is not financing a budget deficit without limits. Instead, it is buying government debt from the long end of the secondary market until a certain money stock and a certain rate of inflation are reached.

26. See Article 101, EU Treaty.

27. For a survey see Bernheim (1987).

28. For discussion of Ricardian equivalence, see Bernheim (1987), Barro (1989) or Tobin (1998, pp. 266ff).

29. That is, if the government does not begin a Ponzi game and start accumulating an ever-growing stock of debt. As this later scenario will ultimately lead either to a debt default or a monetisation of debt, thus making holders of government bonds *a lot* poorer, I will not consider this option further here.

30. Of course, if purchasing power parity (PPP) is assumed for the exchange rate, a fall in prices would automatically lead to an appreciation of the domestic currency, thus leaving the real value of assets denominated in foreign currency unchanged. However, with foreign assets denominated in the domestic currency, as is generally the case for the US, the exchange rate does not matter and the Pigou effect can work – at least as long as there is not a negative feedback via export demand.

31. 'Pure' in this context means the absence of credit. Thus, a system in which money is emitted only in exchange for a specific currency would also qualify as 'pure'.

32. I chose Estonia since the economy knows only a limited degree of dollarisation or euroisation. In addition, as one can observe from the relatively low premiums between interest rates in the Estonian money market and interest rates on the EMU money market, the Estonian currency board has a high degree of credibility. One can expect that there are not very large foreign currency holdings outside the banking system.

33. And therefore even Hall's (1978) argument that individuals live under uncertainty and therefore take the actual income as a proxy for the next period's income becomes meaningless. For all of the individuals it should be clear that a negative demand shock in this period cannot be a proxy for a similar additional shock next period.

34. Empirically, the marginal propensity to consume out of wealth is even lower, ranging between 0.03 and 0.05 (Bernheim 1987, p. 281).

35. A fall in GDP by 1 per cent would equal about €62 billion. For this to be offset, real balances would have to rise by the same amount – roughly one-third.

36. I try to avoid the word 'cause', as it implies a *causal* relationship from an increase in the stock of money to increased investment demand.

37. The US Fed compiles a monetary aggregate L which also includes short-term commercial papers and short-term treasury securities.

38. See for example Woll (1990, p. 469ff) or Mankiw (2000, pp. 541ff).

39. For the deduction of money multipliers, see Woll (1990, p. 469ff), or Moore (1991, pp. 71f), Marquis (1996, p. 133ff).

40. Newer textbooks such as Duwendag *et al.* (1999) or Marquis (1996) still teach the money multiplier, but at least they outline in length the problems connected with this approach.
41. As they are administered by monetary authorities.
42. On p. 73 I will argue that even the monetary base cannot be completely controlled by the central bank.
43. Of course, in an institutional arrangement such as that of the ECB, the monetary base itself cannot expand without the cooperation of the commercial banks as base money is lent to the banks only if they desire additional liquidity. I will treat this special problem on p. 73. However, if the central bank engages in large open market purchases as Svensson (2001) advises the Bank of Japan to do, the monetary base could eventually expand even if commercial banks did not wish to expand their balance sheets.
44. Of course, a legal interest rate ceiling on bank deposits is attributed to the MMMFs' success. Still, since bank deposits were subject to reserve requirements while MMMFs were not, they would have had a comparative advantage even without this ceiling.
45. It is thus ironic that the same economists who in the wake of Lucas' (1976) rational expectation revolution warned against attempts to exploit the Phillips-curve believed in the stability of the relationship between monetary aggregates and real variables.
46. 'The Bundesbank can neither directly restrict expansion of the money supply in any desired way simply by not satisfying commercial banks' overshooting demand for reserves, nor can it offset an insufficient demand for reserves by creating excess reserves of commercial banks. Thus it cannot guarantee that the growth of money supply never runs outside its set target. Instead, due to the complex nature of the process of money creation in which central bank, commercial banks and non-banks interact, the Bundesbank can only indirectly induce the money supply to reach its target by setting interest rates and other conditions for which it provides reserves' (author's translation).
47. Of course, a robust banking system has more benefits than just being an efficient channel for monetary policy. It also supplies non-financial firms with credit so that they can conduct real production and investment.
48. As Goodhart (1994) argues, the endogeneity of the monetary base is not only an institutional fact but also a necessity of a monetary economy with a central bank that provides the monetary base. Because of unpredictable fluctuation in the public's demand for cash, targeting the monetary base would lead to excessive fluctuation in short-term interest rates.

4 Monetary Policy Transmission in a World of Endogenous Money

1. See the overview on interest and profits in Panico (1987).
2. See Bernanke and Blinder (1992) or Sims (1992).
3. See, for example, Clarida, Gali and Gertler (1999), Romer (1999, 2000) and Svensson and Woodford (2000).

4. Of course, in reality, this mechanism is slightly more complicated: money is auctioned off in a tender procedure. In times of expectations of imminent interest rate cuts, this might lead to underbidding by commercial banks and rising money market interest rates. However, the short-term interest rate will not rise above the interest rate charged in the marginal lending facility.

5. See Marquis (1996) and Meulendyke (1998).

6. The expectations theory originated with Fisher (1930) and was further developed by Lutz (1940) and Hicks (1946). For an overview of theories of term structure of interest rates, see Shiller (1990) or Campbell (1995).

7. That is, the absence of systematic expectational errors or $E(E (i_{t-1, t}) - i_{t-1, t}) = 0$.

8. See Figure 4.1 for a graphical representation.

9. See, for example, Hardouvelis (1994) and references in that contribution.

10. See, for example, Kuttner's (2001) re-estimation of Cook and Hahn's (1989) results or Altig and Nosal's (2002) description of interest rate movements in 2001.

11. Though there might be some private information as to the state of the financial sector which the Fed or the ECB has but which is unknown to the financial markets.

12. The quality of the ECB forecasts cannot be tested yet, as the ECB did not publish its forecasts during the first two years of its existence.

13. Note that *affirmative policy actions* are usually anticipated while both *data-revealing policy actions* and *preference-revealing policy actions* come as a surprise to the market.

14. 'Marginal efficiency of capital' in Keynes (1936) or 'natural rate of interest' in Wicksell's (1922) terms.

15. See Tobin (1998, p. 150) who relates his q-theory of investment to Wicksell and Keynes.

16. In a dynamic setting, a q of 1 would mean that both capital stock and real output grew with the natural rate of growth ϕ_0. The investment function would thus become $I/K = \phi_0 + \phi (q)$. See Tobin (1982, p. 179).

17. See Tobin (1998, pp. 150f) and Tobin and Brainard (1977, p. 244) for details.

18. Keynes (1930) calls those profits Q' profits.

19. It should be noted, however, that fiscal policy might be working in situations in which monetary policy is impotent, such as a period of deflation when nominal interest rates have already reached the zero bound and cannot be lowered further, or in situations of high risk aversion in which even a strong cut in interest rates is not sufficient to stimulate investment demand.

20. This is much in line with Collignon's (2002b) claim that fiscal and monetary policy are substitutes in attaining a certain policy mix.

21. This description also bears interesting consequences for the analysis of the business cycle: in times of a boom, when aggregate demand from other components is strong, a higher real interest rate r^M is needed in order to restrict q to its equilibrium value $\bar{q}$. Similarly, in a recession, where all demand components are weak (and R thus low), a very low real interest rate is needed to stimulate investment. The mechanism described here might thus explain the observed procycliality of real interest rates.

22. This mechanism is also reflected in the spikes in the euro overnight index average (EONIA) interest rate at the end of the reserve requirement periods. At this time, commercial banks load up excessive reserves or try to acquire the reserves necessary to fulfil their requirements. See ECB (2001, p. 69f).

23. Bernanke and Gertler (1995) shows that the coverage ratio, the ratio of interest payments by US non-financial corporations to the sum of interest payments and profits, reacts with the US federal funds rate. Bofinger (2001, p. 92) shows a strong correlation between net interest payments and the money market rate in Germany.

24. The debate is known as the 'Cambridge/Cambridge' controversy: while the economists from Cambridge, Massachusetts assumed the existence of an aggregate capital stock which could be aggregated from individual firms' capital stock without too many methodological problems, the economists from Cambridge, UK insisted on the fact that capital prices changed with interest rates and that it was therefore not possible to aggregate capital to a macroeconomic capital stock. For an overview, see Kurz (1987).

25. Which would leave them with a large gross debt, but not a large net debt.

26. The classical savings hypothesis goes even further here: according to that assumption, capital owners do not consume any of their interest income while workers consume all of their income. The effect described here would then be even stronger.

27. This conclusion remains unaffected by the fact that the consumption boom in the USA during the late 1990s was basically sustained by rich households spending a larger share of their income than poor households. The rich households merely had more capital gains from stock holdings, which they consumed. See Maki and Palumbo (2001).

28. Individuals can use their income either as consumption or for bequests to their children. If one considers a chain of individuals from different generations as a single individual with an infinite horizon, as Barro (1974) does, there is an almost linear relationship between permanent income and actual consumption.

29. See Lucas (1988) for a model with deliberate investment in human capital or Romer (1990) for a model with explicit research and development.

30. See, for example, van Els *et al.* (2001).

31. It is assumed that the Marshall–Lerner condition holds. For an appreciation, the argument would be just the opposite.

32. At first sight, the USA seems to be an exception to the rule, as it was able to finance its current account deficit in the 1990s by transferring not bonds, but stocks with no explicit interest or repayment obligation attached. Moreover, as many of the technology stocks acquired by foreigners during that time lost a large share of their value, the US net debtor position now seems to be much lower than it would otherwise have been. The USA basically traded imported Mercedes Benzes for now worthless Worldcom shares.

At this point, given the current weakness in international financial markets, it cannot be expected that the USA will be able to continue financing its current account deficit with technology stocks. With the return of the twin deficits in the government budget and the current account in 2002, it can be expected that foreigners will now again acquire US bonds. The stock market boom in the late 1990s might have thus postponed a correction of the current account, but it did not put it off completely. For an assessment of the US trade deficit's sustainability, see Mann (1999).

33. This is also a result in standard portfolio models for open economies such as the Branson model. See, for example, Gärtner (1997, p. 166).
34. For the USA, the Fed fund target rate is considered, for the euro-zone the ECB's main refinancing rate.
35. For some stimulating ideas, see Shleifer (2000).
36. See Mojon, Smets, and Vermeulen (2001) for a study with the European Commission's BACH database. Chatelain *et al.* (2001) study the investment behaviour of firms in Germany, Spain, Italy and France. See also Chatelain and Tiomo (2001), Valderrama (2001), von Kalckreuth (2001) or the short summary in ECB (2004, p. 49ff).

5 Output and Prices in a World Without the Real Balance Effect

1. In fact, as EMU is only very young and the wage setting mechanism subject to endogenous change (Calmfors 2001), it is difficult to tell for sure how wage setting in EMU works and how it will develop. (See below.)
2. Chapter 4 explores how the central bank might influence the rate of interest relevant for investment decisions while Chapter 6 deals with the restrictions the central bank faces from financial markets.
3. In equilibrium, investment demand changes with the capital stock as more replacement investment is necessary. In disequilibrium, changes in the equilibrium capital stock lead to changes in net investment.
4. Blanchard and Fischer (1989, pp. 376ff) show how to derive this demand function from the consumers' maximisation decisions. See also Dixit and Stiglitz (1977) or Blanchard and Kiyotaki (1987).
5. Note that all firms are faced with the same elasticity of demand η.
6. Alternatively, this interest rate might represent the opportunity costs for not investing in some financial market asset.
7. Again, to make the system solvable, the rate of depreciation is assumed to be constant.
8. Details about the mathematics can be found in Appendix 1 to this chapter.
9. For computational details, see the Appendix to this chapter. This price level can be interpreted in the tradition of Keynes (1930), Riese (1986) or Collignon (1999, 2002a) as an interest rate-related mark-up over wage costs.
10. It should be added that this model abstracts from different kinds of labour or different qualifications among workers.
11. Note that the proceeds from one additional unit are less than the sales price: for a firm facing monopolistic competition, the supply of a unit of production drives down not only the marginal price it gets for its goods, but also the price for all other units produced.
12. As this model is a long-run equilibrium model, it does not distinguish between current and permanent income.
13. The basic results do not rely on the assumption that in this model all profits are saved and only part of the wage bill is consumed. One could easily solve the model for the classical saving hypothesis, thus setting c to 1. In this

case, the multipliers would just get a little larger. Similarly, it is straightforward to assume that profits are also to a certain extent consumed. As is shown in Appendix 5.1, the multiplier in this case becomes a bit more complicated, but output and employment are still not functions of the nominal wage level.

14. This model abstracts from steady-state growth and thus from autonomous investment.

15. The fact that firms do not invest at once so as to meet their desired capital stock can be explained either by technical factors limiting the amount of capital adjustment possible in one period or by adjustment costs. See Romer (1996, pp. 348ff).

16. In this model, it is assumed that one unit of investment embodies the same composition of the single firms' products as one unit of consumption.

17. Not being a function of current income.

18. Remember that $\eta > 1$.

19. This is much in line with the recent findings of Barth and Ramey (2001) who proclaim a cost channel of monetary policy transmission. It does not, however, yet explain the Sims (1992) effect: Sims had found that empirically, an interest rate hike even led to rising prices in the very short term which fall only thereafter. The mechanism explained in this section cannot explain this behaviour because it looks at the long-run equilibrium price level. However, the reaction Sims describes could be explained by the dynamics of the model on p. 130: if demand shows a certain inertia and only reacts with a delay while the firms' input costs react as one, it is plausible that an interest rate hike will lead to an increased price level before demand depresses prices again and pushes the disequilibrium price level down. This reaction is also in line with what Collignon (2002a, pp. 184f) predicts for an economy in which interest rates on credit contracts are changed every time market interest rates change (*a spot market economy*).

20. Details on the determination of the sign of the multipliers as well as proofs for the relationships stated here can be found in Appendix D 5.A.2 to this chapter.

21. This combination between α and η would mean that although the weight of labour in the production function is 0.7, an often-assumed value (Romer 1996, p. 22), labour would earn only roughly 65 per cent of the production.

22. I am well aware of all the methodological problems of the NAIRU concept as described in Galbraith (1997) and other contributions of the Winter 1997 issue of the *Journal of Economic Perspectives*, or which have more recently been voiced by Beyer and Farmer (2002). By using the NAIRU here, I do not want to adhere to this concept, but merely illustrate the different working mechanism between an idealistic atomistic labour market and a labour market with a large, strategically acting wage setter.

23. For computational details, see Appendix 5.2 to this chapter.

24. The proof can be found in Appendix 5.2 to this chapter.

25. The fact that overemployment also enters negatively into the utility function does not change its extrema but is also for convenience so that it is not necessary to define the function over two different ranges.

26. This simplification does not change the basic results. Even if the m firms' influence on the general price level is taken into account, wages in those

firms are set relative to wages in the rest of the economy W_{-m}. However, the resulting terms are much more complicated, so I have chosen the simplification.

27. See Appendix 5.2 for the precise condition and its deduction.

28. As surveyed by Oswald (1982).

29. This is not a problem of the special absolute term introduced in this chapter. Even if one follows standard practice and opts for a quadratic term, this term asymptotically approaches $\gamma_{m2} \, (\bar{N}_m)^2$ while the linear gain from increasing real wages keeps rising.

30. Remember that, for a small union, nominal wage increases translate into real wage increases.

31. See e.g. Bartsch, Hein and Truger (2002, p. 313).

32. The only variable which does not adjust at once is the capital stock, which can be changed only by investment and depreciation.

33. These models in fact focused on *wage* stickiness, but have been reinterpreted by some authors such as Romer (1996, pp. 256ff) and used as a parable for price stickiness.

34. See p. 34 for Hancké's (2002) argument on the role of the French economy, which is usually considered to be an economy without coordinated wage setting.

35. More precisely, the German union which settles on the pilot contract, which is then roughly followed by the rest of the economy. Usually, this used to be *IG Metall*. However, on recent occasions, *IG Chemie* has taken over wage leadership by settling before the metal workers.

36. Calmfors (2001, pp. 340f) claims that the current wage bargaining setup represents only a *transitional phase* (for the next ten-fifteen years) and will then break down. However, he is also only able to speculate about what will be the setup after that time.

37. There are three often-cited periods when the Bundesbank actually tightened monetary policy: the 1974 wage increases after widespread strikes in the public sector (Hall and Franzese 1998), the second oil shock after 1979, and inflationary wage increases after German reunification in the early 1990s. Cukierman, Rodriguez and Webb (1998) also find econometrically that German wage developments had a significant influence on German monetary policy: the Bundesbank usually tightened monetary policy when wage developments were inflationary.

38. The EU Treaty says in Article 105: 'The primary objective of the ESCB shall be to maintain price stability. Without prejudice to the objective of price stability, the ESCB shall support the general economic policies in the Community with a view to contributing to the achievement of the objectives of the Community as laid down in Article 2.' Article 2 formulates as objectives 'a harmonious, balanced and sustainable development of economic activities' and 'a high level of employment'. However, in personal interviews, ECB officials have continuously claimed that this article is to be interpreted as saying that the ECB will promote growth *by* achieving price stability, not promote growth by lowering interest rates when price stability is achieved.

39. Viewing this price level equation within the tradition of Keynes (1930) or Riese (1986) and Collignon (1997), the difference between the disequilibrium

price level (5.60) and the equilibrium price level (5.13) can be interpreted as extra profits or Q' profits. As Collignon has shown, this can also be transformed as an economy-wide Tobin's q of larger than 1.

40. For drawing Figure 5.5, it was assumed that in each period 40 per cent of the remaining shock disappears.

41. Note that contrary to Blanchard and Quah's (1989) approach, both transitory and permanent shocks in this model are *demand* shocks. A transitory demand shock is a shock which can be expected to reverse itself – e.g. increased demand for furniture after flooding. A permanent demand shock cannot be expected to reverse itself. A shift in taste from domestic to foreign goods could be such a shock.

42. This mechanism is basically the same as in Collignon (1999, 2002a), who describes this dynamic process within the framework of Tobin's q theory. Collignon's qs above $\bar{q}$ are the temporary price increases of this chapter. Just as the economy's capital stock increases in Collignon's formulation due to the macroeconomic investment function he formulates, the capital stock in this chapter increases as the single profit-maximising firm reacts to the changes in capital costs.

43. Further parameters are assumed to draw figure 5.6: $\eta = 10$, $\chi = 0.7$, $\delta = 0, 1$, $\alpha = 0.7$ $i^K = 0.05$, $\Delta i^K = 0.01$.

6 The Central Bank: Restrictions in a World of Endogenous Money

1. This is a conclusion completely different from the conclusions in Betz (1993 2001a, 2001b), in which Betz claims that all a central bank can do is execute the financial market's single equilibrium interest rate.

2. Keynes' idea of a central bank as market participant was originally revived by Riese (1986).

3. For discussion of different strands of Post-Keynesianism, see Hewitson (1995).

4. However, in line with Spahn (1993), this assumes high confidence in the banking system's stability.

5. Hoarding of cash is thus not a problem in a world of endogenous inside money. Consequently, stamped money as once envisioned by Gesell (1946) and favourably reviewed by Keynes (1936, pp. 256ff) would be senseless or even counterproductive.

6. Note that Tobin speaks of actual currency while in this chapter all monetary assets are put together into the monetary aggregate M.

7. See also Tobin (1998).

8. Figure 6.1 is a variation of Tobin's (1998, p. 117) Figure 5.6.

9. For a good, concise introduction into portfolio theory and the $\mu - \sigma$-diagram, see Tobin (1998, Chapter 4).

10. Note that even risk averse individuals can end up at point L, where they are credit-constrained if their indifference curve is sufficiently flat.

11. Alternatively, the same can be shown for the assumption of the individual having a quadratic utility function, which unfortunately is not a very plausible assumption as it assumes increasing absolute risk aversion. For proofs of both propositions, see Kruschwitz (1995, pp. 144ff).

However, even if in reality neither returns follow a normal distribution nor do individuals have quadratic utility functions, the mean–variance approach might deliver a good picture of reality, as many investors use a μ – σ-rule (Tobin 1998, p. 71).

12. For computational details, see Appendix 6.1 to this chapter.
13. See Appendix 6.1 for exact values of Φs and computational details.
14. Proofs are in Appendix 6.1.
    The assumption of positive correlation coefficients ρ does not pose any empirical problems: empirically, returns on stocks, bonds and foreign assets are strongly correlated. For Germany, Lapp (2002) estimates correlation between the return on domestic stocks and non-euro-land stocks to be 0.4, the correlation between returns on domestic bonds and foreign non-euro-land bonds to be 0.77 (both measured in DM terms, so taking exchange rate variations into account).
15. As the correlation coefficient cannot be larger than 1, the sum of two covariances of two variables cannot be larger than the sum of their variances.
16. Remember that cov $[r_M, r_M]$ = var $[r_M]$ by definition.
17. Remember that Φ_{den} is also assumed to be negative.
18. 'Direct' here denotes the fact that the demand for the asset is not financed by credit.
19. In fact, this model abstracts from government debt altogether. Adding government bonds either as a distinct additional asset class or as additional credit demand in (6.23) would only complicate the analysis without giving additional insights.
20. *Inside money* refers to money which is not net wealth to the private sector, while *endogenous* refers to the way the money supply is determined.
21. The discussion on p. 172 deals with the dynamics of F via inflows of foreign assets when the current account changes after a change in the exchange rate.
22. This implies the assumption of constant depreciation or appreciation expectations, or – in different terms – of autoregressive iso-elastic exchange rate expectations.
23. In this model, it is implicitly assumed that individuals do not hold real productive capital without either renting it out or using it for their own productive purposes. This is in stark contrast to Betz's (2001b) assumption of productive capital being only alternatively used *either* as store of value *or* as input into the production process.
24. Thus, the conclusion in Tobin (1965) turns diametrically around in a world of endogenous money: Tobin (1965) had argued that, macroeconomically, savings could be held either in real capital or in (outside) money. Given an exogenous share of savings, the economy's capital stock is thus even larger the smaller the share of money in the individual's portfolio (the *Tobin effect* – see also Orphanides and Solow 1990). In a world of endogenous money, this proposition does not hold. Here, it is money which finances (part of) the capital stock.
25. Such an assumption would be plausible if wealth owners perceived the interest rate change as a one-time event not to be repeated in the future.
26. Again, computational details can be found in Appendix 6.2 to this chapter.

27. This is much in line with the mechanism described in Keynes' Treatise (Keynes 1930).
28. The curves' slopes and the directions in which a curve shifts when parameters change are mathematically explained in Appendix 6.2 to this chapter.
29. *More permanently* means until accumulation of foreign assets forces the exchange rate to return to its original level, which might take a very long time as I argue on p. 172.
30. Note that this formula shows a Laspeyres-price index, which means that the initial shares of each good in the index do not change when relative prices change. When taking into account that consumption patterns alter with changed relative prices, the correct price level (with the actual weights in consumption) would be as derived from a model of monopolistic competition in which the individuals choose their consumption pattern given a CES-utility function (see (5.3), p. 99): $P^{Cons} = (P^{dom})^{1-\alpha_{im}} (eP^{foreign})^{\alpha_{im}}$
   However, since this later index implies a drop in the utility level when one of the goods' prices increases, and since it tends to understate price changes, the Laspeyeres-index seems to be more appropriate for the single investor's perception of price changes.
31. If this condition is violated, the conclusions from this model approach those of Betz (1993, 2001b). Then, the central bank has no degree of freedom to change the interest rate, but can execute only a single equilibrium interest rate.
32. See, for example, Okun (1971) or Taylor (1981).
33. These extra profits can be seen in Tobin's q above $\bar{q}$ or in Keynes' (1930) Q profits.
34. Note that validity of the Marshall–Lerner condition is assumed.
35. This paragraph's analysis is only verbal as the portfolio model presented in this chapter assumes a positive stock of foreign assets.
36. This could also be demonstrated in the model presented in Section 6.2. In the perceptions of investors who care about real consumption, a higher correlation between consumer prices and the exchange rate also means a lower variance on the real return of foreign assets var $[r_F]$ and a higher variance on the real return of domestic monetary assets var $[r_M]$.
37. As we know from Section 6.2, a decrease in one assets' variance of returns leads to an increase in its share in the individual portfolio. See also Schelkle (2001, pp. 185ff).
38. The contributions report the home bias only for single euro countries. However, since a part of the foreign equity holdings in those statistics was invested in other euro countries prior to EMU, the home bias in the euro-area can even be expected to be larger (as a French stock held by a German investor has now to be considered a 'home' investment).
39. Tobin's q or Keynes' Q profits.
40. See Gärtner (1997, pp. 157 ff) who uses this approach in a standard Branson (1979) model.
41. This assumption would imply that rentiers own a larger part of net wealth than entrepreneurs do and thus the reaction of the demand for monetary assets to an increase in aggregate wealth is larger than the reaction of aggregate credit demand to an increase in aggregate wealth. This is a plausible assumption.
42. Again, we assume that $A_V^M > Cr_V$ and $A_V^K + Cr_V < 1$.

7   Optimal Policy Pact Mix and Logic of a Social Part

1. Of course, there might be other ways to increase aggregate demand such as changes in fiscal policy. However, they are not covered in this book.
2. Note that 'price stability' does not necessarily mean zero per cent inflation, but rather low and stable rates of inflation which keep the consumption purchasing power from eroding.
3. See expositions in Chapter 2 and p. 27.
4. In fact, the time span since the beginning of EMU is too short to tell for sure how wage bargaining in single euro-zone countries relates to wage contracts in other euro-zone countries. Up until 2002, however, the empirical facts do not seem to prove the Soskice–Hancké-hypothesis wrong.
5. For coordinating monetary policy and wage bargaining targeting consumer price inflation is problematic, since consumer prices include prices for imported goods such as oil which are not only outside the central bank's, unions' and employers' influence, but also highly volatile. Until a change in the ECB's targeted measure of inflation to a more adequate core inflation target (Dullien 2002), economic agents in EMU will have to deal with this target. As it is illusory that wage increases or (in the case of a strong increase in oil prices) decreases can compensate for large and sudden swings in energy prices, the best wage bargainers can do is to base their contracts on long-run trends, thereby ignoring changes in exogenous energy prices altogether and accepting the negative consequences of the central bank's sub-optimal target.
6. ν_0 and ν_1 stand for the more complicated terms $[l_0 - \rho[1 - \alpha]/\alpha + [\rho (1 - \alpha) + \rho_{-1}](1 - \alpha)I]/[1 + (1 - \alpha)^2 I]$ and $[1 - \alpha(1 - \alpha) I]/[1 + (1 - \alpha)^2 I]$ As l_0, ρ, α and I are constants, ν_0, ν_1 are also constant.
7. This type of diagram has already been introduced in Chapter 2.
8. Note that the US target rate of inflation was assumed to be at 3.5 per cent while the rates for both Germany and EU-11 were assumed to be the Bundesbank's target rate of 2 per cent.
9. To be fair, one has to note that the ECB did not yet have much experience in how wage setters would react. Moreover, headlines about high double-digit wage increases in some widely watched cases, such as the Lufthansa's pilots' or Spanish bus drivers' wage bargains, might have caused panic in Frankfurt that a wage–price spiral might be set into motion.
10. 'Stable' here denoting growing at a low pace, as explained in Section 7.1.
11. As shown in Chapter 5, in the model presented in this book, real wages do not depend on nominal wages, but rather on labour productivity and the degree of monopolisation in the economy.
12. Collignon (2001) uses a different terminology: for what this book terms *coordination failure* he calls *strong coordination failure*. What is denoted here as *cooperation failure* he terms *weak coordination failure*.
13. The term 'stability-oriented' is used here to distinguish this kind of wage restraint from a wage restraint that leads to falling unit labour costs and thus produces deflationary tendencies.
14. Though, of course, in the model presented in this book, aggressive nominal wage increases do not change the distributional position in equilibrium.
15. This pattern of payoffs requires a public which assigns responsibility for growth to the central bank. I am not saying that this payoff pattern (also

used in Figure 7.4) is the most likely for EMU, but it is required to show the possibility of coordination failure.

16. The ECB has more recently restricted the interest rate decision to the first meeting in a month.

17. Heise (1999) proposes a different argument for why the central bank moves after the unions' move: as the monetary authority wants to prevent the slightest doubts about its independence, it will move after the other actors.

18. In game theory, complete information implies that both players know the other player's payoffs.

19. Characteristics are from Blanchard and Fischer (1989, pp. 214 ff). For a similar critique of rational expectations as presented here, see Horn (2001).

20. In fact, the central results of this book are an illustration of the fact that different views of basic macroeconomic mechanisms lead to very different policy conclusions.

21. One-month-money has been chosen because one-week-money does not always show the impact of a rate cut or increase due to the date of tender operations of the central bank's refinancing facility. Of course, the spread of one-month-money over the target rate is not a one-to-one indicator for market expectations. A risk premium might apply since in general two meetings of the ECB council fall into that period. However, the magnitude and direction of the spread still give valuable information: a negative spread shows that markets are expecting a rate cut. A spread of over 50 basis points indicates that markets are counting on moves that add up to at least 50 basis points over the next month.

22. For the US, the difference between the Fed funds target rate and one-month commercial papers from financial institutions is considered.

23. In an ECB Working Paper, Perez-Quiros and Sicilia (2002) claim that the difference in predictability between the US Fed and the ECB is insignificant and much smaller than generally perceived. However, their figures show that while cuts are pretty well anticipated for both central banks, market participants were wrong roughly 60 per cent of the times they expected an ECB rate change, while markets never anticipated a Fed rate change which did not materialise (Perez-Quiros and Sicilia 2002, p. 38).

24. Of course, this is true only if the union is not too risk averse and does not have too high a discount rate.

25. Even financial papers such as the *Financial Times Deutschland* and the German paper *Handelsblatt* regularly interpret the same statement of the ECB in different ways.

26. Note that in order to get the payoffs in Figure 7.7, the payoffs for wage restraint/no wage-restraint and for expansionary/restrictive monetary policy need to be added. Thus, the unions' payoff in the situation of wage restraint (–1) and expansionary monetary policy (5) is 4.

27. Rogoff (1985) labels a central banker 'conservative' if she puts a larger weight on price stability than the society as a whole. Ideally, a central banker in Rogoff's model should not put any weight on output stabilisation.

28. If the game were be repeated only n times, both players would have the incentive to betray each other in the last period. As both players know this outcome for the last game, they do not cooperate in the $n - 1$th game either (Myerson 1991). This argument can be extended backwards until the first

game in which there were no cooperation. Thus, from theoretical consider-ations, one could conclude that there would be no cooperation at all in a finite chain of repeated prisoner's dilemmas. However, in real-world experi-ments it is often observed that cooperation does take place by the end phase of the game (Rasmusen 1994); for references, see Axelrod (1981).

29. Upon closer examination, this is slightly oversimplified. In situations in which there is a different probability for wrongly taking cooperation for non-cooperation than for wrongly taking non-cooperation for cooperation (α- and β-errors), the share of retaliation periods will be different from 0.5. However, this qualification does not change the basic result that tit-for-tat action risks significant welfare losses.

30. One example of such a mistake could be the central banker's reaction to a falling oil price. Since with falling energy prices the consumer price inflation falls, the central bank might lower interest rates, which the unions could interpret as a move towards a new cooperation.

31. Von Hagen and Brückner (2001) find that a Taylor rule with particular weight for the economic developments in Germany and France, as the EMU's core economies, as well as an interest-smoothing component aptly explains the ECB's monetary policy.

32. The first two pillars are the coordinated employment strategy (the Luxembourg process) and economic reform regarding the functioning of markets for goods, services and capital (the Cardiff process).

33. Collignon (2001) sees the pact as an instrument of consensus-building which would help the actors coordinate their actions.

34. Such a change would be equivalent to lowering the probability of a player wrongly taking the other's move as non-cooperative and increasing at the same time the probability of a player wrongly taking a retaliatory non-coop-eration by the other player as a cooperative move.

35. Such a behaviour would only be rational, as the defecting (and successfully lying) player reaps the benefits from one-sided non-cooperation in one round without having to bear the costs of being retaliated against.

36. The Appendix gives a short overview of the relevance and consequences of centrally bargained wage agreements in standard neo-classical theory.

37. Heise (2002) cites an occasion on which the meeting of the political level almost did not take place, as the presiding member did not want to spend time on it.

Appendix: Monetary and Wage Policy in Standard Models

1. This remark is not true for some very recent models (Clarida, Gali and Gertler 1999; Romer 1999, 2000) in which the focus lies on the short-term interest rate as a monetary policy instrument – an approach which is in line with what this book presents.

2. This, of course, is not true for those RBC models, such as King and Plosser (1984), which know money only as a passive variable not influenced by monetary policy.

3. It is unclear why this is the case as Keynes himself stresses that the money value of the wealth-owning class's wealth is one of the major forces influencing consumption (Keynes 1936, pp. 92f).

4. However, the Pigou effect is modelled in some extensions of IS-LM, such as Blinder and Solow (1973).
5. See Mayer (1975).
6. Quite a few New Classical formulations do not explicitly explain whether changes in the money supply lead to changes in investment demand or consumption demand. They state only that aggregate demand is a function of real money supply. See, for example, Sargent and Wallace (1976, p. 170) or Felderer and Homburg (1994, p. 271ff). Blanchard and Fischer (1989, p. 518) justify such a short cut with the Clower Constraint and an assumed constant velocity of money circulation. However, with this argument, the transmission of monetary policy becomes a 'black box', as neither the stability of the velocity of money circulation nor the Clower Constraint is deduced from the economic agents' decision.
7. Alternatively, one could interpret the exogenous increase in the money supply as an open market operation by which bonds are directly bought from individuals. In this case, the interest rate falls directly and the process described in this paragraph is skipped. However, the mechanism of an exogenous increased money supply increasing investment remains the same.
8. Hence the term *Pigou effect*, which seems to have been coined by Patinkin (1948, p. 556). Patinkin himself relies heavily on this effect, which he himself later refers to as *real balance effect* (Patinkin 1965, p. 19).
9. I am well aware that in this section, I am using the same variable names for log notation that I used before and will use later for regular notation. I decided that keeping the original model recognisable for the reader was more important than being 100% consistent in my own variable notation.
10. However, it is possible that individuals decide not to work because they have misinterpreted the price signals. In this case, they would have been better off had they worked.
11. Alternatively, one could think of any other negative demand-side shock such as a sudden fall in investment, exports or a cut in government consumption.
12. And, of course, given that the economy is neither in a liquidity trap nor in an investment trap.
13. This approach is commonly known as *Insider–Outsider model*. See Blanchard and Fischer (1989, pp. 438ff); Romer (1996, pp. 465ff).
14. At least if we explain the union's decision making process with some kind of economic reasoning, such as a median union member and not with some ad hoc assumption.

   Franz (1999, p. 302) argues that the Insider–Outsider approach is better suited to explain persistence in unemployment in the wake of a shock than unemployment itself, since otherwise one would have to explain why the insiders accept that some of them will be laid off.
15. Of course, other considerations such as social equity or protection can be brought forward (Burda and Wyplosz 1997, p. 151).

Bibliography

Akerlof, G. A. and J. L. Yellen (1985) 'A Near-Rational Model of the Business Cycle, with Wage and Price Inertia', *Quarterly Journal of Economics*, 100 (Supplement), 823–38.

Altig, D. E. and E. Nosal (2002) 'Why Haven't Long-Term Interest Rates Fallen?', *Federal Reserve Bank of Cleveland Economic Commentary*, March.

Angeloni, I., A. Kashyap, B. Mojon and D. Terlizzese (2002) 'Monetary Transmission in the Euro Area: Where Do We Stand?', ECB Working Paper, 114.

Axelrod, R. (1981) 'The Emergence of Cooperation Among Egoists', *American Political Science Review*, 75, 306–18.

Barran, F., V. Coudert and B. Mojon (1997) 'The Transmission of Monetary Policy in the European Countries', in S. Collignon (ed.), *European Monetary Policy*, London: Pinter, 81–111.

Barro, R. J. (1974) 'Are Government Bonds Net Wealth?', *Journal of Political Economy*, 82, 1095–117.

———— (1989) 'The Ricardian Approach to Budget Deficits', *Journal of Economic Perspectives*, 3, 37–54; reprinted in Snowdon and Vane (1997).

Barro, R. J. and D. B. Gordon (1983) 'Rules, Discretion and Reputation in a Model of Monetary Policy', *Journal of Monetary Economics*, 12, 101–21.

Barro, R. J. and V. Grilli (1994) *European Macroeconomics*, London: Macmillan.

Barth, M. J. and V. A. Ramey (2001) 'The Cost Channel of Monetary Transmission', *NBER Macroeconomic Annual*, 16, 199–239.

Bartsch, K., E. Hein and A. Truger (2002) 'Zur Interdependenz von Geld- und Lohnpolitik: Makroökonometrische Ex-Post und Ex-Ante Simulationen verschiedener Szenarien für die Bundesrepublik Deutschland', in A. Heise (ed.), *Neues Geld – Alte Geldpolitik. Die EZB im Makroökonomischen Interaktionsraum*, Marburg: Metropolis, 303–46.

Bean, C. R. (1994) 'European Unemployment: A Survey', *Journal of Economic Literature*, 32, 573–619.

Becker, G. S. (1993) *Human Capital. A Theoretical and Empirical Analysis with Special Reference to Education*, Chicago: University of Chicago Press; 1st edn (1963).

Bernanke, B. S. (2002) 'Deflation: Making Sure "It" Doesn't Happen Here', Speech on 21 November 2002, Federal Reserve Board.

Bernanke, B. S. and A. S. Blinder (1988) 'Credit, Money, and Aggregate Demand', *American Economic Review*, 78, 435–9.

———— (1992) 'The Federal Funds Rate and the Channels of Monetary Transmission', *American Economic Review*, 82, 901–21.

Bernanke, B. S. and M. Gertler (1995) 'Inside the Black Box: The Credit Channel of Monetary Policy Transmission', *Journal of Economic Perspectives*, 9(4), 27–48.

Bernanke, B. S., T. Laubach, F. S. Mishkin and A. S. Posen (1999) *Inflation Targeting. Lessons from the International Experience*, Princeton and Oxford: Princeton University Press.

Bernanke, B. S. and I. Mihov (1997) 'What Does the Bundesbank Target?', *European Economic Review*, 41, 1025–53.

Bernheim, B. D. (1987) 'Ricardian Equivalence: An Evaluation of Theory and Evidence', *NBER Macroeconomics Annual*, 2, 263–304.

Bernheim, B. D., A. Shleifer and L. H. Summers (1985) 'The Strategic Bequest Motive', *Journal of Political Economy*, 93, 1045–76.

Betz, K. (1993) *Ein monetärkeynesianisches makroökonomisches Gleichgewicht*, Marburg: Metropolis.

———— (2001a) 'Endogenous Money, Liquidity Preference, and the Theory of Interest', Diskussionsbeiträge des Fachbereichs Wirtschaftswissenschaft der FU Berlin, 2001/16.

———— (2001b) *Jenseits der Konjunkturpolitik. Überlegungen zur langfristigen Wirtschaftspolitik in einer Geldwirtschaft*, Marburg: Metropolis.

Beyer, A. and R. E. A. Farmer (2002) 'Natural Rate Doubts', ECB Working Paper, 121.

Blanchard, O. and F. Giavazzi (2003) 'The Macroeconomic Effects of Regulation and Deregulation in Goods and Labor Markets', *Quarterly Journal of Economics*, 118, 878–909.

Blanchard, O. J. and S. Fischer (1989) *Lectures on Macroeconomics*, Cambridge, MA: MIT Press.

Blanchard, O. J. and N. Kiyotaki (1987) 'Monopolistic Competition and the Effects of Aggregate Demand', *American Economic Review*, 77, 648–66.

Blanchard, O. J. and D. Quah (1989) 'The Dynamic Effects of Aggregate Demand and Supply Disturbances', *American Economic Review*, 79, 655–73.

Blanchard, O. J. and L. Summers (1987) 'Hysteresis in Unemployment', *European Economic Review*, 31, 288–95.

Blanchard, O.J. and J. Wolfers (2000) 'The Role of Shocks and Institutions in the Rise of European Unemployment: The Aggregate Evidence', *Economic Journal*, 110, C1–C33.

Blinder, A. S. (1997) 'Distinguished Lecture on Economics in Government: What Central Bankers Could Learn from Academics – And Vice Versa', *Journal of Economic Perspectives*, 11(2), 3–19.

Blinder, A. S., E. R. D. Canetti, D. E. Lebow and J. B. Rudd (1998) *Asking About Prices. A New Approach to Understanding Price Stickiness*, New York: Russell Sage Foundation.

Blinder, A. S. and R. M. Solow (1973) 'Does Fiscal Policy Matter?', *Journal Public Economics*, 2, 319–37.

Bofinger, P. (2001) *Monetary Policy. Goals, Institutions, Strategies and Instruments*, Oxford: Oxford University Press.

Branson, W. H. (1979) 'Exchange Rate Dynamics and Monetary Policy', in A. Lindbeck (ed.), *Inflation and Unemployment in Open Economies*, Amsterdam: North-Holland, 189–224.

Bruno, M. and J. D. Sachs (1985) *Economics of Worldwide Stagflation*, Cambridge MA: Harvard Univeristy Press.

Buiter, W. H. and J. Tobin (1981) 'Debt Neutrality: A Brief Review of Doctrine and Evidence', in G. M. V. Furstenberg (ed.), *Social Security versus Private Saving*, Cambridge, MA: Ballinger.

Bundesbank (1974) *Annual Report*, Frankfurt.

———— (1995) *Die Geldpolitik der Bundesbank*, Frankfurt.

———— (1998) Fünfzig Jahre Dectsche Mark. Monetäre Statistiken 1948–1998, München: C. H. Beck.

Burda, M. and C. Wyplosz (1997) *Macroeconomics: A European Text*, Oxford: Oxford University Press.

Calmfors, L. (1993) 'Centralisation of Wage Bargaining and Macroeconomic Performance – A Survey', *OECD Economic Studies*, 21, 161–91.

———— (1998) 'Macroeconomic Policy, Wage Setting, and Employment – What Difference Does the EMU Make?', *Oxford Review of Economic Policy*, 14, 125–51.

———— (2001) 'Wages and Wage-Bargaining Institutions in the EMU – A Survey of the Issues', *Empirica*, 28, 325–51.

Calmfors, L. and J. Driffill (1988) 'Bargaining Structure, Corporatism and Macroeconomic Performance', *Economic Policy*, 6, 13–61.

Campbell, J. Y. (1995) 'Some Lessons from the Yield Curve', *Journal of Economic Perspectives*, 9, 129–52.

Campbell, J. Y. and N. G. Mankiw (1989) 'Consumption, Income, and Interest Rates: Reinterpreting the Time Series Evidence', *NBER Macroeconomics Annual*, 4, 185–216.

Campbell, J. Y. and R. J. Shiller (1987) 'Cointegration and Tests of Present Value Models', *Journal of Political Economy*, 95, 1062–88.

Chatelain, J. B., A. Generale, I. Hernando and U. von Kalckreuth (2001) 'Firm Investment and Monetary Transmission in the Euro Area', ECB Working Paper, 112.

Chatelain, J.-B. and A. Tiomo (2001) 'Investment, the Cost of Capital, and Monetary Policy', ECB Working Paper, 106.

Chiang, A. C. (1984) *Fundamental Methods of Mathematical Economics*, Singapore: McGraw-Hill.

Clarida, R., J. Gali, and M. Gertler (1999) 'The Science of Monetary Policy: A New Keynesian Perspective', *Journal of Economic Literature*, 37, 1661–707.

Collignon, S. (1994) *Das europäische Währungssystem im Übergang: Er fahrungen mit dem EWS und politische Optionen*, Wiesbaden: Gabler.

———— (1997) 'Unemployment and Monetary Policy in the Single Market: A Dialogue with Franco Modigliani', in S. Collignon (ed.), *European Monetary Policy*, London and Washington, D C: Pinter, 271–89.

———— (1998) 'A Fall-Back Position for Italy', in *The Sustainability Report*, Paris: Association for the Monetary Union of Europe, 121–4.

———— (1999) 'Unemployment, Wage Developments and the Economic Policy Mix in Europe', *Empirica*, 26, 259–69.

———— (2001) 'Economic Policy Coordination in EMU: Institutional and Political Requirements', Paper presented at the Center for European Studies, Harvard University.

———— (2002a) *Monetary Stability in Europe*, London: Routledge.

———— (2002b) 'Reflections on Europe's Constitution', London: mimeo.

Cook, T. and T. Hahn (1989) 'The Effects of Changes in the Federal Funds Rate Target on Market Interest Rates in the 1970s', *Journal of Monetary Economics*, 24, 331–51.

Coricelli, F., A. Cukierman and A. Dalmazzo (2000) 'Monetary Institutions, Monopolistic Competition, Unionized Labor Markets and Economic Performance', CEPR Discussion Paper, 2745.

Cukierman, A. (1992) *Central Bank Strategy, Credibility, and Independence*, Cambridge, MA: MIT Press.

Cukierman, A. and F. Lippi (1999) 'Central Bank Independence, Centralization of Wage Bargaining, Inflation and Unemployment: Theory and Some Evidence', *European Economic Review*, 43, 1395–1434.

Cukierman, A., P. Rodriguez and S. B. Webb (1998) 'Central Bank Autonomy and Exchange Rate Regimes – Their Effects on Monetary Accommodation and Activism', in S. Eijffinger and H. Huizinga (eds.), *Positive Political Economy: Theory and Evidence*, Cambridge: Cambridge University Press.

Diamond, P. A. (1965) 'National Debt in a Neoclassical Growth Model', *American Economic Review*, 55, 1126–50.

Dixit, A. K. and B. J. Nalebuff (1997) *Spieltheorie für Einsteiger. Strategisches Know-How für Gewinner*, Stuttgart: Schäffer-Poeschel.

Dixit, A. K. and J. E. Stiglitz (1977) 'Monopolistic Competition and Optimum Product Diversity', *American Economic Review*, 67, 297–308.

Dornbusch, R. (1976) 'Expectations and Exchange Rate Dynamics', *Journal of Political Economy*, 84, 1167–76.

Dullien, S. (2002) 'The Macroeconomics of a Rising Oil Price: How EMU Governments, Wage Bargainers and the ECB Should Behave', in H.-E. Scharrer and R. Caesar (eds.), *European Economic and Monetary Union: An Initial Assessment*, Baden-Baden: Nomos, 271–96.

Duwendag, D., K.-H. Ketterer, W. Kösters, R. Pohl and D. B. Simmert (1999) *Geldtheorie und Geldpolitik in Europa: Eine Problemorientierte Einführung*, Berlin: Springer.

ECB (1998a) *Monetary Policy in Stage Three. General Documentation on ESCB Monetary Policy Instruments and Procedures*, Frankfurt.

———— (1998b) 'A Stability-Oriented Monetary Policy Strategy for the ESCB', ECB Press Release, 13 October.

———— (1999a) 'The Balance Sheets of the Monetary Financial Institutions of the Euro Area in Early 1999', *Monthly Bulletin*, 55–69.

———— (1999b) 'Die stabilitätsorientierte geldpolitische Strategie des Eurosystems', *Monatsbericht*, pp. 43–56.

———— (2000a) 'Monetary Policy Transmission in the Euro Zone', *Monthly Bulletin*, July, 43–58.

———— (2000b) *Statistical Information Collected and Compiled by the ESCB*, Frankfurt.

———— (2001) *The Monetary Policy of the ECB*, Frankfurt.

———— (2004) *The Monetary Policy of the ECB*, 2nd edn, Frankfurt.

Eichengreen, B. and F. Ghironi (1996) 'European Monetary Unification and International Monetary Cooperation', Working Paper, University of California, Berkeley.

Ellingsen, T. and U. Söderström (2001) 'Monetary Policy and Market Interest Rates', *American Economic Review*, 91(5), 1594–607.

European Commission (1998) 'AMECO – Annual Macroeconomic Database', Version 1998.

———— (2002) 'AMECO – Annual Macroeconomic Database', Version November.

European Council (1999) 'Annexes to the Presidential Conclusions. Cologne Summit 3 and 4 June', Council Document, 150/99.

Felderer, B. and S. Homburg (1994) *Makroökonomik und Neue Makroökonomik.* Berlin: Springer.

Fischer, S. (1977) 'Long-Term Contracts, Rational Expectations, and the Optimal Money Supply Rule', *Journal of Political Economy*, 85, 191–205.

Fisher, I. (1930) *The Theory of Interest*; reprinted New York: Kelley (1965).

———— (1933) 'The Debt–Deflation Theory of the Great Depression', *Econometrica*, 1, 337–57.

Fitoussi, J.-P. and O. Passet (2000) 'Réformes structurelles et politiques macroéconomiques: les enseignements des "modèles" de Pays', in Conseil D'Analyse Économique (ed.), *Réduction du chômage: les réussites en Europe*, Paris. La documentation Française, 11–96.

Flanagan, R. J. (1999) 'Macroeconomic Performance and Collective Bargaining: An International Perspective', *Journal of Economic Literature*, 37, 1150–75.

Franz, W. (1999) *Arbeitsmarktökonomik*, Berlin: Springer.

Franzese, R. J. (2001) 'Strategic Interaction of Monetary Policymakers and Wage/Price Bargainers: A Review with Implication for the European Common-Currency Area', *Empirica*, 28, 457–86.

French, K. and J. Poterba (1991) 'Investor Diversification and International Equity Markets', *American Economic Review*, 81, 222–6.

Freyssinet, J. (2000) 'La réduction du taux de chômage: les enseignements des expériences européennes', in Conseil d'Analyse Économique (ed.), *Réduction du chômage: les réussites en Europe*, Paris: La documentation Française, 97–212.

Friedman, M. (1953) *A Theory of Consumption Function*, Princeton: Princeton University Press.

Gaiotti, E. and A. Generale (2001) 'Does Monetary Policy Have Asymmetric Effects? A Look at the Investment Decisions of Italian Firms', ECB Working Paper, 110.

Galbraith, J. K. (1997) 'Time to Ditch the NAIRU', *Journal of Economic Perspectives*, 11, 93–108.

Gärtner, M. (1997) *Makroökonomik flexibler und fester Wechselkurse*, Berlin: Springer.

Gesell, S. (1946) *Die Natürliche Wirtschaftsordnung*, Lauf bei Nürnberg: Rudolf Zitzmann Verlag.

Gibbons, R. (1992) *Game Theory for Applied Economists*, Princeton: Princeton University Press.

Goodhart, C. A. E. (1984) *Monetary Theory and Practice. The UK Experience*, London: Macmillan.

———— (1989) 'Has Moore Become Too Horizontal?', *Journal of Post Keynesian Economics*, 12, 29–48.

———— (1994) 'What Should Central Banks Do? What Should Be their Macroeconomic Objectives and Operations?', *Economic Journal*, 104, 1424–36.

———— (1997) 'Why Do the Monetary Authorities Smooth Interest Rates?', in S. Collignon (ed.), *European Monetary Policy*, London: Pinter, 119–74.

Goodhart, C. A. E. and H. Huang (1999) 'A Model of the Lender of Last Resort', LSE Financial Markets Group Working Paper, 313.

Green, R. (1987) 'Commodity Money', in M. M. J. Eatwell and P. Newman (eds), *The New Palgrave: A Dictionary of Economics*, London: Macmillan, 496–7.

Grilli, V., D. Masciandaro and G. Tabellini (1991) 'Political and Monetary Institutions and Public Finance Policies in the Industrial Countries', *Economic Policy*, 13, 341–92.

Grüner, H. P. and C. Hefeker (1999) 'How Will EMU Affect Inflation and Unemployment in Europe?', *Scandinavian Journal of Economics*, 101(1), 33–47.

Gurley, J. G. and E. S. Shaw (1960) *Money in a Theory of Finance*; Washington, DC: Brookings Institution.

Guzzo, V. and A. Velasco (1999) 'The Case for a Populist Central Banker', *European Economic Review*, 43, 1317–44.

Hall, P. A. and R. J. Franzese (1998) 'Mixed Signals: Central Bank Independence, Coordinated Wage Bargaining, and European Monetary Union', *International Organization*, 52, 505–35.

Hall, R. E. (1978) 'Stochastic Implications of the Life Cycle-Permanent Income Hypothesis: Theory and Evidence', *Journal of Political Economy*, 86, 971–87.

———— (1988) 'Intertemporal Substitution in Consumption', *Journal of Political Economy*, 96, 339–57.

Hanappi, G. (1995) 'Evolving Strategies – Gaming in Economics', in A. Riedl, G. Winckler and A. Wörgötter (eds), *Macroeconomic Policy Games*, Heidelberg: Physica, 87–102.

Hancké, B. (2002) 'The Political Economy of Wage Setting in the Euro-Zone', London School of Economics, mimeo.

Hansen, L. P. and K. J. Singleton (1983) 'Stochastic Consumption, Risk Aversion, and the Temporal Behavior of Asset Returns', *Journal of Political Economy*, 91, 249–65.

Hardouvelis, G. A. (1994) 'The Term Structure Spread and Future Changes in Long and Short Rates in the G7 Countries. Is There a Puzzle?', *Journal of Monetary Economics*, 33, 255–83.

Hassler, U. and D. Nautz (1998) 'The Link Between German Short- and Long-Term Interest Rates: Some Evidence Against a Term Structure Oriented Monetary Policy', *Jahrbücher für Nationalökonomie und Statistik*, 217, 214–26.

Heise, A. (1999) 'Erfolgsbedingungen einer wirtschaftspolitischen Kooperation', *Wirtschaftsdienst*, 79, 730–8.

———— (2002) 'Der Kölner Prozess – Theoretische Grundlagen und erste Erfahrungen mit dem EU-Makrodialog', *Integration*, 04/2002.

Heston, A. and R. Summers (1995) 'Penn World Table, Version 5.6', http://www.nber.org/pubs/pwt56/.

Hewitson, G. (1995) 'Post-Keynesian Monetary Theory: Some Issues', *Journal of Economic Surveys*, 9, 285–310.

Hicks, J. R. (1937) 'Mr. Keynes and the "Classics": A Suggested Interpretation', *Econometrica*, 5, 147–59.

———— (1946) *Value and Capital*, Oxford: Clarendon Press.

Horn, G.-A. (2001) 'Koordinationsmängel als Ursachen konjktureller Krisen am Beispiel der USA und Deutschland', Habilitationsschrift TU Berlin.

Horn, G.-A., W. Scheremet and R. Ziener (1997) 'Rahmenbedingungen für den Arbeitsmarkt in einer erfolgreichen Wirtschafts- und Währungsunion der Eu-Mitgliedsstaaten', DIW Gutachten im Auftrage des Bundesministers für Wirtschaft.

Issing, O. (1997) 'Comment on Chapter 8 [Goodhart 1997]', in S. Collignon (ed.), *European Monetary Policy*, London: Pinter 175–8.

———— (2002) 'On Macroeconomic Policy Co-ordination in EMU', *Journal of Common Market Studies*, 40, 345–58.

Issing, O., V. Gasper, I. Angeloni and O. Tristani (2001) *Monetary Policy in the Euro Area: Strategy and Decision-Making at the European Central Bank.* Cambridge: Cambridge University Press.

Iversen, T. (1998a) 'Wage Bargaining, Central Bank Independence, and the Real Effects of Money', *International Organization*, 52, 469–504.

Iversen, T. (1998b) 'Wage Bargaining, Hard Money and Economic Peformance: Theory and Evidence for Organized Market Economies', *British Journal of Political Science*, 28, 31–61.

———— (1999a) *Contested Economic Institutions: The Politics of Macroeconomics and Wage Bargaining in Advanced Democracies*, Cambridge: Cambridge University Press.

———— (1999b) 'The Political Economy of Inflation: Bargaining Structure or Central Bank Independence?', *Public Choice*, 99, 237–58.

Keynes, J. M. (1930) *A Treatise on Money*, London: Macmillan.

———— (1936) *The General Theory of Employment, Interest, and Money*, New York: Harcourt Brace.

Kilponen, J. (2000) *The Political Economy of Monetary Policy and Wage Bargaining. Theory and Econometric Evidence*, Bank of Finland Studies, E:19, Bank of Finland.

King, R. G. and C. I. Plosser (1984) 'Money, Credit and Prices in a Real Business Cycle Model', *American Economic Review*, 74, 363–80.

Köhler, C. (2001) *Beschlüsse zu einer fehlentwicklungsfreien wirtschaftlichen Entwicklung in der EWU*, Berlin: Duncker & Humblott.

Kruschwitz, L. (1995) *Finanzierung und Investition*, Berlin: Walter de Gruyter.

Kurz, H. D. (1987) 'Capital Theory: Debates', in M. M. J. Eatwell and P. Newman (eds), *The New Palgrave: A Dictionary of Economics*, London: Macmillan, 357–62.

Kuttner, K. N. (2001) 'Monetary Policy Surprises and Interest Rates: Evidence from the Fed Funds Futures Market', *Journal of Monetary Economics*, 47, 523–44.

Kydland, F. and E. Prescott (1977) 'Rules Rather than Discretion: The Inconsistency of Optimal Plans', *Journal of Political Economy*, 85, 473–92.

Lapp, S. (2002) *Internationale Diversifikation in den Portfolios deutscher Kapitalanleger: Theorie und Empirie*, Berlin: Springer.

Lucas, R. E. (1972) 'Expectations and the Neutrality of Money', *Journal of Economic Theory*, 4, 103–24.

———— (1973) 'Some International Evidence on Output–Inflation Tradeoffs', *American Economic Review*, 63, 326–44.

———— (1976) 'Econometric Policy Evaluation: A Critique', *Carnegie–Rochester Conference Series on Public Policy*, 1, 19–46.

———— (1988) 'On the Mechanics of Economic Development', *Journal of Monetary Economics*, 22, 3–42.

Lutz, F. A. (1940) 'The Structure of Interest Rates', *Quarterly Journal of Economics*, 55, 36–63.

Maki, D. M. and M. G. Palumbo (2001) 'Disentangling the Wealth Effect: A Cohort Analysis of Household Saving in the 1990s', Federal Reserve Finance and Economics Discussion Series, 2001–21.

Mangano, G. (1998) 'Measuring Central Bank Independence: A Tale of Subjectivity and its Consequences', *Oxford Economic Papers*, 50, 468–92.

Mankiw, G. N. (1981) 'The Permanent Income Hypothesis and the Real Interest Rate', *Economic Letters*, 7, 307–11.

———— (1985) 'Small Menu Costs and Large Business Cycles: A Macroeconomic Model of Monopoly', *Quarterly Journal of Economics*, 101, 529–39.

———— (2000) *Macroeconomics*. New York: Worth.

Mann, C. L. (1999) *Is the US Trade Deficit Sustainable?* Washington, DC: Institute for International Economics.

Markowitz, H. M. (1952) 'Portfolio Selection', *Journal of Finance*, 7, 77–91.

———— (1959) *Portfolio Selection. Efficient Diversification of Investments*, New York: Wiley.

Marquis, M. H. (1996) *Monetary Theory and Policy*, Minneapolis: West.

Mayer, T. (1975) 'The Structure of Monetarism', *Kredit und Kapital*, 8, 191–215, 292–313; reprinted in Snowdon and Vane (1997).

McCallum, B. T. (1989) *Monetary Economics; Theory and Policy*, New York: Macmillan.

McCarthy, J. and R. W. Peach (2002) 'Monetary Policy Transmission to Residential Investment', *Federal Reserve Bank of New York Economic Policy Review*, May.

Meltzer, A. H. (1999) 'The Transmission Process', Pittsburgh, PA: mimeo.

Meulendyke, A. M. (1998) *US Monetary Policy and Financial Markets*, New York: Federal Reserve.

Minsky, H. P. (1957) 'Central Banking and Money Market Changes', *Quarterly Journal of Economics*, 71, 171–87.

———— (1986) *Stabilizing an Unstable Economy*, New Haven: Yale University Press.

Modigliani, F. (1997) 'The Shameful Rate of Unemployment in EMS: Causes and Cures', in S. Collignon (ed.), *European Monetary Policy,* London: New Pinter, 242–70.

Modigliani, F. and R. Sutch (1966) 'Innovations in Interest Rate Policy', *American Economic Review*, 56, 178–97.

Mojon, B., F. Smets and P. Vermeulen (2001) 'Investment and Monetary Policy in the Euro Area', ECB Working Paper 78.

Moore, B. J. (1988) *Horizontalists and Verticalists: The Macroeconomics of Credit Money*, Cambridge: Cambridge University Press.

———— (1989) 'A Simple Model of Bank Intermediation', *Journal of Post Keynesian Economics*, 12, 10–28.

———— (1991) 'Money Supply Endogeneity: "Reserve Price Setting" or "Reserve Quantity Setting"?', *Journal of Post Keynesian Economics*, 13, 404–12.

Müller, M. (1998) *Endogenität des Geldes: Eine Untersuchung zum Beitrag des Kredites zur Endogenität des Geldes am Beispiel der Bundesrepublik Deutschland*, Frankfurt: Haag & Herchen.

Myerson, R. B. (1991) *Game Theory. Analysis of Conflict*, Cambridge, MA: Harvard University Press.

Nautz, D. and J. Wolters (1998) 'The Response of Long-Term Interest Rates to News About Monetary Policy Actions. Empirical Evidence for the U.S. and Germany', HU Berlin, SFB 373, Discussion Paper, 78.

Nelson, E. (2000) 'Direct Effects of Base Money on Aggregate Demand: Theory and Evidence', Bank of England Working Paper, 122.

OECD (2000a) *OECD Economic Outlook*, 68, Paris.

———— (2000b) 'Revised OECD Measures of Structural Unemployment', *OECD Economic Outlook* (Paris), 68, 15–168.

Okun, A. M. (1971) 'The Mirage of Steady Inflation', *Brookings Papers on Economic Activity*, 2, 485–98.

Orphanides, A. and R. M. Solow (1990) 'Money, Inflation and Growth', in B. M. Friedman, and F. H. Hahn (eds), *Handbook of Monetary Economics*, Amsterdam: North-Holland, 223–61.

Oswald, A. J. (1982) 'The Microeconomic Theory of Trade Union', *Economic Journal*, 92, 576–95.

Padoan, P. C. (1998) 'Who's Afraid of Italy's Adjustment? Sustainability of EMU as Seen from an Undisciplined Country', in Association for the Monetary Union of Europe *The Sustainability Report*, Paris, 110–20.

Panico, C. (1987) 'Interest and Profit', in J. Eatwell, M. Milgate and P. Newman (eds.) *The New Palgrave Dictionary on Money and Finance*, 1 London: Macmillan, 602–6.

Patinkin, D. (1948) 'Price Flexibility and Full Employment', *American Economic Review*, 38, 543–64.

———— (1965) *Money, Interest, and Prices: An Integration of Monetary and Value Theory*; New York: Harper & Row.

———— (1987) 'Real Balances', in M. M. J. Eatwell and P. Newman (eds),*The New Palgrave: A Dictionary of Economics*, London: Macmillan, 98–101.

Peersman, G. and F. Smets (2001) 'The Monetary Transmission Mechanism in the Euro Area: More Evidence from VAR Analysis', ECB Working Paper, 91.

Perez-Quiros, G. and J. Sicilia (2002) 'Is the European Central Bank (and the United States Federal Reserve) Predictable?', ECB Working Paper, 192.

Pichelmann, K. (2001) 'Monitoring Wage Developments in EMU', *Empirica*, 28, 353–73.

Pigou, A. C. (1943) 'The Classical Stationary State', *Economic Journal*, 53, pp. 343–51.

Ramsey, F. P. (1928) 'A Mathematical Theory of Saving', *Economic Journal*, 38, 543–59.

Rasmusen, E. (1994) *Games and Information: An Introduction to Game Theory*, Cambridge, MA: Blackwell.

Riese, H. (1986) *Theorie der Inflation*, Tübingen: Mohr.

———— (1995) 'Das Grundproblem der Wirtschaftspolitik', in H. Riese and K. Betz (eds.), *Wirtschaftspolistik in einer Geldwirtschaft*, Marburg: Metropolis, 9–29.

Rogoff, K. (1985) 'The Optimal Degree of Commitment to an Intermediate Monetary Target', *Quarterly Journal of Economics*, 100, 1169–89.

Romer, C. D. and D. H. Romer (2000) 'Federal Reserve Information and the Behavior of Interest Rates', *American Economic Review*, 90, 429–57.

Romer, D. (1996) *Advanced Macroeconomics*, New York: McGraw-Hill.

———— (1999) *Short-Run Fluctuations*, Berkeley: University of California.

———— (2000) 'Keynesian Macroeconomics Without the LM Curve', NBER Working Paper, 7461.

Romer, P. M. (1990) 'Endogenous Technological Change', *Journal of Political Economy*, 98, S71–S102.

Roy, T. (2000) *Ursachen und Wirkungen der Dollarisierung von Entwick-lungslän-dern. Ein Erklärungsansatz unter besonderer Berücksichtigung Boliviens*, Marburg: Metropolis.

Samuelson, P. A. and R. M. Solow (1960) 'Analytical Aspects of Anti-Inflation Policy', *American Economic Review Papers and Proceedings*, 50, 177–94.

Sargent, T. J. and N. Wallace (1975) 'Rational Expectations, the Optimal Monetary Instrument, and the Optimal Money Supply Rule', *Journal of Political Economy*, 83, 241–54.

———— (1976) 'Rational Expectations and the Theory of Economic Policy', *Journal of Monetary Economics*, 2, 169–83.

Schächter, A. (1999) *Die geldpolitische Konzeption und das Steuerungsverfahren der Deutschen Bundesbank: Implikationen für die Europäische Zentralbank*, Tübingen: J.C.B. Mohr (Paul Siebeck).

Schelkle, W. (2001) *Monetäre Integration: Bestandsaufnahme und Weiterentwicklung der neueren Theorie*, Heidelberg: Physica.

Schmidt, P. G. (1996) 'Strukturmerkmale des Arbeitsmarktes und gesamtwirtschaftliche Stabilität. Eine vergleichende Analyse der OECD-Länder', *Schriften des Vereins für Socialpolitik*, NF244, 95–148.

Shiller, R. J. (1990) 'The Term Structure of Interest Rates', in B. M. Friedman and F. H. Hahn (eds), *Handbook of Monetary Economics*, 1, Amsterdam: North-Holland, 627–722.

Shleifer, A. (2000) *Inefficient Markets. An Introduction to Behavioral Finance*, Oxford: Oxford University Press.

Sidrauski, M. (1967) 'Rational Choice and Patterns of Growth in a Monetary Economy', *American Economic Review, Papers and Proceedings*, 57, 535–44.

Silvestre, J. (1993) 'The Market-Power Foundations of Macroeconomic Policy', *Journal of Economic Literature*, 31, 105–41.

Sims, C. A. (1992) 'Interpreting the Macroeconomic Time Series Facts: The Effect of Monetary Policy', *European Economic Review*, 36, 975–1000.

Skott, P. (1997) 'Stagflationary Consequences of Prudent Monetary Policy in a Unionized Economy', *Oxford Economic Papers*, 49, 609–22.

Snowdon, B. and H. R. Vane (eds) (1997) *A Macroeconomics Reader*, New York: Routledge.

Solow, R. M. (2000a) 'Toward a Macroeconomics of the Medium Run', *Journal of Economic Perspectives*, 14, 151–8.

———— (2000b) 'Unemployment in the United States and Europe. A Contrast and the Reasons', CESifo Working Paper 231.

Soskice, D. (1990) 'Wage Determination: The Changing Role of Institutions in Advanced Industrialized Countries', *Oxford Review of Economic Policy*, 6, 36–61.

Soskice, D. and B. Hancké (2002) 'Gently Turning. The Political Economy of EMU', Report for project 'Institutionen, Wirtschaftswachstum und Beschäftigung in der EWU', financed by the Hans-Böckler-Stiftung.

Soskice, D. and T. Iversen (1998) 'Multiple Wage-Bargaining Systems in the Single European Currency Area', *Oxford Review of Economic Policy*, 14, 110–24.

———— (2000) 'The Non-Neutrality of Monetary Policy with Large Price Setters', *Quarterly Journal of Economics*, 115, 265–84.

Spahn, H.-P. (1993) 'Liquiditätspräferenz und Geldangebot. Schritte zu einer keynesianischen Kreditmarkttheorie des Zinses', in H. J. Staderman and O. Steiger (eds), *Der Stand und die nächste Zukunft der Geldforschung. Festschrift für Hajo Riese zum 60. Geburtstag*, Berlin: Duncker and Humblot, 245–55.

———— (1999) 'Central Bankers, Games and Markets – A Critical Assessment of the Microeconomic Optimization Approach in the Theory of Macroeconomic

Stabilization', in W. Filc and C. Köhler (eds), *Macroeconomic Causes of Unemployment – Diagnosis and Policy Recommendations*, Berlin: Duncker & Humblot, 379–403.

Sraffa, P. (1960) *Production of Commodities by Means of Commodities*, Cambridge: Cambridge University Press.

Srour, G. (2001) 'Why Do Central Banks Smooth Interest Rates?', Bank of Canada Working Paper, 2001–17.

Staiger, D., J. H. Stock and M. W. Watson (1997) 'The NAIRU, Unemployment and Monetary Policy', *Journal of Economic Perspectives*, 11, 33–49.

Stiglitz, J. E. (1992) 'Capital Markets and Economic Fluctuations in Capitalist Economies', *European Economic Review*, 36, 269–306.

Svensson, L. E. O. (2001) 'How Japan Can Recover', *Financial Times*, 25 September.

—— (2003) 'Escaping from a Liquidity Trap and Deflation: The Foolproof Way and Others', *Journal of Economic Perspectives*, 17(4), 145–66.

Svensson, L. E. and M. Woodford (2000) 'Indicator Variables for Optimal Policy', ECB Working Paper, 12.

Taylor, J. B. (1980) 'Aggregate Dynamics and Staggered Contracts', *Journal of Political Economy*, 88, 1–23.

—— (1981) 'On the Relation Between the Variability of Inflation and the Average Inflation Rate', *Carnegie–Rochester Series on Public Policy*, 15, 57–86.

Tesar, L. and I. Werner (1998) 'The Internationalization of Securities Markets since the 1987 Crash' in A. M. Santomero and R. E. Litan (eds) *Brookings–Wharton Papers on Financial Services*, Washington, DC: The Brookings Institution, 281–349.

Tobin, J. (1958) 'Liquidity Preference as Behavior Towards Risk', *Review of Economic Studies*, 25, 65–86.

—— (1963) 'Commercial Banks as Creators of "Money" ', in D. Casson (ed.), *Banking and Monetary Studies*, Homewood, IL: Richard D. Irwin, 408–19; reprinted in: Tobin (1971).

—— (1965) 'Money and Economic Growth', *Econometrica*, 33, 671–84.

—— (1969) 'A General Equilibrium Approach to Monetary Theory', *Journal of Money, Credit, and Banking*, 1, 15–29.

—— (1971) *Essays in Economics*, 1. New York: North-Holland.

—— (1980) *Asset Accumulation and Economic Activity*, Oxford: Basil Blackwell.

—— (1982) 'Nobel Lecture: Money and Finance in the Macroeconomic Process', *Journal of Money, Credit, and Banking*, 14, 171–204.

—— (1993) 'Price Flexibility and Output Stability: An Old Keynesian View', *Journal of Economic Perspectives*, 7, 45–65.

—— (1998) *Money, Credit, and Capital*, Boston: Irwin/McGraw-Hill.

Tobin, J. and C. W. Brainard (1977) 'Asset Markets and the Cost of Capital', in *Progress, Private Values, and Public Policy: Essays in Honor of William Fellner*, R. Nelson and B. Balassa (eds), *Economic*, New York: Elsevier, 235–62.

Tsiang, S. C. (1969) 'The Precautionary Demand for Money: An Inventory Theoretical Analysis', *Journal of Political Economy*, 77, p. 99–117.

Valderrama, M. (2001) 'Credit Channel and Investment Behavior in Austria: A Micro-Econometric Approach', ECB Working Paper 108.

van Els, P., A. Locarno, J. Morgan and J.-P. Villetelle (2001) 'Monetary Policy Transmission in the Euro Area: What Do Aggregate and National Structural Models Tell Us?', ECB Working Paper, 94.

von Hagen, J. and M. Brückner (2001) 'Monetary Policy in Unknown Territory: The European Central Bank in the Early Years', ZEI Working Paper B18–2001.

von Hagen, J. and S. Mundschenk (2001) 'The Functioning of Economic Policy Coordination', ZEI Working Paper, BO8–2001.

von Kalckreuth, U. (2001) 'Monetary Transmission in Germany: New Perspectives on Financial Constraints and Investment Spending', ECB Working Paper, 109.

Whalen, E. L. (1966) 'A Rationalization of the Precautionary Demand for Cash', *Quarterly Journal of Economics*, 80, p. 314–24.

Wicksell, K. (1922) *Vorlesungen über Nationalökonomie*, Jena: Fischer

Woll, A. (1990) *Allgemeine Volkswirtschaftslehre*, München: Vahlen.

Woodford, M. (2003) *Interest and Prices. Foundations of a Theory of Monetary Policy*, Princeton and Oxford: Princeton University Press.

Wray, L. R. (1990) *Money and Credit in Capitalist Economies: The Endogenous Money Approach*, Cheltenham: Edward Elgar.

Index